1973

This book may be kept

FOURTEEN DAYS

A fine will be charged for each day the book is kept **overtime**.

DEC 12 '74			
GAYLORD 142			PRINTED IN U.S.A.

Sidney's Two *Arcadias*

Pattern and Proceeding

Sidney's Two *Arcadias*

Pattern and Proceeding

by JON S. LAWRY

Cornell University Press

ITHACA AND LONDON

First published 1972 by Cornell University Press.
Published in the United Kingdom by Cornell University Press Ltd., 2-4 Brook Street, London W1Y 1AA.

International Standard Book Number 0-8014-0724-9
Library of Congress Catalog Card Number 72-2360

Printed in the United States of America by Vail-Ballou Press, Inc.

Library of Congress Cataloging in Publication Data
(For library cataloging purposes only)

Lawry, Jon Sherman, date.
  Sidney's two Arcadias.

  Bibliography: p.
  1. Sidney, Sir Philip, 1554–1586. Countess of
Pembroke's Arcadia. I. Title.
PR2342.A6L35   821'.3   72-2360
ISBN 0-8014-0724-9

To my mother, Gladys Moore Lawry

Ἦλθε δ' ἐπὶ ψυχὴ μητρὸς κατατεθνηυίης

Contents

Preface

Like many Neoplatonic and Christian writers before him, Sir Philip Sidney believed that man's "erected wit" or "inward light" can know eternal truth. The essential mark of man, indeed, is his capacity to "discern beauty." But Sidney also believed that most modern men have fallen on evil days. The average man's "infected will" now reduces his power to receive wisdom and to enact it within his own life—politically, in the state, and ethically, in his person. If man is to recover his original high estate, his errant will must be affected and moved. Returning then into active knowledge, man will find that his wit has been purified, his memory or recollection enriched, his judgment "enabled," and his conception enlarged. Only an energizing object of "heart-ravishing" love, however, can sufficiently "strike, pierce [and] possess" his will, thereby converting degenerate passion into something resembling a divine fury. As the political and ethical object for secular admiration, Sidney prescribes the fictional hero, acting within the heroic poem. By admiring and emulating that hero, the reader will regain his own original heroism. During this procedure of "delightful teaching," modern poetry also will have been renewed; for it, too, had fallen from its high estate among the ancients into being the mere "laughing stock of children." A resurgent poetry might thus image as well as move the recovery of man. Sidney also hoped that it would stir a particular and immediate renaissance for England.

These claims for both man and poetry are very high—as high, indeed, as Hamlet's related praise, "What a piece of work is a man!" Sidney was probably right in suspecting that they might fly too high for many of his readers. Today, on the other hand, we are likely to grant that the claims are historically "credible," at least as they apply to his own writing. Sidney exerted a tremendous, if at times unfortunate, influence upon the greatest epoch in English literature. In a sense his works constitute England's literary Renaissance, so forcefully did they simultaneously encourage and represent it. In themselves, they go far toward justifying his general claims: the *Defence of Poesy* is among the two or three best critical essays in English, and the two *Arcadias* (even though little read and much misunderstood) are two of our finest "heroic poems."

This book is concerned primarily with the two *Arcadias*.[1] In order to see them plain, however, it is useful to look first to the *Defence of Poesy*. (It could almost as well have been entitled *The Idea of a Heroic Poem*). Accordingly, the Introduction deals with the *Defence*, Chapter 1 with the *Old Arcadia*, and Chapter 2 with the *New*. In each of the chapters, theoretical consideration of the work's "pattern" and

[1] The *Old Arcadia* is Sidney's first version of the *Arcadia*. Written about 1580, this version was all but unknown until 1907. The *New Arcadia* is a revised version of the first two and a half books of the *Arcadia*, published in 1590. See R. W. Zandvoort, *Sidney's Arcadia: A Comparison between the Two Versions* (Amsterdam: N. V. Swets and Zeitlinger, 1929).

Quotations from the *Old* and *New Arcadias*, as well as those from Sidney's *Defence of Poesy*, derive from *The Prose Works of Sir Philip Sidney*, ed. Albert Feuillerat (Cambridge: Cambridge Univ. Press, 1912; rpt. 1963–1967); Vol. I is the *New Arcadia*, Vol. III contains the *Defence of Poesy*, and Vol. IV is the *Old Arcadia*.

"proceeding" leads into a close reading of the given work. The discussions are intended mainly for the general student of literature, who is likely to know the *Arcadias* more by dim reputation than by direct encounter. For that reason, I have not hesitated to quote extensively, to let commentary closely follow the line of plot, to treat the *Arcadias'* poems more as statement in context than as lyrics in their own right, and to modernize the appearance of Sidney's text while leaving the substance essentially intact. Also, the last footnote for the Introduction and for each of the two chapters is intended to be a "study" note, listing most of the significant modern studies of the works concerned—the *Defence,* the *Old,* and the *New Arcadia.*

Some of the ideas in the book were put forward in papers delivered to the North Central Conference of the Renaissance Society in 1969 and the 1970 MLA Section Four meeting. I wish to thank the Library of Congress, the Folger Library, and the libraries of the universities of Pennsylvania, Virginia, and Pittsburgh for courteous assistance. I owe more particular thanks to the staff of McGill Memorial Library, New Wilmington, Pennsylvania, and to Mrs. Richard Derby, a "Sidney's sister" for our century.

As always, I am grateful to my wife and sons. "Guarded with poverty" though they may have been during this study, they have remained "notable in those [virtues] which stir affection, as truth of word . . . courtesy, mercifulness, and liberality."

J. S. L.

Four Winds Farm
Proctorsville, Vermont

Sidney's Two *Arcadias*

Pattern and Proceeding

The Defence of Poesy:
Sidney's foreconceit
for any heroic fiction

"They that delight in *Poesy* itself should seek to know what they do and how they do," declared Sidney (*Defence,* p. 37).[1] Accordingly, he set down in the *Defence* a prolegomenon for all heroic fiction or "right" poetry. In our turn, we would do well to consider Sidney's definition of poetry before looking to two of his particular "poems"—the *Old* and the *New Arcadia.* If, as seems probable, the *Defence* was written after the *Old* was finished but before the *New* was seriously underway, the critical essay stands in a unique parental relationship to the two works. We suppose that it reflects or predicts as well as defines them. Therefore, a proper study of the two *Arcadias* can begin with a brief consideration of the *Defence.* The source of the two poems, after all, is *"Poesy* itself," and as Sidney stipulates in another context, "The skill of each artificer standeth in [the] idea or foreconceit of the work, and not in the work itself" (p. 8).

Within the *Defence,* the single figure that best represents Sidney's idea of *"Poesy* itself" is the moderator.[2] Together

[1] Quotations of the *Defence,* modernized in spelling and punctuation, are taken from Feuillerat. Parenthetical page numbers placed in the text refer to that edition.

[2] On the moderator, see Elizabeth Dipple, "The 'Fore Conceit' of Sidney's Eclogues," *Literary Monographs,* 1 (1967), 8, and Russell A. Fraser, "Sidney the Humanist," *SAQ* 66 (1967), 91. More broadly still,

with his poem, the poet constitutes a bridge much like Neoplatonic man himself. Poetry can join precept and practice, the universal and the particular, an idea or "foreconceit" and its material manifestation, and higher and lower natures. As "moderator," the poet stands between (and therefore, in usefulness, above) the philosopher with his cold general precepts and the historian with his dead particular facts. If human knowledge is to be both universal and lively, the mediatorial poem is not a mere delight; it is a necessity.

In Sidney's idea of fiction, there is one essential precondition: the proposition that each man's "erected wit" or "inward light" (pp. 9, 19) permits him to know perfect truth and goodness. Eternal truth thus can be "conceived" and in that sense imitated by the human mind. If need be, the mind can then use this general design, pattern, or "foreconceit" to fashion or "feign" a material manifestation of that truth (or some portion of it). By impressing such true patterns upon the raw stuff of nature, including that of his own body or his various bodies politic, man can convert the brazen natural world into a golden one. Sidney evidently found nothing precious or mysterious in this belief. Because it is the mark of man that he can "discern beauty" (p. 30), he can impose the idea of a temple upon a cave and that of a constitution upon the anarchic state. In doing so, he may parallel the creativity of nature by working with the things of nature, but he will never merely "follow" her. It is more likely that he will imitate God, the original designer and maker.

In his original state, Sidney's man is thus a knower and maker—that is to say, a poet. His powers of conception and creation define his humanity.

---

see Ernst Cassirer, *The Individual and the Cosmos in Renaissance Philosophy,* tr. Mario Domandi (Oxford: Blackwell, 1963), pp. 7–45, and Nancy S. Struever, *The Language of History in the Renaissance* (Princeton: Princeton Univ. Press, 1970), pp. 44–63, 90–93.

However, it seemed to Sidney that modern man had increasingly fallen away from his high origins. Erected wit, which "maketh us know what perfection is" (p. 9), had given way to "infected will." In the *Arcadias,* that slide is graphically demonstrated when princes turn idle seducers and a nation degenerates into a mob. It is not that reason (the "erected wit") has withered away, but that passion (the "infected will") has usurped its governing power. When that happens, man becomes less a knower and creator than a blind user and consumer. He is increasingly the slave to things in nature and to fortune and fate within history. Knowledge dwindles into cold philosophy, and action into history's "old mouse-eaten records." If the errant human will is to be converted and the erected wit to be restored, a force as strong as passion must homeopathically oppose passion; men must be brought to love, not merely to "know," truth and goodness.

At this point, Sidney turns to the mediatorial poet. Unlike most other modern men, the poet cannot have severed his intuitive contact with eternal reality; to be a conceiving "maker" at all, he must know and love truth. If he were concerned with himself alone, his only "poem" might be the unwritten (*a-graphos*) conception that results. All about him, however, are men in whom knowledge has declined and love has turned to passion. Partly for their needs, but partly also for the sake of the idea that he loves, the poet will utilize his own communion with eternal truth as the "foreconceit" or meaning which guides him as he fashions a seemingly living manifestation of that truth. This "lively" image of truth will be so admirable that other men may love it and emulate it. They can thereby correct the will, thus enacting as well as knowing goodness. From Sidney's viewpoint, that is the whole reason for fashioning heroic poems:

[Poets] do merely make to imitate, and imitate both to delight and teach, and delight [in order] to move men to take that goodness in hand, which without delight they would fly as from a stranger; and teach to make them know [that is, to realize] that goodness whereunto they are moved; which [is] the noblest scope to which ever any learning was directed [p. 10].

Sidney's central notion of the mediatorial poet intimates that the poet is to be a "conceiving" moderator between man's wit and will; that right fiction, a "speaking picture," is in a sense incarnative, allowing the word to be made flesh; and that the purpose of such a fiction is the redemption and restoration of man to his golden world. It implies a threefold imitation of truth: mediatorial, by the poet; incarnative, by the poem; and propagative, by the reader.

In constructing his apology for heroic poems, Sidney had correctly guessed that few readers might be willing to grant him the height of his definitions of poetry, where "with the force of a divine breath" (p. 8) the poet acts almost in God's "own likeness." He had therefore descended to a more "ordinary opening." Because his two heroic poems are to be justified mainly at that upper level of definition, however, we should continue to particularize the height before descending in Chapters 1 and 2 to "more palpable" truths of description (p. 9).

Perhaps the most troublesome misunderstanding of the *Defence* is that which asserts that Sidney's heroic poet must create his works *ex nihilo*.[3] It suggests the complementary notion that any fiction resulting from such a theory will be either "unnatural" and static or formless and meandering. Depending upon definitions, there may be justice in the latter notion, but there is almost none in the former. Flattering to the poet though the analogy with the Judaic-Christian God of some theologies may be, any *ex nihilo* explana-

---

[3] For this view, see (for instance) Robert M. Durling, *The Figure of the Poet in Renaissance Epic* (Cambridge, Mass.: Harvard Univ. Press, 1965), p. 131.

tion of the origins of poetic matter tends strongly (although not necessarily) to suggest that poems come from nothing and nowhere, that they possess nothing of the "real" or "true," and that they therefore can give the reader nothing and can lead him nowhere. It is an easy step from that supposed precept to the belief that the *Arcadias* in practice must be either mere fantasies or else running internal rejections of pastoral fancy in favor of "real" life in a "real" world. If such truly were the case, Sidney's high claims would be self-defeating and generative of a peculiar surplus of irony. Instead, he holds that the source of poetry is virtuous Platonic and Christian reality, not fancy. That truth is also the object of the erected human wit. It is this reality which poetic wit "images" and in imitation of which it in turn creates seemingly material "images," pictures which movingly speak that knowledge. Truly active knowledge supplies a fiction and its readers not with static contemplation, but with ecstatic ascent into virtue and knowledge and then with ethical and political practice of those ideas.

In the beginning of his *Defence* (itself no mean "poem"), Sidney stresses that ancient sages and scholars, like prophets and oracles, had exercised themselves upon truth which "before them lay hidden to the world" (p. 5).[4] It was not absent, only unrecognized or unrealized, before men "invented" or discovered it. (In Sidney, "invention" does not mean designing a new tool; it means the methodical establishment of the parts of an idea or generalization—the taking of an "inventory," as it were.) Human realization of truth therefore existed long before a writer put it into the poetic apparel which permitted it wide entry into "the gates of popular judgment" (p. 5). Poets seek this general truth, not historical particulars.

[4] Cf. S. K. Heninger, Jr., "Metaphor as Cosmic Correspondence," in *Medieval and Renaissance Studies,* ed. John M. Headley (Chapel Hill: Univ. of North Carolina Press, 1968), p. 14.

They therefore maintain a "high flying liberty of conceit" rather than slavishly accumulating nature's nail parings. Similarly, poetic expression should seek out exquisite, golden "number and measure" (p. 6), for in technical manner as well as "divine matter," poetry is to be most liberal, governing, and excellent. Its own "erected wit" both of matter and manner opposes the decay of "number, measure, order [and] proportion . . . in our time" (p. 27). In much the same way, says Sidney, true knowledge and its methods can prevent "our brain [being] delivered of much matter, which never was begotten by knowledge" (p. 37). Poetry's knowledge and expression thus can hardly derive *ex nihilo*—or even *ex ipso,* from the thinking maker alone.

When Sidney conducts his readers from classic examples to the Hebrew and Christian, he not only slyly abducts unwilling right-wing Puritans to Parnassus but also indicates still more openly the divine or eternal source of "beauty" and knowledge. In David's poems, he says, the poet is found to be a passionate lover "of that unspeakable and everlasting beauty, to be seen by the eyes of the mind . . . cleared by faith" (p. 7). As in other Christian and Neoplatonic statements, such power to "discern beauty" is held to be the peculiar note or gift of man (p. 30). Human knowledge is ultimately "of" that beauty, whether it is described in Platonic, Neoplatonic, or Christian phrases. It offers "infallible grounds of wisdom" (p. 14). In it, or if need be through material representations of it, men may see "the form of goodness" (p. 21), even as in heroic poems such as the *Arcadias* they may witness "the most high and excellent truth . . . magnanimity and justice . . . through all misty fearfulness and foggy desires" (p. 25). Like Italian Neoplatonists before him and like the early Milton of a later age, Sidney all but unites the poetry of "Apollo's Garden" (p. 5) with "the Church of God" (p. 7)—specifically, in David, but by extension, in each poetic "Maker": for to be a poet is to share that divinely "high and incomparable . . . title" (p. 7).[5]

Unlike God, however, the limited poet will be partly dependent upon nature as he creates material representations, whether of the most high and excellent general truth or of lesser, more nearly "historical," truths about more purely human action. Nevertheless, at the very least he will work with or like nature as an equal, not slavishly and at third remove. At best, in a form of true alchemy, he will "creatively" reproduce and restore forms of men to forms of Eden. Like the divine Maker, he knows far more of excellence than material nature can evince. He can therefore "endeavor to take naughtiness away, and plant goodness even in the secretest cabinet of our souls" (p. 13). In both the spiritual pattern and the moral proceeding of poetry, the poet can all but say of his work that which John says of Jesus: *Verbum caro factum est et habitavit in nobis* ("The Word was made flesh, and dwelt among us"). But the praise for poetry ultimately must ascend to the "heavenly Maker of that maker" (p. 8), who continues to wish that his poetic Adam "with the [secondary] force of a divine breath" (p. 8) govern and inform nature by bringing forth "things . . . surpassing her doings" (p. 9). That man can perceive the ideal proves his erected wit, which still knows "what perfection is." That a redemptive, second creation is now necessary as well as pleasant proves his infected will, which stands brazenly between human knowledge and love of perfection, on the one hand, and human practice of it, on the other.

Thus the mediatorial poet functions by "embodying" divine beauty within a poem. The incarnative poem will contain, or even be, a speaking picture—an emblematic or fig-

[5] Henry Olney, in turn, was eager to give Sidney the title "diuine Sir *Phillip Sidney*," deliverer of "sacred pen-breathing works": quoted in *Elizabethan Critical Essays* (London: Clarendon, 1904), I, 149.

urative particularizing of the universal, after the fashion of
Christ's parables in narrative and of hieroglyphics and related
indicators in print, paint, and sculpture. It will manifest or
make "palpable" (p. 9) either the divine, primary, "unspeakable and ever-lasting beauty" (p. 7) or the secondary human
virtues, together with their related but deviant vices. Such
representation will do far more than hold a reflecting mirror
up to nature. Like Shakespeare's definition of drama, and especially like the two pictures with which Hamlet confronts
Gertrude, it will have men "look on this picture, and on this"
in order to see the essential features and images of virtue and
vice. Such pictures may speak either daggers or praises. Thus,
although one may "literally" see only a winning picture of
Ulysses or Cyrus, he will recognize general "exercises of patience and magnanimity" in the one and the "portraiture of
a just empire" in the other (pp. 18, 10). Similarly, in comedy
(such as that of the low figures in the *Arcadias*) he will see
"the common errors of . . . private and domestical matters"
(p. 23).

At the level of human characters, the "speaking picture"
will in most cases be two-sided, like a figure in the Tarot
pack. The same character may tell and show of the erected
wit or of the infected will, depending upon the use he has
made of them; for with a sword, says Sidney, "thou maist kill
thy father [or] defend thy prince and country" (p. 31). Because of the infected will and the great abnormality that it
creates, the "right" poet in the modern world is unlikely to
imitate anew the "unconceivable excellencies of God" (p. 9)
or to reiterate given facts of nature, most of which are ir-
redeemably captive to the seeming "truth of a foolish world"
(p. 18). Instead, with poetic images of vice or virtue he will
reveal the "outward beauty of . . . virtue," which from the
"divine consideration" of a god's-eye view of humanity either

"may be" or "should be" (p. 10). We will then be able to see *"through* them" (p. 15; italics added); like the Byzantine eikon, the image will serve as a "window" by means of which we "see" the invisible reality which the image conveys. The poetic image thus is not a glass through which we peer darkly, but rather a clarifying lens which permits our seeing forms "face to face."

The sole motive for creation is to imitate such "likelihood or necessity" (p. 16). The poet wishes to figure forth, to counterfeit, to "illuminate" (p. 14) the virtues, with their double source in divine and human wisdom, or the vices, with their single source in the infected human will. The manifestations thus created will often multiply significance from one figure upward and outward in an expanding scale of applications: from the microcosm, "man's own little world" (p. 12), through families and public societies, to a "whole Commonwealth" (as in the case of "poems" by Plato and Sir Thomas More), and even to "the general reason of things" (p. 14). In the pattern and proceeding of his two *Arcadias,* Sidney sought out just such a scale.

Yet an imitation of truth by the mediatorial poet and incarnative poem, no matter how excellent it may be, is not the final aim of poetry. Like the third member of the Christian trinity, poetry is intended to move other men with a "desire to know" (p. 19). That desire will lead them to act upon their achieved knowledge, thus propagating truth by them as well as in them. In both the poem and the reader, knowledge and beauty [6] are to be creatively realized in virtue and action.

Such imitative propagation of truth demands action in both the fiction and the reader. If much in Sidney's *Defence*

[6] Cf. the "principle of Transformation" discussed in M. C. Bradbrook, *Shakespeare the Craftsman* (New York: Barnes and Noble, 1969), p. 6.

suggests changeless idea, at least as much also pleads the ecstatic, the morally "moving," the cathartic, even the redemptive, in men's response to idea. Sidney always assumes the quality of liveliness (*energia*) in a poem, but by itself it might be dismissed as a trick of style. More essential is his belief that knowledge (*gnosis*) must be realized in action (*praxis*), of some kind. Three partially obscured principles of movement are inherent in that doctrine.

First, by mediatorially yoking the opposites of Plato's line of knowledge (pure idea, or *noesis,* with imitations of things, or *eikasia*), Sidney supposes a material imitation that will not bar, but rather permit, full sunlight, full insight. The line becomes a place of mutual movement, with each end assisting in the "realization" of the other. The seemingly material image in such a case will be eikonic: a visible "window" through which the invisible is opened to our sight. In this argument, Sidney rather dazzlingly countered Plato's objection to imitation by using Plato's own doctrine of love, in which one rises from love of a beautiful thing to love of beauty itself, as well as Plato's belief that myth can both express the suprarational and stir men to a related ethical progress. He also adds significant shadings from Neoplatonic and Christian employment of ecstatic love and of the hermeneutic interpretation of Biblical stories. Thus, even as David adores his unseen God and as the lover moves from love of physical beauty to that of supersensible beauty itself, so the reader of the heroic poem will make propagative contact with the idea and act of heroism. In Sidney, every degree of knowledge intends such Platonic or Christian elevation of man "from the dungeon of the body, to the enjoying his own divine essence" (p. 11). Like philosophical contemplation or erotic love, the "lively knowledge" of poetry should "strike, pierce, [and] possess the sight of the soul" (p. 14), ravishing man with "the love of [virtue's] beauty" (p. 25). Although the seemingly material object may be transcended in the rapture, it need not be. Movement between human admiration and divine truth can be mutual and continuous, as when a Cyrus who represents divine knowledge is admired by men with such a "divine fury" (p. 45) that both Cyrus and divine wisdom are enacted in their lives.

Next, such a principle of movement "outside" the fiction proper will produce at least a limited narrative and dramatic movement within it—a practice or "action," in the purely literary sense considered by Aristotle. Although "speaking" debates in the *Old Arcadia* and "picturing" narratives in the *New* may seem static, the movement of inter-involving characters among those arguments and pictures nevertheless comprises a significant general action. The characters even come to major reversals and recognitions, as if gradually proving general knowledge within their particular action.

Finally, Sidney considers human knowledge to be sequential as well as intuitive. Although "inward light" (p. 19) might reveal virtue to men at all times, each fictive Cyropaedia trains governors not only to seek direct revelation but also to employ the manifold discoveries that have already been made by other men. Presumably, the careful education necessary to young heroes is also proper to poets; without it, their fictions may be such "matter, [as] never was begotten by knowledge" (p. 37). Furthermore, even the poem itself exists to give "counsel how to be worthy" as well as "desire to be worthy" (p. 25). Such humanistic "knowledges" (p. 28) go far toward equipping men's minds to deal with the ethical choices that they must make in the physical world.

If knowledge becomes "lively" and active in poem and reader because of the virtue that has been realized, imitated, and transmitted by the poet, the whole process of fiction will be heroic. To Sidney, the hero and the heroic signify "new [forms] such as never were in nature" (p. 8). Ardent contact with truth produces a great-mindedness in hero and heroic poem, and in poet and reader. When considering men who heroically contest the infected human will, Sidney thinks directly of the heroic Aeneas, declaring for poem, reader, and poet, as well as hero, *"Hoc opus, hic labor est"* (p. 19).

The maker of heroic poems will be consistently catholic and ideational, caring little about genres [7] but greatly about the order which can impress reflective design and meaning upon a "confused mass of words" (p. 38). For that reason he will poetically imitate the perfect idea of a tragedy (say) *by means of* the work, even as an Oedipus and his action heroically manifest the perfect pattern of a tragic virtue *within* the work.

In considering the *Defence*,[8] we have viewed it as Sidney's

[7] Cf. William A. Ringler, Jr., ed., *The Poems of Sir Philip Sidney* (Oxford: Oxford Univ. Press, 1962), pp. xxxvi–xxxviii.

[8] Studies of the *Defence* appear in several modern editions, including those of Albert S. Cook (Boston: Ginn, 1890); Geoffrey Shepherd (London: T. Nelson, 1965); and Lewis Soens (Lincoln, Nebr.: Univ. of Nebraska Press, 1970). Among other useful studies that bear upon the *Defence* are these: Catherine Barnes, "The Hidden Persuader: The Complex Speaking Voice of Sidney's *Defence of Poetry*," *PMLA*, 86 (1971), 422–427; Cornell March Dowlin, "Sidney's Two Definitions of Poetry," *MLQ*, 3 (1942), 573–581; A. C. Hamilton, "Sidney's Idea of the 'Right Poet,'" *Comp. Lit.*, 9 (1957), 51–59; Virginia R. Hyman, "Sidney's Definition of Poetry," *SEL*, 10 (1970), 149–162; F. Michael Krouse, "Plato and Sidney's *Defence of Poesie*," *Comp. Lit.*, 6 (1954), 138–147; Maurice Lebel, tr. of the *Defence* as *Un Plaidoyer pour la Poesie* (Quebec: Presses de l'Université Laval, 1965); A. E. Malloch, "'Architectonic' Knowledge and Sidney's *Apologie*," *ELH*, 20 (1953), 181–185; John P. McIntyre, S.J., "Sidney's 'Golden World,'" *Comp. Lit.*, 14 (1962), 356–365; Morriss Henry Partee, "Sir Philip Sidney and the Renaissance Knowledge of Plato," *ES*, 51 (1970), 411–424; Annabel M. Patterson, "Tasso's Epic Neoplatonism," *SR*, 18 (1971), 105–133, especially n. 34; Irene Samuel, "The Influence of Plato on Sir Philip Sidney's *Defense of Poesy*," *MLQ*, 1 (1940), 383–391; J. P. Thorne, "A Ramistical Commentary on Sidney's *An Apologie for Poetrie*," *MP*, 54

general literary foreconceit for all heroic poetry. Before moving on to the two works that he created, using that foreconceit, we should grant Sidney the final word upon *"Poesy itself."* Although he thought that the lyric poem was more appropriate to a past religious age than to his own "moral" period, his definition of lyric, if properly scaled down from religious association, can serve for all poetry:

[The] Lord . . . gave us so good minds, how well [lyric poetry] might be employed, and with how heavenly fruits, both private and public, in singing the praises of the immortal beauty, the immortal goodness of that God, who giveth us hands to write, and wits to conceive: of which we might well want words, but never matter, of which we could turn our eyes to no thing, but we should ever have new budding occasions [p. 41].

(1956–57), 158–164; and Paul G. Zolbrod, "The Poet's Golden World: Classical Bases for Philip Sidney's Literary Theory," unpub. Univ. of Pittsburgh dissertation, 1967. In "The Function of Myth in Plato's Philosophy," *JHI,* 10 (1949), 481, Ludwig Edelstein asked if any later authors had risen "to the height of Plato's vision of a new poetry." Sidney must at least have come close.

Chapter 1

The *Old Arcadia:*
"A picture newly made
by an excellent artificer"

The reappearance of Sidney's original *Old Arcadia*[1] in 1907, after centuries of slumber, was itself appropriately Arcadian. At the close of the work, a drugged king similarly arises, also crying out "with a great voice." Unlike its king Basilius, however, the revived *Old Arcadia* was at first greeted in the twentieth century with about as much embarrassment as interest. It seemed to create rather than clear up problems in dealing with the received *Arcadia*—that Siamese twin, partly *Old* and partly *New,* which Sidney's literary inheritors had uncomfortably joined together. Many readers chose to lay the *Old* aside, yet refused to accept the unfinished *New.* Like most recent studies, however, the present discussion unhesitatingly welcomes the *Old,* in its full heroic plenitude.

Whether *New, Old,* or grafted in the center, the *Arcadia* has received fitting attention across the twentieth century in its character as pastoral, as romance (of several descriptions), and as a repository of that which is called "Arcadian"—Arcadian both in the literary tradition that derives from Virgil, and in Sidney's personal style. The emphasis upon convention in those studies probably was unduly great. Although Sidney of course borrowed poetic "apparel" from these and

[1] Page numbers for quotations from the *Old Arcadia* appear parenthetically in the text.

many other conventions, his ultimate commitment in both the *Arcadias* is to the Renaissance heroic poem—that is, to a fiction that figures forth heroism by means of the character and extensive exemplary action of a given hero, or heroes. Emphasis on other issues had tended to conceal that bedrock. Questions of answerable style aside, the apparel of the heroic poem is of relatively slight importance. Only the heroic fiction, together with its great source in truth and great end in action, will matter.

It therefore may be well to "decipher" the *Old Arcadia* swiftly within that context, as Sidney conceives and projects it, before going on to "narrowly . . . examine his parts" (*Defence*, p. 22). As a heroic poem, it contains the determinants for its own pattern as well as for much of its consequent proceeding.

In his life as well as in his fiction and criticism, Sidney was committed to the idea of heroism. Despite his frequent lightness of tone, he eventually stands forth as a profoundly concerned student of politics, a corrective ironist, and a serene, if complex, believer in Christian humanism. Much of that character appears in his definition of the heroic poem—a definition that embraces heroic author, heroic fiction, and heroic reader:

The lofty image of [heroes] most enflameth the mind with desire to be worthy, and informs with counsel how to be worthy. Only let Aeneas be worn in the tablet of your memory, how he governeth himself . . . ; how in storms, how in sports, how in war, how in peace. . . . Lastly, how in his inward self, and how in his outward government, and I think . . . he will be found in excellency fruitful [*Defence*, p. 25].

Ultimately, the *Old Arcadia* and its idea of heroism derive from one great foreconceit or purposive design: the definition of essential man, and of the conditions in which he may enact his essence. The representative hero such as Aeneas will supply a "speaking picture" of that definition, which can make a reader's knowledge of heroism to be "lively" (*Defence,* pp. 9, 14).

In a Sidneian heroic poem, then, it is man who must be hero, and his action, heroism. The *Old Arcadia* images man the hero both in his inward self, privately, and in his outward action, publicly. Despite the "historic" loss of a golden age and the attendant infection of man's will, his essential "erected wit" can still ratify a golden world on earth, both inwardly and outwardly. Such he was created for; such he has possessed; and such, even though men may fall, they may possess again.[2] Man has only to surmount a limiting physical nature, abandon the festering garden of his selfish will, and return to his proper being and action. His ethical and political world is not given him by nature. It is he who creates it, following given universal or divine patterns of perfection. If God is a foreconceiving poet in the great general creation, man the hero is in turn a great secondary poet. In the human self and human state, he can envision (or more exactly, conceive) a golden world, and then proceed to fashion it.

Significantly, the opening lines of the *Old Arcadia* quickly brush past the conventional surface of Arcadia's physical "picture," even though Sidney relishes its "sweetness of air and other natural benefits," in order to reach its inner significance: the "moderate and well-tempered minds of the people" (p. 1). Arcadia as a province is thus originally heroic.[3]

2 See Harry Berger, Jr., "The Renaissance Imagination: Second World and Green World," *The Centennial Review,* 9 (1965), 36–78.

3 In Sidney's handling, the province of Arcadia is not a *locus amoenus* nor a sad Virgilian retreat which mirrors the melancholy mind of a poet. It is partly an ideational *politeia* or Utopia; partly a setting intended to recall the Greek myths of heroism (with Hercules) and love (with Diotima); and partly a real political and geographical

Its people, being in part governors of themselves, unreservedly cherish the greater but related government of human justice and divine providence. Laws—the golden ideas set down by the "good minds" of past princes—are now administered by a central good governor, Basilius (*the king*). Thus in its outward or political part, Arcadia is a symphony of governings, deriving from the rational order of the cosmos.

This heroic kingdom extends also to the "inward" or ethical part of each man. It is upon this rock that the errant Arcadian princes will come to grief. Perhaps for that reason among others, women in the *Old Arcadia* register much of the "inward self." Although Arcadia's princesses have major roles in the outward government (the Arcadian heir-apparent is the princess Pamela), they supply a comprehensive index of the heart and home. Within the royal household, a true pattern of heroism can be seen in the queen's "well-governed

---

place. In the latter function, Sidney's Arcadia often recalls the Ville-hardouins' Achaia. The actual Arcadia had been charted by Polybius and mapped by Pausanias and Strabo. The other provinces of Greece and Asia Minor which are used by Sidney were widely known through writers and heroes as diverse as Alexander, Hercules, Xenophon, Paul, and Tacitus. For that matter, Frankish and Venetian power was maintained in the Peloponnesus almost into the lifetime of Sidney. During his diplomatic journey to Venice, he encountered men fresh from the forlorn battle to save Cyprus from the Turks. Although the *Arcadias* do not imitate history and geography, they preserve many allusive connections with the "real" Arcadia.

See further Elizabeth Dipple, "Harmony and Pastoral in the *Old Arcadia*," *ELH*, 35 (1968), 311; Friedrich Brie, *Sidneys Arcadia: Eine Studie zur Englischen Renaissance* (Strassburg, 1918), pp. 185–221; William A. Ringler, Jr., *The Poems of Sir Philip Sidney* (Oxford: Oxford Univ. Press, 1962), p. 376; George Ostrogorsky, *History of the Byzantine State*, tr. Joan Hussey (New Brunswick, N.J.: Rutgers Univ. Press, 1957), p. 496; and *The Correspondence of Sir Philip Sidney and Hubert Languet*, tr. Steuart A. Pears (London: W. Pickering, 1845), p. xxvi.

youth" and the princesses' excellence "in all those gifts which
are allotted to reasonable creatures" (pp. 1, 2). All of Sidney's
heroes, men as well as women, are thus to be tried not so
much in acts of war and love, as such, as in deeds for the
forum and the home.

Each person and each state thus may be heroic in some
measure, for such was their "high creation." It is that conviction and hope which give rise to the *Old Arcadia*. By its
own imitation of the idea of the hero, the heroic poem will
help to restore and disseminate the idea among living men.

It would be a mistake, however, to consider the heroic
man or state as a simple unit, definable merely by heroism
or its absence. Like man himself, the hero is instead central
in a series of expanding, but interrelated, triads or triplexes.
Drawing ultimately upon Plato, this conception would hold
that the individual man is made up of appetite, will, and
intelligence; that the state is composed of craftsmen, spirited
guardians, and philosopher-governors; and that the cosmos
also reveals a pattern that reaches up from mere body or
surging appetite, through creatural being and action in a
fluid center, to divine goodness and wisdom. Because the
center is almost always a position for choice, Sidney places
extraordinary stress upon the central hero as a mediate exem-
plar. As the heroic and governing Hercules chooses well or
badly at the crossroads, so will many other men choose in
emulation.

The great cosmic triad receives little direct development
in the *Arcadias*. Nevertheless, it suggests the essentially Christian character of Sidney's thought. Without its sense of absolute design and purpose, he would have found even the
most profound philosophical arguments to be insecure.
With it, however, he confidently believes that supreme wisdom supplies not only the foreconceit for man but also
man's own conceiving mind. By means of his knowledge,

man may overcome the seeming direction of mere matter or of fortune, fate, and anarchy.

The political triad, on the other hand, is given commanding attention in the *Old Arcadia*. Although Sidney follows Plato by considering the healthy state to be composed of wise governors, spirited guardians, and honest craftsmen, his interest in the exemplary hero leads him to re-define the center. In his redisposed triad, the three members will reveal eternal truth at the summit; the heroic prince or governor in the center; and the people, below. In this altered model, the prince stands in relation to truth above and people below somewhat as in the *Defence* the poet stands to foreconceit above and reader below. By this means, and without relinquishing his basic humanism, the central ruler takes on the character of a priest, and the secular state a semblance of the medieval church. Not only will the governing hero strive toward the originating divine wisdom, but also, as a secondary, physical object of love and service to his people, he will draw them toward it.

The personal or ethical version sees in each man—whether monarch, martial hero, or shepherd—a similar triad. In varying proportions, he will be composed of a wisdom-loving, an honor-loving, and a desire-loving part. Again, the center is partly redefined in order to accommodate a greatly increased stress. It now appears that the ardor of the honor-loving part, which produces both desire for knowledge and the action attendant upon that desire, is almost as important as the wisdom-loving part. The two are essential to man. Together, they constitute his "erected wit," which can create a golden world. Even the desire-loving part, if properly employed, can increase man's ardor for beauty and goodness. On the other hand, if desire is not controlled by the other parts, it can plunge man downward not only to a Platonic disease of the soul but to Christian damnation.

In the *Old Arcadia,* these three triads are apparent everywhere, but they all gravitate toward the heroic center. Generally, the cosmos is indicated in Apollo, above; Arcadia, at the center; and a dark collocation of fortune, fate, desire, and furies, below. The state, in turn, is officially formed of the royal family, above; counsellors and heroes strong in arms, at the center; and people, below. And the individual man is composed of mind, life-serving "instincts," and appetite. Because the three triads are so intimately connected and transreflective, they eventually may be considered as one. Within that "one," Sidney then fashions a triply-central triad of princes. Not only will this triad demonstrate choice in the person and in the state, but it will also represent man himself within the great universe.

Although the state should have been composed of royalty, heroes, and people, Arcadia proves to have suffered a dislocation at the top of the triad; her governor has abdicated. Similarly, Thessaly and Macedonia are left for a time without their two princely heirs-apparent. These three errant princes are therefore reassigned to the heroic center of the single, general triad. Above them, under these altered circumstances, are placed shepherds who speak for divine wisdom; [4] below them are louts, rebels, and beasts, which represent anarchy. Sidney next fashions a further triad among the three central princes themselves: Musidorus, above; Pyrocles, in the

[4] Whether native or foreign, the Arcadian shepherds are intent upon Urania and the religious or political "shepherd of shepherds," not upon literal sheep. In Arcadia, sheep are always thoughts; even the eclogues have more to do with the *Republic* than with pastoral. Relatedly, the names of the major characters are intended to signify political truth, not suggest a fanciful never-never land. The revival of Greek during Sidney's time would have made the names "Pyrocles" and "Musidorus" seem no more unlikely than Sophocles and Heliodorus. The actual names, in turn, probably would have seemed no less emblematic than those from fiction. Cf. André Chastel, *The Age of Humanism* (New York: McGraw Hill, 1963), p. 25.

middle; and (for most of the work) Basilius, the abdicative ruler of Arcadia, at the base. Then, in order to present this central triad in a private and ethical character as well as a public and political one, Sidney matches each prince with a princess: Pamela with Musidorus, Philoclea with Pyrocles, and the queen, Gynecia, with Basilius. By thus enfolding his central (and doubled) princely triad within both the tripartite state and the triadic universe, Sidney probably felt that he had formed a "speaking picture" for virtually the whole condition of man.

Although the dark imitation of man's infected will must enter the work in due course, the *Old Arcadia* never loses sight of man's original (and recoverable) place in the cosmic triad. It is gloriously celebrated by the king near the end of Act II. He begins in praise of the divine mind, moves to the heroic, judicial creature at the center, and concludes upon the possibility of an arrogant vice, below. In so doing, the fictional king almost recapitulates the author's definition of heroic fiction:

Apollo great, whose beams the greater world do light,
  And in our little world dost clear our inward sight:

. . . . .

Thou God, whose youth was decked with spoil of Python's skin
  (So humble knowledge can throw down the snakish sin):

. . . . .

In travel of our life, a short but tedious space,

. . . . .

Give us foresightful minds, give us minds to obey;
  What foresight tells our thoughts, upon thy knowledge stay.
Let so our fruits grow up, that nature be maintained,
  But so our hearts keep down, with vice they be not stained
                                                    [pp. 127–128].

When erotic love enters Arcadia with the two northern princes, nothing of the well-wrought image called Arcadia need suffer. Because loving intelligence is the bond that unites nature with man, the populace with a prince, and man with higher wisdom, and because for Sidney the loving emulation of a hero can propagate wisdom, any virtuous kind of love can guarantee rather than threaten Arcadia. If love's personal "coupled joys" are framed within man's great "native joys" (pp. 229, 119), Arcadia will be only the more fruitful and secure.

Sidney's golden Arcadia offers to all men a pattern of man's erected wit, in person and the state as well as in the divine foreconceit from which all things human spring. Until this point, the *Old Arcadia* has been considered mainly within its seemingly fixed pattern. The work's related proceeding remains to be seen. We will look first to the triadic "picture" in its aspect of action, and then to the Ramistic "speaking" which charts that action.

Although both the political and ethical triad offer either aspiration upward to pure mind or descent to desire and proud flesh, they nevertheless rest as a fixed paradigm. At first glance, the pattern seems static, more appropriate to expression by a lyric poem than a heroic. Levels of style may seem to reinforce the static character of the fixed triad, what with shepherds' lyrics above, princes' Ramistic debates and self-debates in the center, and the peoples' assenting praise or their comic "low" talk at the base. However, Sidney's emphasis upon *lively* knowledge, to say nothing of the traditional dramatic and narrative character of the epic, demanded a sequential proceeding or "action." It would not do merely to introduce the infected will into Arcadia and watch the triad collapse. Such "action" would be as bad for the heroic poem as the bad man would be for Aristotle's conception of tragedy. Sidney needed an action that would be single (such as that of integration/disintegration/reintegration) while at the same time giving almost simultaneous attention to each of the three elements in the several interrelated triads. And further: if possible, he wanted each of those three elements to show both their political and their ethical characters. Supposedly, the foreconceit from eternal truth had supplied the several triads themselves. It was now left to Sidney, the artificer, to fashion a suitable demonstration of the Arcadian princes "moving" within those given patterns.

And at just this juncture, the would-be "imitator" of Sidney probably should ask some particular patience from his reader. The proceeding of the *Old Arcadia* is a mighty maze, perhaps, but is not without a plan. In bald terms, it must read: *three* vertical or triadic elements, moving in *three* appropriate horizontal or sequential "practices," each of which is multiplied into *two* aspects (the political and the ethical), within *five* conventional partitions of time or movement (Acts or Books). And the sum of all this must be *one* heroic action. Using such a plan, Sidney could attain Aristotelian unity of action with Platonic unity of being, seen in heroes who imitate both.

To meet his own demand, Sidney devised from a number of traditional elements a highly original proceeding, at once intricate and simple. We have already seen how the doubled princely triad (consisting of six princes and princesses) was formed. Each doubled part subsequently moves after this manner: both individually and as a couple, a prince and princess are confronted with interlocking choices of knowledge and will, which necessarily must eventuate in public and private actions. The three parts of the general triad move forward together in one almost simultaneous progression. Their proceeding is embraced on each side, upon occasion, by a level of shepherds above, and of louts below. And in a far greater, cosmic, bracket, all the Arcadians are framed by the opposition of providence above, and fortune or fate below. Although on any particular level the proceeding is moved by free contests of human reason and will, in a larger view the entire suite reveals the massive and sure proceeding of providence.

The one great general action that results is disposed in five conventional partitions.[5] Not only is the work laid out in five Books or Acts (thus harmonizing Homer with Terence, and the narrative with the dramatic), but also the shepherds' choric Eclogues are devised as miniature five-phase proceedings in their own right. In both the whole work and its Eclogues, the first and final "Acts" serve as great frames to display integration and reintegration; by contrast, the three central Acts sink to contest and partial collapse. Perhaps for that reason, the *Old Arcadia*'s general Acts I and V display several great public debates, whereas Acts II, III, and IV are more nearly private.

For Sidney, none of these formulas are straitjackets. He alters them at will. They are never allowed to turn his characters into mere ambulating "stick figures," although it is true that their "fullness" or roundness is made up more of mind than emotions. Not only must each character contain within himself some of each element of the human triad, but also he must to some extent choose which of the places he will finally occupy or honor. In Sidney, choice, not temperament or triadic formula, is destiny.

Finally, by staging much of the work in a theater as well as by dividing it into Acts, Sidney makes his picture theatrically "active." Although he frequently "paints" fixed passions and also openly calls attention to the patterning images which characters represent, in general the *Old Arcadia* is more dramatic than icastic; more theatrical than emblematic. Its primary "picture" is therefore that quintessential "speaking picture," the theater. Its physical settings for the vertical triad are strikingly like that of a playhouse, with a pastoral setting,

[5] See T. W. Baldwin, *Shakespeare's Five-Act Structure* (Urbana, Ill.: Univ. of Illinois Press, 1947); Marvin T. Herrick, *Comic Theory in the Sixteenth Century* (Urbana, Ill.: Univ. of Illinois Press, 1964), pp. 106–107; and R. H. Perkinson, "The Epic in Five Acts," *SP*, 43 (1946), 465–481.

lyrically "above"; two princely lodges surrounded by desert "space" in the center; and a cavern and imitative bowers, "below." Each has its appropriate level of expression. If the disposition faintly suggests the "heaven," stage, and trapdoor of actual theaters, it may also reflect the emblematic character of Vives' Neoplatonic "amphitheater."

However, Sidney is far more direct than this in emphasizing the theater. Not only does he arrange his work in Acts and cause the characters to think often about their roles in a "very stage play," but he also makes the central pastoral meadow both a theater and a picture of Arcadia as it should be:

The fair meadow . . . was indeed a place of great delight, for through the midst of it there ran a sweet brook. . . . The meadow itself yielding so liberally all sorts of flowers, that it seemed to nourish a contention betwixt the color and the smell. . . . Round about the meadow (as if it had been to enclose a theater) grew all such sorts of trees. . . . In most . . . of which trees, there had been framed by art such pleasant arbors that it became a gallery aloft from one tree to the other . . . [p. 42].

Complementing that meadow is the final great court setting, a place of trial fixed in the "midst of the green, before the chief lodge." In the sweeping circular movement of the *Old Arcadia,* characters proceed from the great integrative theater out to disintegrative caverns and back again to the reintegrative place of trial. The vernal "O" of the theater has reflected that circle. The great speaking "debates" both identify and move the action: in Act I, princes demand the course of passion over reason; in Act II, the characters speak directly of a similar self-division; in Act III, the deceit and seduction in passion are revealed; in Act IV, Everlasting Justice begins to oppose the arguments of a crumbling state; and in Act V, a human trial of passion finds reason to be so cold that providence resolves the action back toward the golden foreconceit.

Although the part played by the theatrical "picture" in the *Old Arcadia*'s structural proceeding is fundamental, it is somewhat obscured in our actual reading by another principle of movement: the "speaking." Debates and dialogues very nearly constitute the work, in the narrative sections as well as in the eclogues. In public and in private, and in contests both between and within individual characters, dialogues are so continuous as to be the main voice of the *Old Arcadia*. If Sidney's use of dialogue looks all the way back to Plato, his great set speeches look forward to those of Shakespeare and Racine. Although the general character of such speaking is relatively familiar, the specific working-out of the average speech probably is not. In order to understand Sidney's characteristic disposition of the work's "speaking," therefore, it is useful to look briefly to Ramistic logic.

As is the case with almost every other intellectual system he met, Ramism was for Sidney only one element in his wide-ranging thought. Although he was a proponent of Ramus's system, Cambridge a Ramist university, and Sidney himself a friend of refugee Protestant Ramists, he himself was not to be contained in so methodical a circle. Nevertheless, Ramist influence offers a convenient way of describing the *Old Arcadia* and thus for differentiating the proceedings of the two *Arcadias*.

Twentieth-century studies, both sympathetic and otherwise,[6] have helped to renew Ramism as a force important for

[6] See Perry Miller, *The New England Mind: The Seventeenth Century* (New York: Macmillan, 1939); Norman Nelson, "Peter Ramus and the Confusion of Logic, Rhetoric, and Poetry," *Univ. of Mich. Contrib. in Mod. Phil.*, No. 2, April, 1947; Walter J. Ong, *Ramus: Method and the Decay of Dialogue* (Cambridge, Mass.: Harvard Univ. Press, 1958); and Rosemond Tuve, in both *Elizabethan and Metaphysical Imagery* (Chicago: Univ. of Chicago Press, 1947), p. 351, and "Imagery and Logic: Ramus and Metaphysical Poetics," *JHI*, 3 (1942), 365–400.

literature, if not for philosophy or logic. Given Ramists of such note as Sidney and Milton, it would indeed be surprising if it were not so. Briefly put, Ramism begins with the universal or general. Proceeding as in an outline by twin branchings, it moves downward in particularizing twin components as far as it is useful (or possible) to carry the process. At the most general level, it consists of two steps: first, an "invention" or inventory of separate "arguments"—that is, of individual words or phrases which indicate concepts; second, a disposition or judgment of the arguments that have been invented. Frequently, such disposition involves moving the arguments into a sentence in which the more general "argument" is the subject and the twinned component arguments appear as predicate(s). Fixed twinning principles of opposition, conjunction, and adjunction guide the thinker in "inventing" the separate arguments; fixed principles of classification, especially that of affirmation as against negation, guide their disposition. In most instances, the disposition of arguments is completed by the formation of the simple sentence described above. For more complicated cases, a syllogism or paragraph of two or three interrelated sentences may be necessary. Even in the syllogism, however, Ramism continues to seek the twinning principle, preferring the extremely quick and absolute service of the either/or syllogism to the more discursive kind approved by Aristotle.

By its nature, Ramism appears to be dogmatic, taxonomic, and non-discursive. It seeks the simple conception or the "axiomatic" sentence, not argument or meditation. It is therefore less supple and dramatic than the "Socratic" dialogue which appeared everywhere during the Renaissance. Although Plato would have disliked its rigid method, he probably would have found the basic Ramist reliance upon idea and intellection acceptable. In demanding a brief but profound form of statement, Ramism is often the verbal

equivalent of the Renaissance emblem or motto—and, perhaps, even of the individual artistic work when it is considered to be a "speaking picture."

As Rosemond Tuve has shown, Ramist dialectic is compatible with the metaphysical conceit as well as with the
familiar opposites from Petrarch, such as the fire and ice of
love. It is not alien to the spirit of the *débat* or a *psychomachia,* although such kinds of work find no direct place
within its system. In theory, it could offer Sidney a foreconceit
or argument of government from which twinning "dispositions" would proceed. Characters (especially those at different
levels of the Neoplatonic triad) could embody the disposed
arguments, and debates by those characters could then "be-
speak" them. In practice, Ramism helps to account for the
twinning devices so prominent in Sidney's more mannered
prose. (The somewhat less dialectical poems of the *Arcadias,*
on the other hand, are likely to isolate three or more characteristics for each noun or verb during the course of the poem
and then to recapitulate them within a concluding *collector.*)
Ramistic pairings begin even with the first sentence of the
Old Arcadia:

Arcadia among all the provinces of Greece was ever had in
singular reputation

partly for the sweetness of the air and other natural benefits	but	principally for the moderate and well-tempered minds of the people,

who, finding

how true a contention is gotten by following the course of nature	and	how the shining title of glory so much affected by other nations, doth in deed help little to the happiness of life,

were the only people, which as by their justice and providence

gave neither cause nor hope to their neighbors to annoy them,	so	were they not stirred with false pride to trouble others' quiet.

In passing, we should note that in itself Ramism probably would have led Sidney to restraint rather than indulgence of rhetoric.[7] Ramism is committed to truth in an almost plain style. However, it will produce a twinning so open and continuous that to the uninitiated its style will seem elaborate, ornate, and even precious. It is also possible that a desire for coherence as well as respect for classical figures of speech may have led Sidney to the related, highly mannered "twinning" of verbal and phonal recurrences, which can join otherwise separate arguments and sentences. In any case, Sidney's "Arcadianism"—insofar as the distinct style exists at all—probably can be identified in considerable measure with Ramism.

Even though in theory the tightly methodical Ramistic system may seem foreign if not downright hostile to the artistic imagination, in practice it offered several interesting possibilities to literature. In the first place, as a conceptual system it honored the concepts of fiction equally with those from any other source. Not only did Ramus deliberately choose most of his illustrations for arguments from classic poets, but also his simple or complex arguments would receive full and equal credit in fictional as well as extra-fictional settings. By virtue of its gravitation to the noetic or intuitive, Ramism was fully at home in "golden" worlds such as those of Christianity and Platonism. With proper use (including graded training) of the

[7] See David Kalstone, *Sidney's Poetry: Contexts and Interpretations* (Cambridge, Mass.: Harvard Univ. Press, 1965), p. 85; and Neil Rudenstine, *Sidney's Poetic Development* (Cambridge, Mass.: Harvard Univ. Press, 1967), pp. 132–133.

mind, the Ramist writer as well as the Christian or Platonist could attain to an erect perspective upon supposedly eternal truth. Ignoring the fallen brick of this world, he could recognize concepts that were themselves golden and which, if properly put to use, might bring back at least an intellectual or political age of gold. If the Ramistic writer were also a Sidneian poet, he would hope to work directly with concepts and images of the golden world—a world existing as it *should* be, in truth and pure reason, or as it *might* be, in judicial paradigms for actual existence. And by using the forces of literary liveliness and movement, he might activate as well as envision a golden world within the brazen.

Unexpected principles of movement thus appear within what at first seemed to be a rigid, diagrammatic system for knowledge.[8] Even a merely "conceptual imitation," which seems to involve only knowledge rather than action, must "move" slightly as it sequentially disposes arguments and methodizes them. If Ramism were to encounter a situation such as that in the *Old Arcadia* in which several Ramistically twinned characters were set disputing their partly valid but partly erroneous inventions and dispositions, it would not merely ask, but demand, that syllogistic interjudgments bring order and truth out of the confusion. And if it were assumed that one purpose of dialectic was the presentation of truth to another person, instructively, his progress from ignorance to truth would also offer a kind of "action."

Later, in its final flowering at Harvard, Ramism managed to achieve even something of the classical and Renaissance insistence upon virtue-in-action. It then declared that knowledge must lead "automatically and irresistibly to . . . *prattomen*"—a direct accomplishment of a moving moral action. In

[8] The diagrammatic is compatible with the emblematic. See Angus Fletcher, *Allegory: The Theory of a Symbolic Mode* (Ithaca, N.Y.: Cornell Univ. Press, 1964), p. 100.

his *Defence,* Sidney assumes that practice will spring from an emulation of fiction's models, such as that of the piety for which the character Aeneas is only an adjective or "adjunct." In this way, ethical and political as well as purely literary action might ensue even from the seemingly static arguments of Ramism. If it were assumed that truth not only could be known by men, but that "justice and providence" desired that men know it and therefore moved them to it, then the divinity that either was truth, or guaranteed truth, might also actively shape its ends in men. In the *Old Arcadia,* a hint that such a proceeding might be inherent in the Ramistic pattern appears in inventions such as this one, upon love:

Love . . . is engendered betwixt lust and idleness. . . : his adjoined companions be, unquietness, longings, fond comforts, faint discomforts, hopes, jealousies, ungrounded rages, causeless yieldings; so is the highest end it aspires unto, a little pleasure with much pain before, and great repentance after [p. 17].

In the work as a whole, almost all the characters possess within their erected wits and their fervent wills the idea or argument of the perfect polity. Because Ramism can work by twinnings of dissimilarity as well as likeness, aspects of that ideal foreconceit can immediately be placed against their fallen contraries whenever the princes abdicate reasonable roles in either their persons or the state.

In the early parts of the *Old Arcadia,* an external counsellor is likely to support the idea of the state against the Ramistically dissenting arguments of a vagrant prince. Similarly, the narrative debates of each Act are grandly opposed, as well as reflected, by the concluding Eclogues. Near the center, as real isolation increases despite generally perverse couplings that look like love, the wit of each person is likely to argue real love, Ramistically, against his own lustful will. At the close, the flawed argument by which an ideal human judge tries to restore Arcadia to its proper foreconceit reckons too little with one final, complex opposing argument— that of providential mercy. It is an argument more nearly "shown" than spoken, however, in that a higher justice converts what had been a perverse oracle into truth, and fulfills a central vow by the deluded king of Arcadia to return from private passion to public governance.

In the end as well as in the most general foreconceit, Sidney's *Defence* supplies the best summary for the pattern and the partly Ramistic proceeding of the *Old Arcadia*. All of its princes at last show that they know, and will increasingly perform, actions not "of lies, but of true doctrine; not of effeminateness, but of notable stirring of courage; not of abusing man's wit, but of strengthening man's wit; not banished, but honored by Plato" (*Defence,* p. 35). For that reason, heroism recovers on all fronts: the state is restored, the king is "resurrected," and the princes and princesses are united within "coupled joys." The dialectical "speaking picture" can then be veiled, for men have been returned to the beauty and wisdom that are beyond debate.

"To have his counsel and allowance": The First Book or Act

The *Old Arcadia* begins not in a lost golden age but with a timeless golden foreconceit: the noble inward and outward state of reasonable and well-tempered man, acting within the complementary "course of nature" (p. 1). Nowhere in the work is that pattern discredited or fully discarded. In his direct and indirect appearances in the work, the author himself obviously cherishes it as the special precept of his fiction. His choric shepherds' minds are always open to this "high conceit." Most of his other characters honor it, if at times only in defining their departure from it. And the proceeding of the work, having been initiated in that pattern of Arcadia, strives always to regain it. Given this humanistic paradise, what would move men in that happy state to fall away?

The easy answer (which is correct, as far as it goes) is, of course, *passion;* the brazenness of humanity's infected will is allowed to outweigh the gold of its erected wit. Much of the action supports this view. It is true that a triad of "political" princes in Act I and a closely related triad of "ethical" princesses in Act II show the corrosive effects of self-love. It is also true that Arcadia as well as the noble Arcadians therefore slides downward from the shepherds' "high conceits" toward the base mentality and frequent violence of louts, beasts, and anarchic rebels.

Looked at more comprehensively, however, the issue is not solely that of reason *versus* passion. In the first place, although love as mere desire is a passion that may topple the state and degrade a man, "right love" is a virtue that can bind together separate elements of the state and lead men to love reason itself. On the other hand, a reasonable virtue such as friendship may become a vice if it merely pities passion or acts as its accomplice. Practice, not mere definition alone, is the proof of vice and virtue. In the second place, behind the somewhat limited, principally human issue of reason and passion, there looms a cosmic extension of the same question: is the universe "free," at least within the operations of golden human reason and divine providence, or is it "fated," bound helplessly to fortune and fate within a brazen nature? To be free in this broad sense is also to be ordered, governed, and predictable, whereas to be fated is to be controlled by restless natural passions and fortune. This universal issue begins almost with the book itself. In foolishly seeking to know and prevent the future, the Arcadian governor manages only to bind himself and his family more thoroughly to its "fate."

Similarly, in taking a wrong, un-Herculean path when dealing with desire, the two visiting princes (and later the three
native princesses) only the more certainly surrender to it.
Thus in the *Old Arcadia* the author's focus upon the seemingly limited contest of reason *versus* passion almost always
increases until it discloses the tremendous question of providence *versus* fortune or fate.

In the active proceeding of the work, providence and human reason gradually prove their strength directly within the
seeming power of fate and fortune. Although in the episode
mentioned above the Delphic prophecy had been improperly
sought and "furiously" delivered in darkness, it is nevertheless "true." All of its elements are golden and reasonable.
They will reunite the king and queen, bring noble young
princes and princesses together in marriage, and introduce
the Macedonian monarch to Arcadia in a visit of alliance.
It is only the "fatal" attempt to bind or thwart the course of
reason and governed nature that creates a painful deviant
progress for those elements. Even in the worst rough-hewing
by men in the *Old Arcadia,* however, the governed operation
of nature under true human wit eventually opposes and erad-
icates the fault. Within the self-destructive turbulence of
fortune, excess itself can become a form of order and even
the furious sibyl will indirectly serve a rational Apollo.

Of the two *Arcadias,* the general proceeding of the *Old,*
with its "simple" Achillean formula, displays more of self-
corrective fate, whereas the *New,* with its "complex" Odyssean action, gives more attention to resistible fortune. Both
works, however, celebrate the corrective concurrence of human reason and divine design. Although such correction
comes to the righteous characters partly because of their return to reflective reason, it comes mainly from the action of
providential liberty itself. In the spectacular *coup de théâtre*
which closes the *Old Arcadia,* for example, the rigors of hu-

man justice are displaced by the unexpected, life-avowing miracle of a natural "resurrection." As human reason and divine providence together supply the foreconceit of the *Old Arcadia,* they also bring about the last golden laugh. It is as gentle as it is serenely confident.[9]

Although the structure for this pattern and proceeding is likely to seem unmistakable once it has been stated, it obviously was not clear to many readers in the past, as Hazlitt, Virginia Woolf, and Eliot demonstrate.[10] For that reason, in the following discussion Acts I and II are given somewhat closer reading than the three remaining Acts. In them, the structural "determinations" of the general pattern and action can be most fully inspected.

The *Old Arcadia* begins and ends with a governor. He tends to stand for all human reason. To reject reason's control, at any level, is to reject "an even tenor of happiness"— that inward and outward state of perfectness which is the emblematic meaning of the original Arcadia. The rejection must be wilful; it will never be thrust upon a person. As the elder prince will counsel his cousin, "There is no man suddenly either excellently good, or extremely evil, but grows either as

[9] Much Sidneian comedy resembles the pastoral humor described by Richard Cody, *The Landscape of the Mind: Pastoralism and Platonic Theory in Tasso's Aminta and Shakespeare's Early Comedies* (Oxford: Oxford Univ. Press, 1969), p. 17. In general, comedy, as well as the theme of justice, argues against the sense that divinity is inimical to men which occasionally appears in W. R. Elton, *King Lear and the Gods* (San Marino, Calif.: Huntington Library, 1966), pp. 55–62. Sidney is a Platonic optimist in the skin of a Puritan activist.

[10] William Hazlitt, Lecture VI of "Lectures on the Dramatic Literature of the Age of Elizabeth," *Works,* ed. P. P. Howe (London and Toronto: Dent, 1931), VI, 320; Virginia Woolf, " 'The Countess of Pembroke's Arcadia,' " in *Collected Essays* (London: Hogarth, 1966), I, 19–27; T. S. Eliot, *The Use of Poetry and the Use of Criticism* (New York: Barnes and Noble, 1933), p. 51.

he holds himself up in virtue or lets himself slide to vicious-
ness" (p. 16). If a man chooses evil, he will have traded reason's
"perpetual mansion" for "this poor bating place of man's
life"; and like Philip of Macedonia, he will discover only
terror when he also exchanges reason for fortune-telling.

The Arcadian representative of all men who exchange
reason for passion is Basilius (*the king*). Although Sidney does
not propose an Adam and a garden but only a Basilius and
others in Arcadia, a fall from the golden world nevertheless
occurs. Thus, although the name "Basilius" is not translatable
into Everyman, it may still be legion.

"The manner of . . . determination": Government *versus* self, in Philanax with Basilius

The *Old Arcadia* having begun upon the given human pattern of right reason and good government, only to see it
abandoned for the disjunctive pattern of furious soothsaying
and abdication of all government, its proceeding in Act I
displays the full arguments and effects of those seeming opposites. The contest of reason *versus* passion, which involves
each of the triadic Arcadian princes in turn (the governing
prince of Arcadia, the heroic prince of Macedonia, and the
more intellectual prince of Thessaly), is in each case so
nearly a Ramistic argument that in the long run arguments
are effects, and words *are* deeds. The public "doing" of passionate abdication therefore also seriously threatens the private being of the prince.

If truth were given a fair field in the debates of Act I, the
correct side of the disjunction—which is also the side of divine providence and human reason—would never lose. Not
only are the arguments of the counsellors for reason incomparably more strong, but also even the defenders of passion
cannot abdicate their "erected wit" entirely, even when they

seem to dissolve it within infected wills. But the field of dispute is not fair. Passion characteristically pleads for pity, usually in the virtuous name of friendship. Its defendant will say that if passion is a disease, the reasonable friend should help, rather than merely abandoning the victim to his fate. Once reason has been wheedled into defending passion, it will have to abandon much of its governing, and erected wit will have been weakened not only in the original victim of passion but also—as future effects will reveal—in the current champion of reason. Under that double jeopardy for essential, liberating reason, a man, his family or community, and his state are all laid open to the tyrannous attacks of fate and fortune.

In the first and most representative of the three contests in Act I, Arcadia's governor idly abandons the proper foreconceit of humanity, together with its several manifestations in Arcadia's laws, social structure, and geography. They should have defied augury. Into its place he thrusts mere fancies, on the one hand, and attempted foreordination, on the other, thus managing to imitate both fortune and fate. His consequent abdication is more "plurisignificant," though much less moving, than that of Lear. In the single person of the abdicating Basilius, the state, the family, and the prince all tumble from wise government toward folly, fragmentation, and tyranny.[11] The state devolves upon louts and rebels, the family is isolated and surrendered to the government of fools and

---

[11] See Edwin A. Greenlaw, "Sidney's *Arcadia* as an Example of Elizabethan Allegory," *Kittredge Anniversary Papers* (Boston and London: Ginn, 1913), pp. 327–337; Sir Fulke Greville, *Life of Sir Philip Sidney*, intro. Nowell Smith (Oxford: Oxford Univ. Press, 1907), p. 11; and S. K. Orgel, "Sidney's Experiment in Pastoral: The Lady of May," *JWCI*, 26 (1963), 202. For related discussion, see A. R. Heiserman, *Skelton and Satire* (Chicago: Univ. of Chicago Press, 1961), pp. 75–88, and John J. O'Connor, *Amadis de Gaule and Its Influence on Elizabethan Literature* (New Brunswick, N.J.: Rutgers Univ. Press, 1970), p. 201.

the vagaries of released passions, and the wise prince becomes a stumbling *senex,* the pawn of a superstitious sibyl or a supposed Amazon. Although Sidney probes the effects of passion in each of his triadic princes by staging three separate considerations of reason and passion, the contest placed first in order is also primary in general effect.

The counsellor to whom Arcadia's governor turns for "confirmation of [his] fancies" (p. 3) is the model Philanax (*friend of the king*). The counsellor is partly at a loss even before he begins answering the king's arguments for passion. In the king's decision to elevate the lout Dametas into a position of trust, Basilius had already begun to misjudge stupidity as plainness and honesty.[12] In an Arcadia thus being turned upside down, Philanax' attempt to correct rather than confirm errors is likely to receive less than a fair hearing. Nevertheless, he gives Basilius counsel from the depth of his judgment, not a sycophant's agreement "for fashion's sake" (p. 3).

At the beginning of their representative debate, human counsel is squarely equated with humanity's foreconceit. Its wisdom is to be sought not after, but before, an act such as Basilius' scouting of Delphos and his virtual abdication, even as a king's proper seers are not sibyls, but his own "wisdom and virtue" (p. 4). They alone can supply "a way of proceeding" (p. 4) that will sustain both inward comfort and outward prosperity. The fancies of "soothsaying sorcerers," like the pressures of each man's infected will, reveal either that which is totally untrue or that which, by virtue of those very fancies, has become so utterly fated that it cannot now be prevented. To the good governor Basilius it should have been a death, to say nothing of a massive folly, to dream of abandoning Ar-

---

[12] Dametas is emblematically converted into "Demaenetus" in Thomas Moffett, *Nobilis: Or a View of the Life and Death of a Sidney,* tr. V. B. Heltzel and H. H. Hudson (San Marino, Calif.: Huntington Library, 1940), p. 74.

cadia to tyrannous fancy when both he and his people needed the security of reason. "Why," demands the counsellor, "should you deprive yourself of governing your Dukedom for fear of losing your Dukedom, like one should kill himself for fear of death?" (p. 4). Folly thus discloses itself to be the herald of fate.

Similarly, good counsel warns the prince that his folly will assure, rather than prevent, the prophesied degradation of his daughters. If he reduces them from their former liberty, he will all but force them, in their curiosity or rebelliousness, to seek the very thing they supposedly were being protected against. Whether having to do with future prospects or present secrets, things hidden or proscribed must "catch men's fancies" and thus defile their minds. Then each such person, even though he may have been infected at second hand, will have to repeat Basilius' degrading descent into the obscure Delphic cavern, trying in darkness to discover golden truth. (The central episodes of the *Old Arcadia* do in fact take place in dark caves and suspect bowers.) By placing his elder daughter and heir in the keeping of a misjudged lout and thus forcing her to wear shepherds' clothing, Basilius is not only fomenting dangerous resentment in her, but also providing a terrible general sign of Arcadia's metamorphic degeneration. Ignorance has become the "mother of faithfulness" (p. 5), not its servant. Philanax sees in Dametas a figure for the general contest of ignorant, fortunal passion with eternal reason: "Oh no, he cannot be good, that knows not why he is good, but stands so far good as his fortune may keep him unassayed; but coming to it, his rude simplicity is either easily changed, or easily deceived. And so grows that to be the last excuse of his fault, which . . . might have been the first foundation of his faith" (p. 5). But as the counsellor's diagnosis ruefully suggests, it is already too late. When his fine peroration urges the prince, "Stand wholly upon your own virtue, as the surest way to maintain you in that you are and to avoid any evil which may be imagined," the prince sophistically replies that one must give way in a wind, and bend like a reed before an enemy or a storm; when Philanax retorts that man should reason from the strength of rocks, not the weakness of reeds, the governor only turns over the state to him, weakly hardened in his fatal "determination" to retire (p. 6). No longer the firm Shepherd King, he will idly play at being a shepherd. Friendship is now bidden to endorse such "fashion," even as reason has been ordered to confirm fancy.

Determined in folly, the lapsed governor is thus no knight of courtesy, flying from court to cot. He is more nearly a Lear who, in the prime of his governing, has surrendered to fancies at once luxurious and timorous. As the rule of reason—that ultimate governor, under providence—has seemed to topple, so now goes the man, the family, and the state.

"The exercise of virtue": Physical heroism *versus* physical love, in Pyrocles with Musidorus

As reason is an image of the governor in man, so Basilius had supplied an image of the political governor in his private and public action. That image is shared by the two northern princes, who are introduced into Basilius' Arcadia after it is already partially "fallen." Because they are in turn introduced to love in this infected site,[13] their mistakes in love are understandable, although not therefore excusable.

Despite the similarity of their contests, the three princes are separate members of a triad. Now at the base, most unhappily, is Basilius, who has wilfully transformed himself from gov-

[13] The condition of Arcadia may help to explain some of the anomalies in the princes' views of love and their somewhat contradictory disguises. See Walter R. Davis, *Idea and Act in Elizabethan Fiction* (Princeton: Princeton Univ. Press, 1969), p. 63.

erning prince into a *senex* governed by fateful foolishness. In the center is the more spirited and physical of the two young princes, Pyrocles of Macedonia. At the summit is Thessalian Musidorus.

The two young princes bear a distinct resemblance to the two brothers in Milton's *Comus*. Their characters within the triplex are suggested or emblematized not only by their names (Pyrocles, *fire and glory;* Musidorus, *gift of the muses*) but also by their coloring and by the related disguises that they choose in Arcadia. The brown Musidorus chooses shepherd's weeds, whereas the "red-and-white" Pyrocles takes an Amazon's martial dress. Together with Basilius, they once might have presented the three "souls" of a prince—spiritual, intellectual, and spirited, which approximately reflect the faculties of understanding, reason, and love. However, in the present Arcadia the virtue of each part of that princely soul, once defined and sustained by both reason and nature, may be converted into a related vice. Basilius has shown the way by sliding from wise governor into foolish recluse. In turn, Pyrocles can transform heroic handsomeness into secretive, effeminate seduction, and Musidorus can alter liberal philosophy into ambush and crude force. Even more strongly than was the case with Basilius, however, the reduction of each of the younger princes by infective passion is resisted by himself and opposed, with great and true strength, by the reason of a counsellor. For the intellectual Musidorus, that counsellor quite properly is himself. Also, in the latter two contests each prince is opposed not by a counsellor from a lower level but by another prince. Their debate thus is ultimately a defense of the idea of a prince.

Before they came to Arcadia, neither of the young men had seemed in any peril of being less than a prince. During their adolescence, the idea of a prince had been set before them as a speaking picture by Evarchus, king of Macedonia and father to Pyrocles. As his name suggests, in his governing Evarchus may have been superior to Arcadia's Basilius; he had never measured greatness except by goodness. Although the two young princes had grown up together in Pindar's Thessaly, it being safer than the warring Plutarchian Macedonia, in either province the example of Alexander or Hercules would have supplied additional heroic images of the prince. Their honorable emulation in the "exercise of virtue" (which soon ironically becomes the cause for a princess' "exercise of patience") had been guided by the knowledge "that the divine part of man was not enclosed in this body for nothing" (pp. 6, 7).

Like young Cyruses or Alexanders, then, the two young princes had cultivated the reasonable "knowledges" that would always be their best ministers, even when, as monarchs, they might have men such as Philanax to be their counsellors (p. 7). Sidney charts their double Cyropaedia with great seriousness. In narrative, he eventually takes them to Cyrus' Asia Minor. Refusing the lure of romantic epic, however, by saying "it is a work for a higher style than mine" (p. 8) and reserving that matter for the *New Arcadia,* he instead swiftly conducts his heroes to Arcadia. It should have been the conclusion of their Grand Tour: "and so taking Arcadia in their way, for the fame of the country, they came thither . . . after that this strange solitariness had possessed Basilius" (p. 8). If they elect to linger in this land of the newly infected will, the young princes will be exercised not in prudent openness of knowledge and action but in the obscurities of blind Cupid and Basilius' fanciful midsummer-night's dream. To their increasingly benighted eyes, Basilius may even come to replace Evarchus as model of a prince, much as their own princely governments also will threaten to slide away because of their virtual abdication or exile.

For the two young princes, the warning note that reason is

now in doubtful dispute with passion sounds first in Pyrocles, the more physical and therefore the more susceptible of the two. It occurs in Diotima's own city, Mantinea. As he stares at a painting of the royal family, young Pyrocles sees only Philoclea (*lover of glory*). Because the picture is comely, he is right to be moved; however, in itself such an emblem may speak either *in malo* or *in bene*. Like the sword of the *Defence,* love, too, may kill a father or save a nation. During the course of the *Old Arcadia* it will seem to do both.

As is often the case in Sidney, Pyrocles' vice, passion, is associated with a virtue, pity. He is first led toward love by the chivalric cause of a woman wronged, familiar to him from Asia Minor. Not understanding the difference between past pity and present curiosity, Pyrocles, like the king before him, follows unknown desire rather than known virtue. He successively assures himself that he wants to see the "architecture" of her lodge; then, to see the model for the painting; finally, with increasingly "uncertain wishes" and "unquiet longings" (p. 9), to see Philoclea herself. His progress could have represented good Platonism or good mental penetration of an emblem. In Pyrocles, however, the movement has been from the spiritual to the physical, as it was for Psyche with Cupid. Still resembling Basilius with the oracle at Delphos, then, he commends "his whole estate" into a woman's cause (p. 9), and indulges his desirous fancy with the same "great speed and secrecy" (p. 10).

Although Pyrocles offers token opposition to his own metamorphosis into an "Amazon," for the most part he continues to follow Basilius; he strives to justify the change, not to oppose it. Curveting in sophistical parodies of pedagogy and philosophy, he resists all "betterings" on the grounds that they surely must break a mind. Then, spinning almost full circle, he insists that the "betterings" undergone in love actually expand the mind into contemplation. When even he cannot quite stomach such excuses, he shifts from defence to praise—first, of the physical Arcadia and its "goddess" (who must be good, for they are a "perfect model of the heavenly dwellings"), and then of woman, the sex he intends to "become" in order to be fully a man. It seems to Musidorus that in every debated point Pyrocles deliberately plunges down the triad from mind to matter and from intelligence to appetite. The great debate between them therefore moves between Pyrocles' defence, and Musidorus' dispraise, of matter and desire.

Like the king's counsellor before him, Musidorus eventually gives way. His arguments are vitiated first by pity and then by a form of charity that forbids further argument, lest friendship too should fall. Apart from that slight reserve of reason, however, passion carries the day.

In the first stage of Musidorus' representative counsel against passion, he uses the sad example of Basilius and Arcadia as a warning to Pyrocles against altering from his essential princeliness:

A mind well-trained and long-exercised in virtue . . . doth not easily change any course it once undertakes, but upon well-grounded and well-weighed causes. . . . I have marked in you . . . a relenting, truly, and slacking of the main career you had so notably begun and almost performed. . . . You now leave [knowledge, arms, and exercise] undone, you let your mind fall asleep . . . you subject yourself to solitariness, the sly enemy that most doth separate a man from well-doing [pp. 10–11].

Pyrocles' arguments similarly suggest that even his words are no longer "knit together to one constant end but rather dissolved [each] in itself, as the vehemency of the inward passion prevailed" (p. 13). Such atomization into fortune and fancy suggests to Musidorus not the governing of a prince but the anarchic dreaming of poor poets and of their principal "fantasical, mind-infected characters," the contemptible creatures whom "children and musicians call lovers" (p. 14). Applied to his cousin, Musidorus' condemnation profits from the guilt of each new association. Although Sidney the ironist sees a cherub who watches Sidney the writer of this same "vain amatorious poem," Sidney the maker knows that the *Old Arcadia* is much more than a mere love story.

Sidney's young prince Pyrocles is no such ironist. Accepting each of his cousin's definitions, stating his design of becoming an Amazon (in a very peculiar imitation of Hercules), and crying out, "The question is not now, whether I shall love or no, but whether loving I shall live or die" (p. 15), he silences advice with the claim of pity. Although his lips beg for wise counsel, his eyes ask only for permission. His cousin cannot find a way to refuse it. In spite of Musidorus' warning that any change of the outward man argues a correspondent blemish upon "the face of so excellent a mind," and his admonition "if reason direct it, we must [and] will do it . . . to say I cannot is childish, and I will not, womanish" (p. 16), his pity has already conceded part of the battle against "womanish" and "unnatural rebellion."

The second stage of the two princes' debate becomes progressively embittered, until charity halts the contest. As Pyrocles had formerly babbled of a green Arcadia, so he now says that woman is better than man; because she is mother and source of all that is fine in man, he says, effeminacy must be the truest manliness, and matriarchy the best possible state. "Transported with a little vehemency," he does not hear the Swiftian sting when he says that women are "capable of virtue." He is too intent upon saying that, "If we love virtue, in whom shall we love it, but in virtuous creatures, without your meaning be, I should love this word of *Virtue* [merely] when I see it written in a book" (pp. 18, 19). To himself, he seems a good Platonist. To Musidorus, he appears as a man who loves only the vulgar Venus while claiming to love the celestial. He warns the younger prince that "as the love of heaven makes one heavenly, and love of virtue virtuous, so doth the love of the world make one become worldly, and this effeminate love of a woman, doth so womanize a man, that, if you yield to it, it will not only make you a famous Amazon, but a launder[er]" (p. 17). It is thus the object of love which largely determines the kind and quality of the lover. In Pyrocles' case, a seeming divine fury reveals only "lust and idleness," even as he himself threatens to slide from "reason . . . to sense, and man to woman" (p. 17).

When the plainant for passion responds, he confirms the older prince's belated fears. With a wink, Pyrocles declares that "there is nothing I desire more, than fully to prove myself a man in this enterprise." He also holds that Philoclea must already have "joined [him] and love together" in a form of marriage. He even usurps Sidney's emphasis on action by vowing, somewhat rakishly, "rather in deeds to perform than in words to defend [his] noble desire" (p. 20).

Before the replacement of reason by desire, reasonable counsel stands helpless. When Musidorus would act Odysseus with one of Circe's beasts, pleading, "Let your own brain disenchant you," he is told that the heart is already too far "possessed" (p. 20). Harshly judging that his cousin is therefore interested only in the "white and red" of physical beauty —an attribute that Pyrocles has properly despised in himself—Musidorus decides to abandon the field. Unwittingly imitating the abdication of Basilius, although motivated by a seeming virtue rather than by vice, he would end his role as counsellor rather than witness his cousin's fall. With him, of course, would go friendship [14] and cousinly relation. Such

[14] For the theme of friendship, see R. W. Zandvoort, *Sidney's Arcadia: A Comparison Between the Two Versions* (Amsterdam: Swets and Zeitlinger, 1929), pp. 143–145; Laurens J. Mills, *One Soul in*

an anticipatory polarization between judge and defendant would be worse, almost, than that which separates men into condemning judges and condemned criminals near the end of the *Old Arcadia*.

However, the pity that Musidorus eventually will demand from Evarchus and which, ironically, has qualified his present counsel, now prophetically wards off such division. If Pyrocles' plea for pity had at first been made cynically, it now becomes a sincere request. In Musidorus' response, a merely permissive pity therefore alters into something like Portia's unstrained mercy.

Moving gradually from jest to earnest, the young hero Pyrocles is at last brought to tears by his cousin's harsh dismissal. He begs, "Have you all the reason of the world, and with me remain all the imperfections?" (p. 21). As a matter of fact, Pyrocles *is* partly in the right, especially in his judgment of the occasional priggishness and self-righteousness of his counsellor. He also is so honestly pained that he falls into an anticipatory faint when he believes that he must suffer loss of friendship even as he undergoes the tidal pull of love. He thus anticipates the *Old Arcadia*'s final appeal from a double human jeopardy, under which a man first experiences a largely unwelcome passion and then suffers from a justice that condemns without curing that passion.

Reassuringly, charity aids reason in Musidorus' reply. After being caught for a moment "in such sort, as might well paint out the true passion of unkindness" (p. 22), the elder cousin is moved to share the defendant's trouble, even though he certainly will not support his argument. In a prophetic act of restorative friendship, he concludes the debate. With the grave smile that is the mark of Sidney's comedy, he judges,

Bodies Twain (Bloomington, Ind.: Principia, 1937), p. 219; and Fritz Caspari, *Humanism and the Social Order in Tudor England* (Chicago: Univ. of Chicago Press, 1954), p. 165.

"Since you are unperfect . . . it is reason you be governed by us wise and perfect men": and commands Pyrocles to love Philoclea, "with all the powers of [his] *mind*" (p. 22; italics added).

Unlike the mere fall that was intimated in Basilius' earlier debate, this second great assay of reason with passion has played out in miniature something of the *Old Arcadia*'s total design. Originally heroic in his reason, every Pyroclean man may become "sick, and sick to the death" (p. 21) in passion. While he is fastened in his brazen world, he may remain unmoved or unaided by either severe judgment or soft pity. On the other hand, mercy, friendship, and images of true virtue may point his way back to a golden world. Whether or not they effect a restoration of the man, those comforters may at the least avoid the creation of new vices by the supposedly "wise and perfect men" of counsel.

Thus the friendship of the cousins, although not their concurrence in reason, is at the last moment significantly renewed. Pyrocles is pleased to commit himself to Musidorus' ambiguous commandment to love Philoclea with his mind. He laughingly says that such an order proves his cousin "far fitter to be a prince, than a counsellor" (p. 22). Unhappily, however, this response defines a prince in terms of Basilius' permissiveness to passion, not in Evarchus' control of it. Musidorus ruefully concurs in the definition, at least as it applies to Pyrocles; counselling no other course, he promises in the name of friendship to remain nearby for help. He unwittingly associates himself with the redefinition, moreover, by promising "to be partaker of any evil may fall unto you" (p. 23). When comic irony brings him to his own encounter with love's "evil," his advance definition will cause him, too, to meet it as a new, transformed, Basilian prince.

At the end of their debate, the altered definition of a prince is also declared by Pyrocles' self-knowing device: an eagle disguised as a dove, yet lying under another dove in love's delicious pain. After the Astrophilian author smilingly announces his own partial complicity because of "compassion for [Pyrocles'] passion," it is small wonder that Pyrocles revises his cousin's charge that the young hero is a "notable philosopher of fancies" to read, instead, an "astronomer [of] heavenly fancies" (pp. 24–25). Both may be right, again; in love, it is possible to be either a selfish Narcissus or an aspiring Pygmalion (p. 24).[15] With that question left open, Pyrocles, in the Amazonian disguise that for a time abdicates heroic manhood, moves toward the lodges that are also, in their way, Arcadian disguises or retreats from proper statehood.

When he is once again alone with himself and his own reason, however, the broadly representative Pyrocles cannot so easily disguise himself from himself. He designs the first poem in the *Old Arcadia*. Not only does it announce the theme of the whole work, but it also stresses much of its Ramistic method—a method as prominent in some of the poems as in the narrative debates. Using twinning partition, he fully acknowledges the two contestants within him. Al-

---

[15] Rosemary Syfret, ed., *Selections from Sidney's Arcadia* (London: Hutchinson, 1966), p. 266, emphasizes that the princes *should* fall in love. Mark Rose, in *Heroic Love* (Cambridge, Mass.: Harvard Univ. Press, 1968), pp. 11–12, develops the conventional association of *hero* and *eros*. The question is not really whether, but how, the princes will meet a passion which may also be a virtue. Similarly, although in Mark Rose's "Sidney's Womanish Man," *RES*, 15 (1964), 353–363, the submission by a man to a woman intimates the unnatural *haec-vir*, such translacing of woman and man—a *condispositio*—might also be good; see John Charles Nelson, *Renaissance Theory of Love: The Context of Giordano Bruno's* Eroici furori (New York: Columbia Univ. Press, 1958), p. 252. Even Amazons might be praiseworthy: see Celeste Turner Wright, "The Amazons in Elizabethan Literature," *SP*, 37 (1940), 442.

though the condition he describes produces not remorse but rather a "determination" in the speaker himself, the poem nevertheless speaks truth for all the principals in *Arcadia;* for the courtiers and shepherds who are affected by the governing Arcadians; and for the reading audience, which will have suffered its own, similar infections:

> Transformed in show, but more transformed in mind,
>   I cease to strive, with double conquest foiled;
> For woe is me, my powers all I find
>   With outward force, and inward treason, spoiled.
>
>   .   .   .   .   .
>
> What marvel then I take a woman's hue,
> Since what I see, think, know, is all but you? [p. 25]

True to Sidney's doctrine of poetry, the overhearing Musidorus is moved (again, to pity), "so lively an action doth the mind, truly touched, bring forth" (p. 26). Within or without the *Old Arcadia,* imitation always is understood to be propagation. The immediate question is whether Musidorus in his way will next imitate the sliding Basilius. If he does, the diagnosis in Pyrocles' lyric will have been triply confirmed: "reason to his servants gives his right,/Thus is [its] power transformed to [man's] will" (p. 25).

"As though his fancies strove to mount up higher":
Celestial *versus* infernal love, in Musidorus alone

When kings turn recluses and heroes become Amazons, it also becomes increasingly apparent that golden Arcadia, both in its general form and its particular agents, can be the victim of inversion or parody. When reason seems weakened or abandoned at the summit, passion, rising from the base, is eager to turn the world upside down. Just before he reveals the transformation of a third hero, Musidorus, Sidney fully displays a possible new pattern for the sliding princes. Up from the lowest part of the human triad climbs the lout Dametas, together with his ungainly wife and unseemly daughter. Because the princess Pamela has been delivered into their care, they now make up a comic but terrible parody of the royal family.

Almost a speaking picture of the passion and folly which now infect Arcadia and of the infected will in general, Dametas has long since been taken up by the credulous king. He lives only by his "dull senses." At his best, he can do no more than lie "upon a sunny bank . . . gaping as far as his jaws would suffer him" (p. 26). (But then, Basilius, too, even now lies sleeping: p. 30). In the past, Basilius had credited the man's bluntness as plainness, his silence as wit, and his ig-norance as virtuous simplicity. In sardonic cross-reflection, if not in virtual identity, the king's credulousness and the subject's stupidity threaten to merge. In much the same way that Pyrocles became a woman for a woman's sake, royal folly has contrived in Dametas "a creature of his own making [and likes] him more and more" (p. 28). Dametas has thus become not only the "principal herdman" but also, almost, the prince.

Although Dametas bawls out a challenge to the truly Her-culean Pyrocles "like him, that plays Hercules in a play," God knows, says heroic Sidney, that Dametas "never had Hercules' fancy in his head" (p. 28). Similarly, whereas Pyrocles' song had moved the princely Musidorus to pity, it has brought Dametas only to obscure rage. Even beauty draws only a curse from this mixture of Chaucerian miller and Shakespear-ian Malvolio.

The question of love, soon to be elevated to the Neopla-tonic empyrean by Musidorus, is also ironically inverted or contested by Dametas. On the principle of marrying for love, which the starry-eyed Pyrocles had just celebrated, Dametas had married the nauseous Miso. Like had led to like, in marriage and parentage; even as Miso displays a "wretched body [and] a froward mind" (p. 27), their daughter is the grisly perfecting of them both. When Pyrocles laments that his pearl, Philoclea, should be kept by such a "vile oyster," he unwittingly describes the plight of Arcadia generally and of himself, more particularly. All Arcadia is now abandoning Apollo and clear reason for sibyls, enigmatic passions—and Dametas.

Despite the lout's stupidity and cowardice, he shows a kind of prescience in challenging Pyrocles as "Thou woman, or boy, or both" (p. 28). In a new version of the king's surrender to a furiously inspired woman, however, Dametas cannot long enjoy his courage. Not only does the disguised Pyrocles confront him like Latona with the churls but also his own two women, either of whom is enough to make any man comically "blind . . . in love" (p. 29), rush out to overwhelm him. Suffering all the dubious rewards of the matriarchy Pyrocles and Basilius have championed, Dametas thus becomes both a splendid comic foil and sober warning, agonizing, "Here is foreign wars abroad and uncivil wars at home, and all with women; now . . . the black jaunders and the red flux take all the wrabbed kind of you!" (p. 30). Gibbering like a Caliban made Dogberry, "making faces like an ape that had newly taken a purgation" (which constitutes a perfect picture of "what a deformity . . . passion can bring a man into, when it is not governed with reason" [p. 30]), he lumbers off to Basilius for help.

Still within the brief interlude before Musidorus' transformation, Pyrocles is introduced to Basilius as the Amazon "Cleophila." Unlike his man, Basilius leers toward the supposed princess. As he had stumbled into identifying himself with Dametas in the past, Basilius also manages to bring the altered Pyrocles into association with himself. Having pointedly commented upon "her" companion solitude in his solitary place, he hardly need attend Pyrocles' huffy retort, "They are never alone . . . that are accompanied with noble thoughts" (p. 31). Nor does it do for Pyrocles to declare virtuously that he must maintain the manners of his (Amazonian) country "in all places," or to celebrate a hero's "private, as . . . public virtues" (p. 32), or to treat of himself as an Odysseus who suffers shipwreck and wandering; because he speaks all this in the character of an Amazon, it is only just that Basilius treat him not like Odysseus but like a "young Siren" (p. 33).

The unfortunate passional association between the old king and the young hero continues when the royal ladies enter, for Pyrocles reacts in the recent Basilian way to Philoclea's black eyes and teasingly clothed body. In another largely questionable sense of identity, Philoclea's garments resemble "her" own, even as her name and his pseudonym "Cleophila" are one. Pyrocles stands transfixed for a moment, like a "well wrought image." Then he takes her hands "by force." Although he addresses her as "Divine Lady," the delight they "conceive" in each other can as yet be only dangerous and seemingly lesbian. Because Pyrocles is "possessed" and given to sensual foreimaginings that fall far short of golden foreconceits, Philoclea is haunted by irony and a fatal, Delphic fancy in courteously saying to him, "Well, I find you an invincible Amazon, since you will overcome in a wrong matter" (pp. 34, 35).

And using some associative irony of his own, the author invites his supposed audience of listening ladies to serve as index to these falls: do they not sometimes feel the passion of envy, or perhaps that of love? With that question, he shifts to Musidorus, the highest, because most intellectual, of the three princes. Love will now contest with reason at an intellectual summit. It is not necessarily a moral summit as well, however, as later events will show.

The third contest of governing reason with passion occurs

for the most part within the individual prince, Musidorus, and is therefore disposed in narrative rather than dialoguic "drama." The interlude with Dametas and the royal family having provided an interval sufficient for Musidorus' offstage transformation, the presently most reasonable and aspiring of the passion-stricken princes is then reintroduced. His new apparel supplies a "picture" of his inward state. As the transformations of Basilius and Pyrocles had been sharply sketched by an emblematic external property—the solitary desert, for Basilius, and the clothing of a woman, for Pyrocles—so Musidorus' transformation is indicated by his shepherd's attire.

In the latest contest, however, a prince's altered clothing is not so much a deceitful disguise as an imitation of the state to which his princess has been reduced. Although she remains a princess, Pamela has been humbled into association with Dametas' family. Because she now must wear "shepherdish apparel," pastoral associations cluster around her: her breasts excel the "fair mountainettes" of Tempe in Musidorus' own Thessaly, and her impresa shows a "perfect white lamb tied at a stake, with a great number of chains, as if it had been feared lest the silly creature should do some great harm" (p. 33). Although the meaning supplied by a motto for the picture is usually the "life of an impresa," as Sidney notes, Pamela's picture instead wittily "took silence as the word of the poor Lamb, showing such humbleness, as not to use her own voice for [the] complaint of her misery" (p. 33). If her impresa expresses some anger with her father and disdain for Dametas (after all, her shepherdish dress is cut from russet velvet), in the main it serves to show not only the pastoral form of her degradation but also an inherent Christian exaltation. The latter possibility is developed movingly and at great length in the *New Arcadia*. In the *Old*, Sidney's major emphasis continues to be fixed upon the degeneration that occurs when princes, properly the Shepherds of their people, become mere rustic clowns.

As the princess Pamela, whose state and emblems have anticipated those chosen by Musidorus, had been humbled by
politics, the gazing prince Musidorus is humbled by love of
her. He too has now been chained and rusticized. Even as
Sidney was elevating Pamela and Musidorus to a Platonic
and Christian height, then, he was also preparing a dialectical
revenge upon the sententious young Troilus/Hippolytus.
Iconographic values aside, it is not necessarily worse to be a
transvestite Amazon than a sacrificial sheep in chains. In
neither case is Macedonia or Thessaly served. Were transforming love to be well used, however, it might yet serve the
ends of humanity, and therefore of providence.

As the younger prince had entered the work upon the question whether love was good or evil fortune, so Musidorus is
seen "with his eyes sometimes cast up to heaven, as though
his fancies strove to mount up higher; sometimes thrown
down to the ground" (pp. 35–36). These gestures stress the
"disjuncts" of his personal debate. In a lyric paralleling Pyrocles' song of transformation, he confesses that shepherd's
dress, like Amazon's clothing, is the external sign of an inner
change. However, instead of repeating Pyrocles's claim that
the lover is "with outward force, and inward treason spoiled,"
the loftier Musidorus envisions a probable Neoplatonic ascent. Because love gains the assent of his will, he reverses
Pyrocles' terms: "Yield outward show, what inward change
he tries" (p. 36). Yet even Musidorus throws himself upon
the currents of his "destinies" as if he were a Basilius with
the oracle rather than a reasoning man with providence. His
new sense of helplessness probably is not altogether bad. Insofar as he acted the Hippolytan prig with Pyrocles, he has
now been usefully, humanly humbled into a semblance of
Pamela's lamb.

Despite some wavering, his sharp intellect has not yet been
reduced. It shows itself not only in some fairly acute psychology (Musidorus wonders, disjunctively, whether love has

proved so powerful in him because it would be "bravely revenged on him," or because "his very resisting made the
wound the crueller"), and in the inquisitiveness proper to
desire, but also in the somewhat chilly use he makes of
Menalcas, the good shepherd from whom he borrows clothing: having hired him to go to Thessaly, Musidorus will arrange that he be arrested and detained "till [his servant in
Thessaly] heard his further pleasure" (p. 37). Such usage anticipates his later projected use of force against Arcadia. As
was the case with Pamela, then, his shepherdish attire cloaks
some regal hauteur. If his disguise is more honorable than
that of Pyrocles, especially in being associated with the Arcadian shepherds' high doing and thinking, it is thus not
without its own deceitfulness.

On this occasion, when Pyrocles learns of the latest fall
from Musidorus, the conference of a second prince does not
bring counsel, but only the amused sense of a common fate or
sophisticated complicity. Pyrocles' question about "the goddess of those woods" who can thus transform men (p. 37),
however, is essentially serious. Is love's power to be that of
Cottyto, Circe, Flora, or Venus? Has the old law "that love
is a passion, and that a worthy man's reason must ever have
the masterhood" (p. 38) been transcended, or has it only
been ignored? Must the disjunctive argument indicated in
Musidorus' address to love—"Celestial or infernal . . . heavenly or hellish" (p. 38)—be resolved only into damnation?

Whatever the issue may be, Pyrocles in his turn comes to
a permissive pity, as a "lively" expression of grief by the
speaker once more creates a Sidneian impression in the
hearer. For a moment the two princes move forward together
again in their original, representative friendship. They are
now somewhat blindly "led by the common course of humanity," however, rather than by knowledge and heroism.
Using that image of a common way, they find it possible to

"lament their own mishaps." So much the worse for themselves and their people, if in the "common course of humanity" the princes can find brazen approval for the ethical transformation of the one "in sex" and the political metamorphosis of the other "in state" (p. 39). Supposed human nature would then be asked to excuse a fatal breach of humanity.

With the transformation of the third prince of the masculine, largely political triad completed, Sidney draws the narrative of Act I to a symphonic close. Because the Act has been an emblem and an argument as well as one part in a "very stage play of love" (p. 50), the principals are associated with a summary emblem and argument at the curtain: the eruptive attack of wild beasts upon Arcadia, where "such beasts had never before been seen" (p. 42). Having shown the depth to which Arcadia may fall, the Act itself then proceeds to a complete close with a radically different lyric "action," presented by choric shepherds.

Association or identification of the principal characters with beasts—all of them, that is, except Pamela—both precedes and follows the actual attack. The two men who are primary causes of Arcadian weakness are handled first. In swift summary strokes, Dametas is prophetically shown to be fooled by gold, his senses having always been "masters of his silly mind" (p. 40), and Basilius, in debate with himself ("a sufficient eclogue in his own head," p. 41), is seen to let honor fall before lust. Just as the party nears the pastoral theater, they are attacked by a "monstrous lion, with a she-bear." [16] The two princes, reverting to their proper characters as true heroes, soon destroy the animals. But it is now the turn of Pyrocles and Musidorus, who have launched a concealed erotic attack

[16] See Giordano Bruno, *The Expulsion of the Triumphant Beast*, tr. Arthur D. Imerti (New Brunswick, N.J.: Rutgers Univ. Press, 1964), pp. 113, 129, for association of both animals with Arcadia.

upon Arcadia even as the princesses have "wounded" them, to be associated with the beasts. Although the lion actually attacked Philoclea, Pyrocles almost as brutally desires her. In a rather terrible form of the Pyroclean sequence *see-think-know,* the queen, Gynecia, also demonstrates the pull toward bestial longing: "Doubt framed a desire in her to know, and desire . . . a longing to enjoy, [reducing] her whole mind to an extreme and unfortunate slavery" (p. 44); soon, imitating the she-bear, she will hate her own daughter. Because Pyrocles' description of the lion as an "unnatural beast, which contrary to his own kind would have wronged Princess' blood" (p. 44) approximates the charge to be laid against him in Act V, Philoclea can be described as a secretly willing Arethusa, fleeing Alpheus. Even Musidorus has all but duplicated the bear, which would have tendered Pamela a "mortal embracement" (p. 47); when she swoons, he anticipates his later near-rape by "softly taking her in his arms [and seizing] the advantage to kiss and rekiss her a hundred times" (p. 48). Finally, when the Falstaffian Dametus rushes from hiding to kick the dead bear, complaining that "such beasts should be suffered in a commonwealth," precedent and consequent identifications of the principals with the beasts is complete.

Among the Arcadians, only Pamela has resisted the general pull toward beastly passion. She alone, in pushing away the "newcome shepherd" Musidorus with "great disdain" (p. 48), has made "open war upon herself, and [obtained] the victory." Otherwise, all Arcadia seems adrift like Dametas, whose "heart was framed never to be without [immoderate] passion" (pp. 48–49). In the meantime, the golden eclogues have been delayed past darkness by the general eruption of disorder.

Yet even at this worst, heroism and heroic love can reassert themselves. When the royal women nurse Pyrocles, we are reminded that they have learned medicine in order to "minister to virtuous courage; which in those worthy days,

was even by ladies more beloved, than any outward beauty"
(p. 46). Partly for the same reason, Gynecia associates Pyrocles' feat with that of Hercules with the Nemean lion. Although the great virtues have been vitiated or abandoned,
they have not been erased.

At the end of the narrative portion, Sidney makes a somewhat misleading gesture toward both historicity and a distancing *in illo tempore* by pretending to report from "ancient records of Arcadia" (p. 47). He probably intended it as
a quick bow to Aristotle, who had recommended using heroes
known to history or legend. However, he never really shifts
his ground for imitation: the *Old Arcadia* is *of* an idea, and
for an audience. Sidney frequently associates the actual "fair
ladies" of his immediate audience with the tale. His still
more general audience is thereby reminded that they also
inhabit this timeless "stage play." Although the stage may
now be framed by fortune on one side and by man's common
"unquiet imaginations" (p. 50) on the other, the horizon
within remains unlimited.

"We shepherds are like them that under sail": Youth *versus*
    age, upon love

Sidney's eclogues are astounding performances. They await
a full study in their own right [17]—one that is almost certain
to find infinitely more to praise for their accomplishment
than to censure, because they failed to make classical metre
speak in English. In the present discussion, they will not be
considered for their poetry but for their contribution as

[17] See the impressive beginning by Elizabeth Dipple, "The 'Fore
Conceit' of Sidney's Eclogues," *Literary Monographs*, 1 (1967), 3–47,
as well as Ringler, *The Poems of Sir Philip Sidney*, pp. xxxviii–xxxix,
and John Thompson, *The Founding of English Metre* (New York:
Columbia Univ. Press, 1961), pp. 139–155.

choric statement within the *Old Arcadia*'s broad pattern and proceeding.

In pattern, the eclogues stand lyrically with the golden foreconceit from which man, including the characters of the *Old Arcadia,* has been fashioned. It had once been imaged in the ruler. Because the shepherds who sing the eclogues treasure the original form of man so much, its seeming loss in the present Arcadia induces both yearning celebrations and general laments. Formally, although the set that closes each Act comprises a small action in its own right (even to the point of moving in approximately five "acts"), the four sets of eclogues taken together constitute a vast, responsive chorus, moving parallel with the narrative. It celebrates the original golden Arcadia and mourns the threat to it of "unlawful desires" (p. 53). If the Arcadians could hear, it would offer them counsel, in a great debate with the narrative sections. Unhappily, the princes react like the court at Hamlet's dumb show.

Considered in their entirety, the eclogues present a hymn to heavenly beauty, and an elegiac lament that men have fallen away from it; a tribute to heavenly and human love, and a condemnation of their lustful parodies; praise for the good governor and his peace, and scathing satire upon Basilian irresponsibility; and a high Platonic overview of mortal toils, together with a hushed, sympathetic awareness of mortal griefs. Although the eclogues are in one sense the most conventional materials in the two *Arcadias,* seeming to fix the works in the pastoral-romantic line of Sannazaro and Montemayor, even they are often put to radical, experimental use. Like many Greek choruses, they offer themselves as being simultaneously above all human time; aware of it in its most general, mythic dimensions; and involved both judicially and emotionally in the local events of the narrative present.

Perhaps the best introduction to the general achievement of the eclogues is Philisides. At first, he seems to be no more than an autobiographical figure out of Sannazaro. The character Philisides, however, has little to do with Sidney, but much to do with a broad philosophical and literary *methexis* (the participation by an audience in a fiction). Like some of the eclogues themselves, in the course of the work Philisides grows from comic snappishness to profound melancholy. And like the "true" Arcadian shepherds, he thinks and feels about divinity and man in the most comprehensive and Platonic way. His vision includes man's fall—a fall which involves Philisides, too, because of his distance from an adored golden idea. A portion of the human fall that he sings in the Third Eclogues is not only a demonstration of Sidney's integral use of shepherds and eclogues but also the literary and ideological center of the *Old Arcadia*. In it, he praises the God who sits "beyond the heaven, far more beyond our wits"; lowers his gaze to a paradisal "harmless empire" enjoyed by cooperative animals; sees lordly man enslave them, even as he enslaves himself with bloody appetites; and finally warns tyrannical man that a "plaint of guiltless hurt doth pierce the sky," while at the same time encouraging the mild sufferers "in patience" (pp. 237–242). To all this, Philisides' auditorial "sheep" have listened for love, not acquisition of knowledge. But of course, as the *Defence* insists, to receive right poetic delight is also to receive wisdom.

Such a song radically joins universal with particular, even as it "translaces" fiction with life and life with fiction. Not only is the image of a true idea as applicable in "real" history as it is in contemplative ethics and politics, but also the little myth supposedly is reported from Sidney's real-life mentor, Languet; is sung to Arcadians, within the fiction; and is heard by auditorial "sheep," and read by his "flock" in a real audience, on still other planes of time and being. And if

Sidney himself seems to look out from his work "as a painter of old Italy [would] set his face in a dark corner of his canvas," [18] he does so not to step out into life but to invite the living reader into the fiction. Philisides, like all the rest of Sidney's fiction, is an image of the divine idea, whereas life in itself is now only a "poor bating place." Pastoral such as that of Philisides and the shepherds, or that of "Lycidas" and "Arcades," employs fictive reflections from both actuality and literary conventions first to define, and then to transcend, them. Because such fiction ultimately is an image of divine reality, it can open the eyes directly to visions of that truth.

For that matter, the shepherds of Arcadia are not mere workaday shepherds, as the transformation of Musidorus into their kind has already suggested. He is never more truly one of them than when "his fancies strove to mount up higher" (p. 35). They themselves are far more like Athenian citizens than rustic clowns. No "base shepherds" (p. 52), they own their flocks and thus may serve as images of monarchy and priesthood. Together with some visiting strangers from "great houses" they had flourished under Basilius' shepherd-like care, which was manifested both in international peace and in personal artistic patronage. Sometimes, their eclogues under "hidden forms" (resembling those of the *Old Arcadia* itself) treat of the loftiest matters, divine as well as human. For the most part, therefore, pastoral complaint and contest have been transformed by Sidney into meditative lyric and political and ethical dialogue. As is usually the case in Sidney's *Arcadias*, the fair Grecian attitude is more nearly that of the temple, academy, and stoa than of the pasture or fold.

The eclogues commence under Dametas' direction; in theatricals as in politics, he has assumed management. Reflecting

---

[18] James Joyce, *Ulysses* (New York: Viking, 1961), p. 209. See André Chastel, "Le tableau dans le tableau," in *Stil und Überlieferung des Abendlandes* (Berlin, 1967), I, 15–29.

the tides of attraction and jealousy that are coursing within the noble audience, the first exercise is a dance to Pan. It proceeds into a ring dance in which half the company sings, "We love, and have our loves rewarded," to which the other half responds ("as in a choir") with the leaden echo, "We love, and are no whit regarded." "All joining their voices," they conclude with reintegrative concord: "No music kindly without love" (pp. 53, 54).

The experience of the princes in Arcadia had already raised the question of whether love is Heaven or Hell. The shepherds have now thrust the question into the center of the first eclogues. It is not resolved here. Instead, it proceeds across the four sets of Eclogues, debated all the way by youth and age, the two major ages of man. During that extended contest, cocky youth loses it callowness and joins the general choric voice of humanity. Similarly, grouchy age abandons its mirthless cantankerousness.

In the immediate present, however, the rivalry of youth and age within the Eclogues is a standoff. Each party is guilty of some folly. As such, they offer obvious mirrors to the young princes and to old Basilius.

Responding to the troubled heroism of the principals and thereby joining the prose and verse sections, the older shepherd Lalus *(speaking, singing)* begins the eclogues. He observes that young Musidorus (now known as a shepherd, "Dorus") is noble, but sees in him the "extreme tokens of a troubled mind." He therefore asks that love be brought "to a more large expressing" (p. 54). He is certain that if the idea of love is fully known by means of a "signifying" song, the shadows of discord and isolation will flee away. In their contest, Musidorus, whose fancies have reached as high as heaven, properly achieves a noble victory in style.

On the natural level of Pan (and Pyrocles), Lalus celebrates "health" in love and friendship among one's fellows. Pan is "too mean a match," however, for Musidorus' more nearly divine "infection" (p. 55); he and his muse (no less than Urania, for the moment) have celestial objects. If Musidorus had once argued that the "love which lover hurts is inhumanity," he now wisely finds such lower "reason vanished" into erected wit. In it, even a *Liebestod* in the body fould not be unreasonable. Only cruel honor (specifically, that which arises from Musidorus' seeming to be of a different class than Pamela) keeps his merit unregarded. And if on the natural level Lalus and Pan would weave a charming circle around a lover, Musidorus and the Muse would leave Pamela as free and masterful as the sun. In place of Lalus' gift of sheep and myrtle bowers, the spiritual lover vows high adoration: "I have no shows of wealth, my wealth is you,/ My beauty's hue, your beams; my health, your deeds" (p. 58). Such spiritual ardor almost inevitably produces torment along with ecstasy:

> I find no shade, but where my sun doth burn;
> No place to turn, without, within it fries.
> Nor help by life, or death, who living dies [p. 59].

In contrast, the shepherd Lalus is happy to be a tame cat in love. Musidorus knows, however, that he himself can exist only through the demanding vision of celestial love, for in all things else he is an emblem of self-division.

Once the double laud of love is completed, a Marvellian Dicus (*justice*) demands the floor. His song is a Ramistic dissentany that expresses absolute hatred for erotic love. His picturing device shows Cupid as a bestial hangman—Argus-eyed, horned, ass-eared, darkness-seeking, cloven-hoofed. Familiar from emblem books, this monster controls as his creatures "a goodly man and an excellent fair woman" (p. 60), who stand for Adam and Eve as well as each later human couple. He lures all mankind to come to him and be hanged. If Dicus can degrade the Pan of Lalus into such a Cupid, he will find no place at all for Musidorus' Platonic fancies; they are all dismissed as "vain conceits" and "deceits" (p. 61). In all of Cupid's several ages, he adds, he is cruel: in his generation, beast upon beast; in his proceeding, partly Oedipal, involving "father's death, and mother's guilty shame" (p. 61); and in his promises, doubly lustful, seeming always to manifest two desires, complementary to his two horns and his cloven feet:

> To narrow breasts he comes all wrapped in gain,
>   To swelling hearts he shines in honor's fire,
> To open eyes all beauties he doth rain,
>   Creeping to each with flattering of desire [p. 62].

For Dicus, love is not only the world's great tempting courtier but also its tyrannical executioner. Both wanton boy and Father Time, love leads on the dance of lust, which is also the dance of death.

By implication, at least, the topic of love has been exchanged gradually for that of the differing temperaments of youth and age. That issue fuels the next contest. Before Geron (*age*) and Philisides (*starlover*) take up the poetic combat, however, sour Dicus is answered with a long prose narrative by "a young shepherd named Histor" (*history;* p. 62). This story contrapuntally interrupts lyrics here, as poems earlier were set into the narrative prose. It also provides some account of the two young princes in their past heroism.

In Asia Minor, where the younger Musidorus and Pyrocles had once exercised their unclouded virtue, the princess Erona (like Dicus in the eclogues, and like the early Musidorus in

Arcadia) had rebelled against love, going so far as to cast down her city's images of Cupid. Cupid is revenged when she falls in love with a base, Dametan man. In a clear warning to Arcadia in the present, her country is soon weakened by her love. After it is conquered by Persia, her base husband is executed. She herself must be burned at the stake at the end of this "fatal year" unless the two princes return to save her. Thus not only Macedonia and Thessaly, but also Asia Minor, needs the princes to be active heroes, not languishing, "transformed" lovers.

Emblematically, the case of Erona (*love*) shows not only the torment of love but also the need for its being governed; her private passion clearly should have been tempered and reconciled with public action. In the *New Arcadia,* this kind of reflective instruction will dominate the direct narrative. In the *Old,* the princes do not really respond either to the lesson or to her summons, resolving only "as soon, as this their present action (which had taken full possession of all their desires) were wrought to any good point, they would . . . take in hand that journey" (p. 67). The issue presented by her need of the princes is never really resolved in the *Old Arcadia.* However, a poet like Spenser might have judged the two princes idling in Arcadia to be dangerously like Verdant, with Acrasia, at the Bower of Bliss.

Histor had promised to repeat a song that was concerned with the tale of Erona—a song of lamentation sung by her later true lover, Plangus (*lamentation*), to the "wise shepherd Boulon" (*counsel;* p. 63). Irritated by all youth and its longwinded love melancholy, Geron interrupts. Too heartily clapping Philisides on the shoulder, he says that "sweet tunes do passions ease" (p. 68). The abstracted young Philisides retorts that the flammable oil of expressing love can scarcely cool youth's fire. Their debate, which enlarges upon the issue between Boulon and Erona's lover, proceeds from that distinction: age recommends a somewhat chilly self-control, whereas youth asserts its ardent, yet fatal, control by love.

Somewhat like all the counsellors in Act I, Geron begins by chiding that advice becomes difficult when a victim tries "all his force against himself" and makes every conception serve that cause. He urges rebellion against the "tyrant love" and the concepts that surround it: "Let not a glittering name thy fancy dress/ In painted clothes because they call it love;/ There is no hate that can thee more oppress." Philisides must begin by "raising up, upon thy self to stand," so that he is never mastered by either love or fortune (p. 69).

Believing himself to be pestered by a Polonius, the young Philisides barks out, "O Gods, how long this old fool hath annoyed/ My wearied ears!" (p. 70). He cannot believe that young people in Geron's time possessed the recommended "hearts of brass, wise heads, and garments trim." As for the question of age in itself, no one wants old houses, rams, or horses; what one wants, regardless of years, is the "oldest mind/ With virtue fraught, and full of holy fear" (p. 70). In his response, Geron really agrees: man is to be defined not by old or young beasts but by "strongest soul." The proof of his strength must come from his purging fancy and love, which cause a man "to be a player of [his] own annoy." A return by Philisides to general knowledge and government would "let special care upon thy flock be stayed." The impatient (and inattentive) Philisides cuts off the debate by saying that "one look of hers" is all his government (p. 71); the question is thus closed before it was broached. The young Histor appends a smug coda: "Thus may you see how youth esteemeth age" (p. 72).

The attractive ardor of Pyroclean youth seems to have triumphed over the sententious caution of age. Geron, thoroughly "out of countenance," appears to admit as much by hastening on to the next poem, so that he can savage youth.

However, the general Arcadian context, in which good counsel so often has had to give way before wilful passion, suggests that Geron has the better of the argument, although seeming to lose the immediate debate.

Disgruntled, Geron seeks some comfort in consorting with Mastix (*scourge*), "one of the repiningest fellows in the world" (p. 72)—though scarcely because of love's melancholy. In a reminder of the beast emblem that closed Act I, they find Geron's Virgilian dogs better than young men, because they are both more governed and more governable. Geron is in part right to scold two passionate young men for abandoning their flocks; Macedonia and Thessaly, to say nothing of Asia Minor, even now await the doting princes. Mastix, by finding the fault to be general, implicates Basilius as well:

> What marvel if in youth such faults be done?
>   Since that we see our saddest shepherds out,
> Who have their lesson so long time begun,
>
>   .   .   .   .   .
>
> Either asleep be all, if nought assail,
>   Or all abroad, if but a cub start out [p. 73].

He is sure, however, that discordant, beastly faults will work "justice"—if only because men will "their own faults disclose" (p. 73). Among such, youth (and most of the present Arcadia) is judged to be "woemen, manwould, and men effeminate" (p. 74). The satire always available to pastoral has struck very close to home; it also has virtually repeated the terms of the Delphic oracle.

Frightened, Geron urges proper caution in speaking of the powerful: parrots can get cages for talking in "great men's bowers" (p. 74), whereas swans turn to safer, if more melancholy, silence. (The melancholy Philisides now might have warrant to be amused at a political swan.) Becoming cynically politic, Geron further advises that madness in great ones go entirely unwatched. That disclaimer does not really hold, however, when he finally asks, "Who makes us such judges over all?" (p. 75). The stance that Mastix and Geron have taken with the general foreconceit of humanity qualifies them to be judges, even if they are sourly old and grouchy.

The present Arcadian audience, refusing all application of the debate to themselves, laughs the old men off the stage. The final set of poems therefore goes to the two disguised princes, who either directly or complicitously should have stood to the judgment of being "woemen, manwould, men effeminate."

The general judgment proper to the choric eclogues is reduced somewhat in the self-serving princes. Whereas all of the shepherds (even the most comical) were open to the exalted conceptions of divine wisdom, the two princes, who by nature should have the same conceptions and whose minds by training should reach to heroic knowledge as well, in some measure alter the "hidden form" of the shepherds' fictions into disguises, and use the eclogues to make concealed declarations of love. Excellent though love may be, concealment can make it as suspect for them as it is for Viola in *Twelfth Night*. Wracked "betwixt fear and desire" (p. 75), Musidorus enacts a new "woeman" Paris, baffled by Nature, Fortune, and Love. The "effeminate" Pyrocles plays gracefully with the conceit of a wasteful death in love unsatisfied, as opposed to a resurrection in love satisfied. In alternating strophes, they sing together a long laud of the love which, although it must be pastorally disguised in the woods, is as fine as that of the palace. Even as they rhetorically bless love's "mishaps," however, they find its fortunate falls to remain "veiled in a contrary subject" (p. 78).

The general judgment asked by the *Old Arcadia* takes note of the contradiction, holding that if Nature is partly opposed to abdication and disguised love, then the princes who praise such mishaps "do seem to rebel, seem fools in a vain suit" (p. 78). Furthermore, the seemingly humble attitude of Musidorus may be as questionable as Basilius' exile, together with his choice of Dametas:

O glittering miseries of man, if this be the fortune,
　Of those fortune lulls, so small rest rests in a kingdom,
What marvel though a prince transform himself to a pastor?
　Come from marble bowers, many times the gay harbor of
　　anguish,
Unto a silly cabin, though weak, yet stronger against woes

　　　. . . . .

Then, do I think indeed, that better it is, to be private
In sorrow's torments than tied to the pomps of a palace [p. 82].

And Pyrocles responds in kind. Although his rhetorical proceeding intends to justify his conduct, the general pattern reproves it—largely, again, because of its similarity to Basilius' political weakness:

Jailor I am to myself, prison and prisoner to my own self,
　Yet be my hopes thus placed, here fixed lives all my recomfort,
That that dear diamond where wisdom holdeth a sure seat
　(Whose force had such force so to transform, nay to reform me)
Will at length . . . pity the wound festered so strangely within
　me [p. 85].

Having made love secretly to their employment in making love to their mistresses, Pyrocles and Musidorus also retire from the eclogues. They pointedly remind the princesses that the high conceits of the songs should be penetrated by "the parties meant" (p. 86).

With the eclogues completed, the actors all melt into a sleep. It is no reformation, however, but only the "elder brother of Death" (p. 86). It breeds the passionate schemes that will lead directly to a seeming death by poison. Nevertheless, the original pattern for Arcadia, together with its representation in the reason of counsellors and the precepts of the shepherds, offers a final speaking picture for love: "Love is better than a pair of spectacles to make everything seem greater which is seen through it; and then is it never tongue-tied . . ." (p. 86).

"Desire holds the senses open, and love's conceits [are] very quick" : The Second Book or Act

In order to create an image of man in his ethical as well as his political part and thus to show the fair as well as the brave, in Book I Sidney had matched each of his triad of princes with a private princess of like faculties. Had Arcadia remained golden, each such union would have been perfect in its kind. (In the reintegrative marriages that close the *Old Arcadia,* they actually become so.) Each would also have been a token of the union of state and household, although any of the lovers in himself will of course transverse those seeming boundaries as princes become husbands and fathers and princesses remain potential monarchs. But in Book I, the world of Arcadia had degenerated from gold into brass. Book II thus must follow a darkening action in which each of the princes had in some measure abdicated reason and "outward government." After compromising his political being, each has assumed a private role or disguise—burgher, Amazon, shepherd. This duplicity has falsified or infected his private dealings with the princesses, even as it has made for a division within his own "inward self."

Thus Arcadia's princesses, who in their triad represent womankind, do not have the chance to meet love openly and "heroically." Like the politics of Book I, the ethics of Book

II suffers from Delphic obscurity. The earlier metamorphoses of Basilius, Musidorus, and Pyrocles will now be paired with similar degenerations in Gynecia, Pamela, and Philoclea. The insistent parallels of the two Acts will extend also to an emblematic rebellion at the Act II curtain and to love laments in the Second Eclogues. Because clouds from Act I lower across all of Act II, love's labor in Arcadia must be severely jeopardized, if never quite lost.

In many ways, the principally feminine and ethical concerns of Act II are more problematical than the political issues of Act I. The three princes had acted in full knowledge of what they were doing, all their claims about fate to the contrary. A simple act on their part, even now, could still enfold love within the primary pattern of reason, where it would serve, not oppose, political and personal honor. But for the Arcadian women, on the other hand, there can be no such direct knowledge or will. Because their lovers are disguised, love itself is obscure. Healthy natural attraction is forced to work against duplicities even of sex. Therefore the noble but bewildered princesses slide willy-nilly into roles and attitudes that are demeaning or compromising.

Whereas the descent of the hero had proceeded from encounters with passions opposite to the heroic, the alteration of the loving women occurs, far more wrenchingly, within the province of love itself. If the princes think of the women as being at once the objects of Platonic-Petrarchan adoration and also the objects of sly lust, and if their related disguises make the princesses seem to themselves both faithful princesses and women raging with abnormal erotic appetites, then the context for love will make the princesses at once commanding, and dependent; conventionally cruel mistresses, whose confidence has nevertheless been rakishly abused; bold, and abject. Thus, love turns Gynecia into a kind of Phaedra, Philoclea into a seeming lesbian, and Pamela into a possible

Basilian deserter of her royalty. In their several falls, each woman is shamed by the form her love takes and yet at the same time lured into the unknown by its very obscurity. Largely as a result of Basilius' related concealment of Arcadia from itself, the pattern for love flies from proper mystery to wholly improper isolation and desperate secrecy.

For such reasons as these, the "speaking" of Act II is far less a matter of public dialogue than of private, interior debate, which is pointed by the rhetorical figure *anthypophora*. These self-contesting monologues frequently are overheard by one of the princes, however, and on such occasions provoke a secret revelation of identity. Although recognitions should provide enlightenment, such partial and secretive disclosures serve only to increase the general conspiratorial obscurity. When love's truth is disclosed in covert, seductive fragments, it becomes almost a falsehood.

If the men in Book I had at times railed against a pleasing passion that could reduce public heroism to private servility, so much more must the noble Arcadian women lament the Euripidean pain of their reduction. However, they are not free from duplicity of their own. No matter how ardently they may pray for a pattern of honesty, their private judicial proceeding is uncertain. Although reasonable judgment tells them what they have been, fancy—not entirely the princes' deceit—disturbs the prospect of what they may, or ought, or must now be.

"In shame there is no comfort, but to be beyond all bonds of shame": Gynecia, and the disclosure of Pyrocles

Because Sidney seeks lively images in which to "incarnate" permanent ideas, his way is not that of allegory. Basilius was not a personification of monarchy, but a representative monarch. Similarly, although her name suggests that she is to be that abstraction called *woman,* Gynecia is instead a representative for women. The royal Arcadians thus are manifestations or embodiments of the idea of the governor of a state and the mother-governess of a family, struggling with passions that oppose those functions; they are not Ideas.

Like the public Basilius of Act I, with whom she is parallel in order of treatment as well as in age and temperament, Gynecia has had long practice in good domestic government. Neither the king nor the queen can attribute passion to youth or inexperience. When Gynecia penetrates the disguise of Pyrocles, she therefore knows that her emotion is desire. Would it have occurred without Basilius' abdication and Pryocles' disguise? Probably not. As Philanax had warned, idleness and obscurity "catch men's fancies" and defile them (p. 5). Thus, although Gynecia is partly the victim of political circumstances, she knows far more of what she is doing than her inexperienced daughters can. She must therefore know quite well what she does to herself and her daughters in blindly following desire. She has to reverse the direction Sidney had pointed out in the *Defence:* whereas he had pictured a person in whom reason "hath so much overmastered passion, as that the mind hath a free desire to do well" (*Defence,* p. 19), she exists in the tormented state of one in whom desire has overpowered the will, even though reason remains urgent. She cannot fool herself, as the princes had; she cannot command herself, as Pamela will; and she thus becomes a grand Racinian expression for the tension of knowledgeable reason and knowing passion.

As is his custom, Sidney does not give us a physical description of the queen. It probably is unneeded, as is knowing the color of Lady Macbeth's slippers or the design of Jocasta's brooch. Although readers will find Gynecia far less "realizable" than such figures, partly because her dramatic situation is incomparably less circumstantial and urgent, in one way she is fuller than they are. Whereas we envision them within the full pressure of tragedy, we see her in the preceding pressure of deliberation. If they become great exemplars of given kinds of passion, she is an anatomist of the passion that knows itself. If they are magnificent gestures, she is a great analytical voice.

Act II unfolds, emblematically, at night. Darkness has brought only envenomed restlessness to the queen, who speaks for "womankind" (p. 88). Even remembered virtue is an agony, because it can offer no antidote to an infected will. When her "eyes of judgment" play the counsellor to her, she sees all the "evils she was like to run into . . . the terrors of her own conscience . . . her long exercised virtue, which made this vice the fuller of deformity." "No small part of her evils was that she was wise to see her evils," in full envy of Apollo's "unspotted light" and unaltered course. Yet when wisdom stands in "imperfect proportion" to such a will, it resembles the pity of Act I; it becomes almost an accomplice to evil. Much as she may apostrophize the universe, asking that it hate "an overthrown worm," a heart "[full] of wild ravenous beasts" (like those in Act I), Gynecia refuses any foresight that might also prevent such horrors (pp. 87–88). Instead, collapsing upon fate or fortune as Basilius had done, she contends that destiny must have commanded her solitude and then impelled Pyrocles upon her.

Yet the queen is not utterly swept away by her passion or its "furious," sybilline rhetoric. Her acute mind remains capable of objective irony, even though irony, too, confirms the intensity of her desire. Thus when it appears to her that Pryocles' "foretaken conceit" of disguise is really directed to her daughter, she fears that the worst part of erotic fortune may be that it will not include her at all! Jealous fear, the adjunct of passion even in Basilius' abdication, poisons the mother in her. Now more savage than the she-bear, she vows that if Philoclea is her rival, "the life I have given . . . I will sooner with these hands bereave thee of, than my birth shall glory she hath bereaved me of my desires" (p. 88).

It is a shocking rhetorical aria.[19] Although it closely resembles the masculine speeches of transformation in Act I, it quite lacks an external opposing counsellor. Instead, at its close Gynecia hears from an anticipatory "little arbor" (p. 89) only a secret "whispering note" (p. 88), the words of which are teasingly indistinct. This kind of voice is the present obscure substitute for counsel. In a song directed to the expressive lute—a device which in the *Arcadias* always indicates a speaker's rueful objective analysis of his own emotions and actions, and which often therefore briefly retrieves the original human foreconceit—the speaker, like Gynecia, bewails man's removal from seeing, thinking, and knowing into "hasty sight," fiery heart, and treacherous reason; yet it also ambiguously wishes that "to this strange death [it might] vainly yield [its] life" (p. 89). Such discordant song, speaking for an altered Arcadia, can no longer either ease or conceal pain: "The time is changed, my lute, the time is changed" (p. 89).

Thinking to seek company for her misery, Gynecia moves forward, only to discover her misery's cause: the disguised Pyrocles. The twisting ambiguity of a love that must be hated wrings from her a cry which not only speaks for all the characters' erotic compulsion but also again anticipates the problems of justice in Book V: "Dost thou offer me physic, which art my only poison? or wilt thou do me service, which hast already brought me into eternal slavery. . . . [I] make thee judge of my cause, who art the only author of my mis-

[19] Appreciation of Gynecia has come largely from the continent. See J. J. Jusserand, *The English Novel in the Time of Shakespeare* (London: Unwin, 1890; repr. New York: AMS Press, 1965), p. 247, and Franco Marenco, *Arcadia Puritana* (Bari: Adriatica, 1968), p. 103.

chief" (p. 90). She demands at least the end of disguise: "Take pity on me . . . , and disguise not with me in words, as I know thou dost in apparel" (p 90). She also asks for "counsel." For an instant, confusion seems about to work an end to confusion, bringing all Arcadia to welcome recognitions and reversals. However, Gynecia and Pyrocles are so much alike in desire that her words take on a familiar ring. In Act I, he, too, had asked for pity and counsel but wanted only approval of his passion. Under such direction by desire, words are primary disguises of truth, not its vehicles.

That glum truism is illustrated by old Basilius, whose near approach interrupts the conference of his queen and their would-be lover. Passion is no less anarchic when it is orchestrated for bassoon, however. Even though Basilius fetches a senile "little skip" (p. 91) in extending the comedy of age from the First Eclogues, his passion is still strong enough to lie. In praising the constancy of age, he carefully ignores his abdication from Arcadia and his wish to trade his aging queen for a young Amazon:

> Let not old age disgrace my high desire,
> O heavenly soul in human shape contained.
>
> . . . . .
>
> Old age is wise and full of constant truth,
> Old age well staid from ranging honor lives [p. 91].

Thus, no reversal can yet occur; passion continues to be destiny. In its obscurity, the queen resolves only to "stir up terrible tragedies rather than fail of her intent" (p. 92). Pyrocles, in a very similar case, finds himself no "nearer to quench the fire that consumes [him]." And the princess Philoclea, heavily concerned in their hatred and love, also finds "strange unwonted motions in herself" (p. 93). So, says Sidney in quick summary, "in one lodge was lodged each sort of grievous passion."

"The lively image of a vehement desire": Pamela, and the disclosure of Musidorus

In a rapid leap up the triad, the investigation shifts from Gynecia, who now represents almost uncontrolled desire, to Pamela, who maintains intellect. The setting makes a similar removal, changing from the lodge of Basilius to the "demeaning" lodge of Dametas. Pamela's reasonable, constant virtue is to be tried against her own strong attraction to love, and also against Musidorus' pleas for humility and charity. Like Pyrocles' request for pity, Musidorus' wish for charity in love can be another name for mere permissiveness.

Despite their distance from each other in the triad, Pamela and Gynecia are alike not only in their quite proper accessibility to love but also in penetrating the princes' disguises or emblems. Unfortunately, because such awareness must be kept secret, the princesses' proud ability makes them accomplices to the princes' deceit. Knowledge, whether passionate or reasonable, may lead to a very similar self-betrayal. Musidorus' revelation of his identity should work against disguise, but it only doubles the number of persons involved in the fraud.

Although she represents the third and uppermost part of the soul, Pamela lives in a partially fallen Arcadia. She must therefore take love, as she has had to take her political station with Dametas, at a decidedly lower rate. In part, love comes to her as it had come to the more sensual Pyrocles—through the eye. She had been attracted to the heroic Musidorus when he saved her from the she-bear. However, she fully recognizes the "baseness" of his birth, which seems to associate him with the loutish, immoral Dametas. When she feels "no small stirring of her mind towards him, as well for the goodliness of his shape, as for the excellent trial of his courage" (p. 93), Pamela labors to oppose the urgent call. She has no will to be a Gynecia.

But love, in a brazen Arcadia, is replete with craft on the one hand and irony on the other. When its irony smites Musidorus, he falls back upon its craft. Chagrined that the pastoral disguise intended to lead him to Pamela has actually severed them, the elder prince, too, for a time seeks out Basilian "desert places . . . counsel [to] his miseries." As soon as he recovers from finding his "service . . . lightly regarded, his affection despised, and himself unknown" (p. 94), he contrives a clever ruse: he will come to Pamela under the guise of courting the ugly, stupid Mopsa. Unfortunately, love takes on some of the mean character of the ruse. The trick leads even a Pamela into dog-in-the-manger possessiveness toward the supposed shepherd, after which she is the more willing to attend the "second meaning" and "cloudy fancies" [20] of his song (p. 95).

Despite the questionable device of her lover, the intellectual Pamela is sufficiently stirred by the song. Musidorus can therefore hint at his true identity. This second unmasking of a prince begins as he commends the height of his thoughts. They complement the "divine spark" of Pamela's mind, as signalled by her outward beauty. He pleads that her mercy and charity form a bond between his thoughts and that spark. Like a prince Odysseus disguised as a shepherd, he then relates his "tragedy" for her (p. 98). By lauding the "well-doing" of his past heroism, "from which no faint pleasures could withhold him" (p. 99), he increases the pathos of his being overthrown on the "stage" of Arcadia. In its "charmed circle," heavenly beauty has produced "hellish agonies"—a

[20] See Edgar Wind, *Pagan Mysteries in the Renaissance* (New Haven: Yale Univ. Press, 1958), p. 72.

"maze of longing and a dungeon of sorrow" (p. 100). If charity and mercy are being stirred by his imagery, so is the anticipation of a future near-rape in a concealed bower.

Although Mopsa nods to sleep during the tale (much as Dametas had resisted Pyrocles' song), Pamela receives from the cloudy narrative, and the disguised narrator, the "lively image of a vehement desire in herself" (p. 101). She at once acts to govern even a divine frenzy, warning herself, "Pamela, take heed; the sinews of wisdom is to be hard of belief; who dare place his heart in so high places, dare frame his head to as great feignings" (p. 101). She correctly fears that he may be not an artist but a charlatan; just as correctly, probably, she consigns the fears and their cause to the "high place" of a reasonable judgment.

Seeing Pamela retreat toward true reason, Musidorus hastens to lull her back toward fancy. His song, which balances the last song of Pyrocles, speaks of exalted matters, but its intent is partly seductive:

> My sheep are thoughts which I both guide and serve,
>   Their pasture is fair hills of fruitless love;
> In barren sweets they feed, and feeding starve;
>   I wail their lot, but will not other prove.
> My sheephook is wanhope, which all upholds;
>   My weeds, desire, cut out in endless folds;
> What wool my sheep shall bear, while thus they live—
>   In you it is, you must the judgment give [p. 102].

Although Musidorus is basically honest, his appeal to judgment in this context hopes to undo her judgment, even as his vow of constancy invites her beyond the "great constancy she would fain have overmastered" (p. 102). She is now led into the ironic position of debating love with Musidorus exactly as he himself had contested it with Pyrocles in Act I. When she asks, should not love purify a prince's desire as fire purifies the salamander, he replies that the prince would prefer to bear away such "fire" with him (p. 102). But why, she asks, should the "fire" consent? Out of virtuous gratefulness, she is told, as well as in hatred of her unworthy bondage to Dametas. Musidorus has craftily added the political to the ethical in his persuasion.

Her conscience almost too much consenting, Pamela is in no way dissuaded from a possibly worse bondage by the princely jewel then given to her. Its "device" is an altar of gold, dedicated to Pollux but actually honoring Castor. Its "legend" is the Sidneys' own *Sic vos non vobis*. This attestation from Musidorus' own "integrated" heroic past (which is not strictly applicable to the partly seductive present) impresses Pamela's mind with "a great testimony of the giver's worthiness" (p. 103). His related gift or seizure of erotic "fire," however, is not judged; nor does the given judgment receive a sounder public trial than that which had led Basilius to abandon Arcadia.

"Impossible to resist, as . . . deadly to yield": Philoclea, and the disclosure of Pyrocles

Providence aside, in the Sidneian triad much—perhaps all —of the proceeding depends upon the center. That is the position of man in the universe, of the guardian in the state, and of will in the polar human triad which reads intelligence/will/desire. It is in this position of the princely triad that Sidney places Philoclea, alongside Pyrocles. Although more depends upon Pyrocles, Philoclea is the author's announced favorite among all the characters. Given a little more nerve, she might have been a favorite to a Shakespeare, as well. As it is, she is intended to compose a center between her sister's cool intelligence and her mother's driven desire. She represents so much for men as well as women, moreover, that the author confesses that he will have to accuse her of faults he feels in himself—and which he no doubt infers in the infected *hypocrite lecteur*. It is for such reasons, along with her warm "natural" innocence, that Sidney says it is to Philoclea "principally [that] all this long matter is intended" (p. 103).

And so to Philoclea falls the second Act's third major contest of a princess with her own passion. In it she wrestles, alone, with the direction of her past, present, and future. Although the struggle eventually causes Pyrocles to reveal his identity to her, the circumstances of her love remain secret and vaguely shameful. Her future seems predicted not so much in their love as in either a terrible dream of Gynecia's, in which love is almost identified with death, or in a rebellion that is the political equivalent of private desire.

Philoclea's representative struggle calls into question the contest of innocence with experience. Sidney would contend that man may be the better for "not knowing of evil," yet he would add that such innocence may find it "the easier to fall, because it hath not passed through the wordly wickedness" (p. 103). Having had no impressions of evil, Philoclea cannot draw upon a preventive judgment of it. Like a peaceful state assailed by an unsuspected army, she is therefore wholly surprised by her passion.

In her turn, she moves into a dangerous solitude, unable to admit even to herself how far desire has mastered her. Like Basilius, she lets wandering thought feed the flame of love. Within the general proceeding of abdication, she seeks out a shadowed bower, which may also resemble a "little chapel" (p. 105). The description is a useful reminder that love, and even solitude, can still have a fair face. There she steals away from the past innocence of her parents' care and her own chaste vows. Although hurrying beneath Diana's moon, she is no longer under Diana's protection nor Apollo's clear foreconceits as she returns to a monumental white marble stone. In the past, she had written on it her faithful compact with the goddess, as well as with all the other "living powers" of nature:

> This vow receive, this vow, O gods, maintain,
> My virgin life no spotted thought shall stain.
>
>   .   .   .   .   .
>
> O Chastity, the chief of heavenly lights,
>   Which makes us most immortal shape to bear,
> Hold thou my heart . . .
>   Such life to lead, such death I vow to die [p. 104].

Her past vow had been the equivalent of Pyrocles' past dedication to heroism and Basilius' allegiance to Arcadia. Her somewhat guilty removal into private ethical quandaries is mirrored in the present worn and blotted condition of the verses. The change is like that of Pyrocles the hero into "Cleophila" the Amazon. The blots confess a blotted writer, even as the constancy of the white marble judges her own inconstancy.

Although the alteration appears to contain a cautionary judgment, Philoclea is like her mother in condemning herself but doing nothing to free herself from willing servitude. Such action leads her into verses that are almost as ambiguous, and even seductive, as those just murmured to Pamela by Musidorus:

> My words, in hope to blaze my steadfast mind,
>   This marble chose, as of like temper known:
> But lo, my words defaced, my fancies blind
>
>   .   .   .   .   .
>
> My words full weak, the marble full of might,
>
>   .   .   .   .   .
>
> My words black ink, the marble kindly white,
>   My words unseen, the marble still in sight,
>   May witness bear how ill agree in one,
>   A woman's hand with constant marble stone [p. 105].

As her soft hand had once shielded her eyes, so now she would hide herself from her inward seeing, thinking, and knowing. As is always the case in Sidney, she cannot wholly prevent the knowledge, even though it as yet supplies little direction. She now recognizes, however, that "poisonous heat" (p.105) has invaded her heart, despite the supposedly benevolent, yet fatal, influence of chaste planets. If at first she partly accuses her stars even while asking their aid, she eventually blames only herself. When she wishes that "Cleophila" might be "a young transformed Ceneus" (p. 106), she has moved not only toward true nature but also beyond the comfort of ordinary fear, all but recognizing, as Gynecia had before her, that her greatest present fear is not of love, but its lack: "And yet are these but childish objections. It is the impossibility that doth torment me, for unlawful desires are punished after the effect of enjoying, but impossible desires are plagued in the [very] desire itself" (p. 106). She has thought her way to a distinction like that between sin and psychosis. Involved in it is the realization that erotic love between women, such as hers appears to be, seems contrary to nature. Thus Pyrocles' Amazonian disguise has created wild work for the princess he loves.

As the scene ends, a cloud passes over the chaste moon. It images to Philoclea once more the blot on her character. Although the subsequent "high climbing" of the moon suggests a possible ascent in love, at present the moon can only direct her back to her lodge. And there she finds her parents mooning in quite another way over the "woman" whom she, too, loves.

Before her love can receive recompense of a sort in Pyrocles' revelation of his identity, the two lovers must run the gauntlet of Basilius' foolish love and Gynecia's tragic desire. The two have now become "disastered changelings" from their marriage (p. 107). In this envenomed midsummer

night's fancy, Pyrocles, who like Philoclea speaks for the
center of the human triad, feels pursued by "two wakeful
eyes of love and jealousy" (p. 108). Ruefully, he mourns a
love that is both surplus and dearth of love. It is a general
indictment of desire:

> What I call wrong, I do the same and more,
> Barred of my will, I do beyond desire.
> I wail for want, and yet am choked with store [p. 108].

Pyrocles charges all these comic contradictions to the blind
Cupid: although love may claim to be as young and fresh as
Philoclea, he is in reality "thousands old" (p. 109), like Dicus'
Cupid.

The diagnosis of desire is at once proved in action. To
serve his concealed love, Pyrocles enlists Basilius to act as
paternal pander. In a scheme Epicure Mammon would have
found piquant, the father is to loose his daughter to Pyrocles,
supposedly in order to plead the father's case. As Pyrocles
says, somewhat ignobly, "Desire holds the senses open, and
lovers' conceits [are] very quick" (p. 110). Even Philoclea,
for all her innocence, is afflicted with "a new field of fancies"
(p. 111) in all this; she cannot avoid knowing that both of
her parents are in some perverse fashion her rivals.

The increasingly desperate, if frequently comical, nature
of the night's desire is almost at once indicted and emblematized in Gynecia's fascinating Penelopean dream. It is the
new oracle, to which the *Old Arcadia*'s proceeding has come.
Within a wilderness that suggests both the Arcadian "desert"
of abdication and a phallic character in its thorns, she sees
Pyrocles upon a possibly yet more phallic "fair hill" (p. 111).
However, love's possible Zion is as yet only a Golgotha. The
figure at the summit is a corpse, reeking of death. Yet she
takes the corpse for her rest—not because of love, really, but
because of shameful contagious corruption. When she awak-

ens, she finds that Basilius may have stolen even that shame from her; he has sent his daughter through the night to the disguised young guest.

The comic love and frantic jealousy of the king and queen represent the conditions of love in an infected world. Those conditions haunt the meeting of Philoclea with Pyrocles. It will be difficult for their love to escape the present Arcadian context. Nature and relative innocence nevertheless manage to create one vulnerable harmony in this night of discord. Here, as at the close of the *Old Arcadia,* Sidney discovers much divine justness within candid human love.

Philoclea comes upon Pyrocles when he is (questionably) mirroring his love in swift water and writing flowing verses in sand; his "inward grief" is perhaps only too closely associable with those "outward" pictures (p. 113). However, his eventually fiery breath might have come from Philoclea's "own mouth" (p. 113). Thus united in feeling, he reveals to her, his conqueror and "judge," that he is Pyrocles, reduced by her to this "fall of fortune and unused metamorphosis." Despite that lament, Pyrocles also elevates himself into being a Sidneian "living image and . . . present story of the best pattern, love hath ever showed of his workmanship" (p. 114).

Similarly, if Philoclea is swept by Pyrocles' "manifesting of his being" (p. 115) into a total frankness that is all but total surrender, she nevertheless brings residual judgment from other days, when love was not disguised and princes not transformed: "If I had continued, as I ought, *Philoclea,* you had either never been, or ever been, *Cleophila;* you had either never attempted this change fed with hope, or never discovered it, stopped with despair. But I fear me my behavior, ill governed, gave you the first comfort. . . . I was glad to yield, before I was assaulted" (p. 115). Because her virgin vows are blotted and the better monument of marriage vows has not been mentioned, she can offer only honesty of word. From him, she asks a triumph unlike those of arms in Asia Minor: "Thou hast then the victory, use it now with virtue" (p. 116).

In lieu of such a promise, the enraptured Pyrocles—like Musidorus, immediately before him—gives his lover rich jewels. Although "their souls" do truly desire "to meet" (p. 116), it is not honied love or their virtue, but only the galling passion of Gynecia, that holds them from a literal playing-out of her "assault" and his "victory." A walking emblem of "jealousy . . . the sister of envy, daughter of love, and mother of hate," Gynecia would convert love into death, even as her dream had intimated. She is willing to sacrifice not only her daughter but "all the works of earth and powers of heaven" to obtain her desire. Caught between desire and jealousy, she cries out in song that "their flames mount up, my powers postrate lie:/ They live in force, I quite consumed die" (p. 117).

At once, Act II moves to a close upon a translacing emblem from the political world: poisonous ethical rebellion is closely mirrored in the state, in a contrapuntal balance for the emblematic attack by beasts in Act I. Because Basilius' abdication had released every citizen into his own will, a "violent flood" of villeins rises. Like passions among the noble Arcadians, among the mob "every one commanded [but] none obeyed; he only seemed to have most preeminence, that was most ragefull" (p. 118). Inflamed by wine and crowd psychology, the worst among them suggest regicide. The onrushing rabble is met by Musidorus, Philisides (who in a sharp poem has roused Musidorus from lyrical retreat), and Pyrocles—most notably, by that last, mediate young prince. Having announced himself a man (if only privately) and having shown possibilities of princely love, he now again shows himself a hero and governor, in both deeds and words. Primary emphasis falls upon his judicial, reintegrative governing of the rebellion. With reason, he puts down the "unbridled use of words" (p. 121); from the governor's own "judgment seat," which will figure so largely in Act V, he restores the rebels from being a mob into being "wise and quiet Arcadians," free from the Platonically predictable "tyrannous yoke of your fellow subject" (p. 124).

During the time that Pyrocles was acting the true prince, his various lovers remain unaltered in their agony. In comparison with that private confusion, the public insurrection was easily put down. Basilius thinks the oracle is fulfilled, now, when to each clause he adds the name "Cleophila." If that change implies the death of the queen, even as the mob's passion had sought his, "such is the selfness of affection [that] he thought the gods in their oracles did mind nothing but [his love]" (p. 127). The queen has similarly considered the death of Philoclea. Thus, the yearly hymn to Apollo, which closes the narrative section of Act II, is in large part a revelation of the Arcadians' distance from Apollo's clarity, wisdom, and heroism. The hymn's conceits gradually aspire to an all-but-Christian virtue in place of desire and disguise:

Apollo great, whose beams the greater world do light,
   And in our little world dost clear our inward sight,
Which ever shines, though hid from earth by earthly shade,
   Whose lights do ever live, but in our darkness fade.

·   ·   ·   ·   ·

Let this assured hold our judgments ever take,
   That nothing wins the heaven, but what doth earth forsake
      [pp. 127, 128].

The approaching shepherds with their eclogues also help to alter the image of atomistic rebellion into that of a serviceable circle. In their lyrics, passionate rhetoric also is replaced by a reflective, judicial consideration of reason and passion.

"To heavenly rules give place": Reason *versus* passion

The *Old Arcadia*'s Eclogues are invaluable reductive mirrors for both the proceeding and its great pattern. Within the total proceeding, they not only mirror the five general Acts formally, in their own five-step movements, but also mirror the entire action ideationally, reducing it to a scale in which it can be readily "seen." And for the general pattern or fore-conceit, they are a continuing, concentrated manifestation and voice. In the Second Eclogues, the five steps—which move through contests of aged reason with youthful eroticism; boisterous lovers in praise of their girls; reason with extravagant grief; hope, with echoing despair; and complicitous secrecy, openly considered by the two young princes—are in turn reductively mirrored or framed by an opening dance. It embraces both the general and particular proceedings within the eternal pattern.

The summary eruption of rebellious political passion in Arcadia provides the direct occasion for the reflective pastoral dance. In it, seven "reasonable" shepherds oppose seven of their "passionate" fellows. When reason calls passion a rebel, passion merely retorts that reason is a tyrant; all passions, it says, must be "free" (p. 129). Similarly, if reason demonstrates passion's bondage to nature, death, confusion, and blindness, passion loftily redefines them as joy and sweetness. To this point, the dance has imitated the Arcadian proceeding. It next mirrors the stable idea from which reconciliation and reintegration may be expected. In the end, a merciful reason and a weak, but still-protesting, passion agree that "instead of fighting [they must] embrace one another." And they yield both present judgment and future government to "heavenly rules" (p. 130).

Although the emblematic dance might have discovered

the good for all the Arcadians in their perilous flood, in them the related "skirmish betwixt reason and passion" continues unabated. The king and queen lean upon Pyrocles; he "convoys" his mind and eye to Philoclea; and Musidorus probably was saved from such direct abuse of reason only by a challenge to enter the first contest. Even in it, however, he aggressively stands up for passion. In recapitulation of the dance and of much of the *Old Arcadia* itself, he will "love love's contemplation," no matter what broader or higher conceits reason may oppose.

When the well-meaning but anti-erotic Dicus hopefully inquires why Musidorus has ended his lamentations in love, thinking that perhaps love itself has evaporated, Musidorus is greatly offended. He swiftly "skirmishes" in love's praise. By arguing his constancy to love in its present infected condition, however, he necessarily speaks mostly for passion. If Musidorus can still say of love's proceeding,

> Sight is his root, in thought is his progression,
>   His childhood, wonder; prenticeship, attention,
> His youth delight, his age the soul's oppression,

then Dicus (acting as judge of such questionable passion) may be right to reply,

> Thy safety sure is wrapped in destruction,
>   For that construction thy own words do bear—
> A man to fear a woman's muddy eye,
>   Or reason lie a slave to servile sense [pp. 132–133].

When Musidorus berates the judge for blasphemy against love, Dicus (like the opening dance) retires toward heavenly rules. He hopes that his compassion may offer "some help, or change of passion" to his young friend, so that Musidorus may regain "a quiet mind" (p. 133). But he misses the mark.

Like the princesses in Act II, Musidorus is not complaining about the change, but only its lack of success. Without love, therefore, a quiet mind "should most of all disquiet [him]" (p. 134). The partial Pyrocles of course applauds such a "changeless heart" in love, as the first set closes.

To continue the assault of youthful passion upon a seemingly aged reason, two "jolly youngkers"—cousins, no doubt, to Spenser's Cuddie, and fairly obvious reductions of Pyrocles and Musidorus at present—rush forward to take up rhetorical cudgels against Dicus. Madcap voices for brisk concupiscence, Pas (*whole*) sets out to better Pan, and Nico (*victory*) to outdo the "aged" Apollo. Perhaps in a veiled warning to the princesses, they refer thematically to metamorphoses not of princes, but of Syrinx and Daphne. After discomfiting "Dicus old," they frolic into praise of their Leuca and Hyppa. The stakes are Nico's cat against Pas's dog, "Catch":

Nico.   O if I had a ladder for the skies,
      I would climb up and bring a pretty star,
    To wear upon her neck that open lies.
Pas.   O if I had Apollo's golden car,
      I would come down, and yield to her my place
    That shining now, she then might shine more far [p. 138].

Although one accuses the other of bleating and receives a fit insult in return, both friendship and love are really only roistering good fun to the boys. They juggle a riddle about the familiar beast with two backs—he "that hath four legs and with two only goes," and has "so strange lives, that body cannot rest/ In ease, until that body life foregoes"—until the amused but more sedate Dicus cries, "Enough, enough . . . / Let cat and dog fight which shall have both you" (p. 138).

As a mirror for the noble young Arcadians, the otherwise

agreeably comic "youngkers' " version of love and friendship
is demeaning In a quick shift, Pyrocles diverts the third set
of Eclogues to a complaint, related by Histor, which the
love-sick Plangus (from the First Eclogues) had made to "the
wise Boulon." As their names suggest, a private or ethical
complaint in love is now to be tried for permanent public
value. It also represents a general trial, by judicial reason,
of the allied passions of love and grief. It anticipates the *Old
Arcadia*'s narrative proceeding in Acts III and IV, as well
as the conclusive judgments of Act V.

The third set of poems is central not only to the Second
Eclogues but to the entire *Old Arcadia*. Plangus's complaint,
borne forward from the prose interval of the First Eclogues,
begins with a despairing argument for suicide: "Alas, how
long this pilgrimage doth last,/ What greater evils have now
the heavens in store/ To couple coming harms with sorrows
past." It then anticipates Fulke Greville's complaint against
the condition of humanity: "Ah where was first, that cruel
cunning found,/ To frame of earth a vessel of the mind/
Where it should be [to] self-destruction bound,/ What
needed so high spirits such mansions blind?" (p. 139). As if
finding the mixture of elements in man to be hopeless rather
than creative, Plangus rejects man as a "player placed to fill
a filthy stage" and as "this talking beast, this walking tree"
(p. 140). Disappointment in love produces like disappointment toward man and the universe.

Although Boulon quietly replies that the pleasant physical
face of Arcadia argues correspondent "good haps" that will
maintain such a "perfect state," his stand with the original
Arcadian foreconceit may have taken the Arcadian fall too
little into account. His mild words impel Plangus further
into despairing blasphemy:

O heaven, if heaven there be,
Hath all the whirling course so small effect?
Serve all thy starry eyes this shame to see?
Let dolts in haste some altars fair erect
To those high powers which idly sit above,
And virtue do in greatest need neglect [p. 141].

The cry of Plangus is by extension the lament of all the Arcadians who have been brought fatally (although often comically) under love's control. It anticipates their cry when love brings them to shame and the threat of death. The medicining reply of Boulon is therefore of universal applicability:

Blasphemous words the speaker vain doth prove,
Alas, while we are wrapt in foggy mist
Of our self-love (so passions do deceive)
We think they hurt, where most they do assist [p. 141].

This doctrine of Boulon, although not the merit of his verse, suggests that of *Samson Agonistes*. It implies that even the folly of Basilius and the dangerous passions of the young lovers will yet prove to be "well." Even the mists of self-love may lead the Arcadians into clear love for others. Boulon now serves as a better oracle than the furious woman. Much that he suggests here is dramatically effected at the regenerative close of the work. Once the old drivel Cupid has been revealed as diabolical old self-love, a more general, more nearly Christian, love may rise. Like the fortunate fall, such scourging use of a vice to create a virtue will have "beat [men] on to bliss" (p. 141).

In the meantime, Boulon judges desire as being tyrannical and disproportionate. He urges that man refuse service to "female lamentations"; man should instead hold, with "some grammar," to a broad sense of cosmic congruities (p. 143). If Plangus still rejects such ordering syntax and conception, which involve all "wise discourse, sweet tunes[,] poet's fiction, . . . moral rules," in favor of a sweeping "malediction" upon fate, Boulon in turn must condemn a will that associates love with death. It merely heaps inward woe upon unavoidable outward trouble, a fault closely related to the Arcadians' recent movement outward toward fatal commitments.

Doleful thinking on events, Boulon finds, leads to misapplied demands for pity. Those cries serve to conceal from a man his Musidoran collapse into moral inertia:

> Betwixt the good, and shade of good denied,
> We pity deem that, which but weakness is;
> So are we from our high creation slided.

However, like the appealing young lover himself, the Arcadians in attendance reject the medicine of Boulon for the "passion of Plangus"; it all too well appears to each of them as "the balance of his own troubles" (p. 144).

Because Musidorus had been associated with Plangus in Asia Minor, Pamela, who now is also led by "vehement desire" (p. 145), asks for Plangus' story. It begins in emblem and ends in a present demand for the princes to be heroes, not mere languishing lovers. In Paphlagonia, then, two maids and two youths (equivalent to the Arcadian lovers) had been sacrificed to a Giant (equivalent to passion). The actual princes, acting as a twinned Theseus or Perseus, had dispatched the monster. When they went on to arbitrate a quarrel between two local brothers, the princes had shown their might in wisdom as well as arms; they were patterns of princely "wit, liberality, and courage" (p. 146). At that point, however, the encounters had changed. In anticipation of the Arcadia to come, the princes next moved into the periphery of feminine passions. Such trials were quite unlike the clear, simple demands of arms and justice. The full story is dis-

cussed in the next chapter. It involves a nymphomanic Andromana of Palestine and her peer, an Egyptian stepmother
who resembles both Potiphar's wife and Medea. Having
dealt with those two erotic "monsters," the still-heroic princes
had come to Arcadia.

In the *New Arcadia,* such tales from the heroic past will
be told in the endangered present in order to preserve the
future. In the *Old,* the lovers have ears to hear but will not
listen. Unlike Odysseus, who wept to hear his own history,
the princes only rejoice that their ladies have heard so
much of their valor. And the two women, with never a
thought to the warnings conveyed by erotic monsters in
Asia Minor, smugly find "contentment" in this public, yet
concealed, tribute to "their lovers" (p. 151). The even more
resembling Gynecia meanwhile "only saw [Pyrocles,] she
heard nobody but [him,] and thought of nothing but of
[him]: so that Histor's discourse passed through her ears
without any marking, judging . . . that it should nothing
appertain to the party" (p. 151).

Thus the Arcadians have dealt with the tale's instruction
much as Plangus had dealt with the judgment of Boulon;
they have ignored it. Basilius, in his incredible but characteristic fear of the absent or the future, even tries to distract the
disguised Pyrocles' mind from the story, lest "she" fall in
love with the story's Pyrocles! Accordingly, the company
turns with Basilius to Philisides—who, under a mask, is also
the maker of both those fictive Pyrocleses.

With a wholly different kind of attention to that which is
materially absent, Philisides has all this while "sat so melancholy as though his mind were banished from the place
he loved, to be imprisoned in his body" (p. 151). Not only
has he never forgotten the first lesson of the *Old Arcadia*—
that human life on earth is not an eternal mansion, but only
a bating place—but he also stresses that the infected will

must be overcome if one is to attain, or maintain, that eternal mansion. In an echo song, he will therefore show that the present Arcadian self-love answers itself with real despair.

With Philisides' song, the *Old Arcadia* considers love not as a contest of passion and reason but as one of a higher and lower form of love. With an almost holy aspiration toward a Venus Urania, Philisides wills to love the One or its higher manifestations; he wants to be at least an Il Penseroso. However, because he is seemingly divorced from the ideal and fixed in Arcadia's bating place, he now sings not to a Stella or Urania, but to himself. As had all but happened with the selfish lovers of Act II, in this context echo answers aspiring questions with negatives deriving from the words of the questions themselves. Such is the disorderly "grammar" to which love has come. Eventually, as in the Narcissus legend and Gynecia's dream, such love will find that death was its predicate or complement. If men ask, "Then to an earnest love, what doth best victory lend?" the heavy echo replies, "end"; if they demand, "Doth the infected wretch of his evil the extremity know?" they are told, "No"; and if they protest "Horrible is thy blasphemy unto the most holy," they are dryly corrected: "O lie" (pp. 152–154).

Philisides has presented a dark night of self-knowledge, resembling that of Act IV. Although the company applauds him, neither he, whose mind is fixed elsewhere, nor they, whose minds are too thoroughly fastened upon their lesser loves, actually attend that instructive echo. It is left to prepare groundswells for the future.

Like a song to one's own lute, songs answered by echo can hardly be self-deceiving. Man's own ardent self-delusions, however, carry no such penalty. In the last set of the Second

Eclogues, Pyrocles takes the stage, almost bursting to express
that very consuming "ardor" (p. 155) which Philisides' song
had found to be acrid and Histor's account had condemned.
Is the young singer, who is both hero and prince, to

> . . . sing the fall of old Thebes
> The wars of ugly Centaurs
> The life, the death of Hector

in works that imitate heroism, or should he instead sport with
a literary Amaryllis, and

> Recount the rape of Europe,
> Adonis' end, Venus' net,
> The sleepy kiss, the moan stale?

He instead turns to a new and very modern kind of echo:
"The singer is the song's theme" (p. 155). Love in turn is
the singer's song, rejecting the claims of the "other"—reason. Love thus becomes fatality, not transcendence:

> Nature, sovereign of earthly dwellers,
> Commands all creatures to yield obeisance
> Under this her own, her only darling.
> Say then, reason; I say, what is thy counsel?
>
> .   .   .   .   .
>
> Thus, sweet pain, I do yield whate'er I can yield.
> Reason, look to thy self: I serve a goddess! [p. 157]

Although such a lyric, urging love's infection, may be only
another unattended echo song, it can also indicate a history
as shameful as that of Asian Andromana. A song of "myself"
is a celebration, not a judgment.

The answering asclepiadics of Musidorus are little more
hopeful. Although they seem to praise the soul and contemplation, together with the wise thoughts of man when be-
holding "what the creator is," they turn to another (femi-

nine) soul "closed in a mansion/ As sweet as violets, fair as a lily is" (pp. 157–158). The fair hope for a golden world is thwarted by disguise, self-deceit, and materialism.

Within that shadow, the passionate Arcadians leave the theater and counterfeit sleep. Reason is no better served next day, when Basilius goes "to continue his Apollo devotions, and the other[s] to meditate upon their private desires" (p. 158). It is plain that they all worship either a self within or, in part, a blind god or goddess without; and also that for a time, a dry, mocking echo must be their only oracle.

"Darkling into his chamber": The Third Book or Act

The doubled triad of Arcadian princes and princesses having removed or been seduced from reason, the *Old Arcadia* must now show prince accompanying polity down into darkness. In a central cave of passion and Platonic error, the lovers perform in fortune's puppet show. Gradually, the glamorous secrecy of the love-bower discovers the ashen tomb. The complaints that had once thrillingly described desire as a *Liebestod* had been right. Soon thereafter, the ambiguous disclosures of identity from Act II begin to shriek in the public ear. Thus, ironically, the state that had seemed to dissolve in the face of passion also begins to move toward renewal by means of that identical passion.

As a "stage play of love," the *Old Arcadia* in its critical third Act looks backward to its setting out and forward to the completion. Looking backward, it recapitulates the princes' friendship, but sees them again abandon it for love; it repeats Basilius' abdication, as he leaves even the oracular Apollo himself for an Amazon; and it again brings the alien princes into the two lodges, although they now will try to separate the princesses from the two families. Looking ahead, Act III sees these several loves hasten into a selfish criminality that must collapse of its own weight, thus serving "Everlasting Justice." Contrary to the lovers' hopes, the cave of passion does not supply a new universe. Instead, all the isolative paths that had led into it also lead out into a great public center. Shadowy error thus rises surely into the light. In the *Old Arcadia,* there has been no travel except on a radius of the foreconceit.

As beasts and rebels had supplied emblems of degeneration in the first two Acts, so in Act III a cave of assignation serves both as setting and as "speaking picture." All of the princes descend into the haunts of blind Cupid, the furious sybil, and passion. The two young princes who force these proceedings act less like vernal kings of May than like Don Juans. If they bring love to Arcadia, they also bring the threat of death; extending the preceding beast imagery, each comes to resemble a tiger. And in no compliment to their princesses, the young men's former blazons of beauty now become near-pornographic inventories.

But at the outset, the noble Arcadians seem about to attain their urgent desires. Only gradually is love seen to be a "dark but pleasant" vault (p. 169), signalling not only a trysting place but also the grave. The end of the desire once called treason, then, seems to be death. For that reason, it is a mercy when the permanent pattern of reason demands revelation and judgment. Although human judges may err even as the human lovers have erred, providence will not.

"The division of these two lodges": Musidorus *versus* Dametas' lodge, for Pamela

Friendship, like any other of the heroic virtues emanating from man's erected wit, does not buckle to passion without a struggle or a backward glance. For an instant as Act III begins, the princes again couple "their souls in . . . mutuality either of condoling or comforting." They look back upon the past "as in a clear mirror of sincere good will." In recollection, however, they immediately run upon themselves as shepherd and "counterfeit courtesan" (p. 159). Passion and transformation have come to seem an inevitability.

Regardless of its ultimate result, such passion will seem joyous in success. Musidorus displays a glove he has won not in tilts of honor, but of love; and his songs, which once celebrated Petrarchan aspiration, now wink publicly at a more sensual enjoyment ("O sweet glove, the witness of my secret bliss"—p. 160). He buoyantly plans to spirit Pamela to a nearby seaport, under oath to offer "no force unto her till he had invested her in the Duchy of Thessalia" (p. 163). However, it will still be a political rape. And even the personal side is compromised when he promises to bring help to the less lucky Pyrocles: he will invade Arcadia and force Basilius to give up Philoclea to his cousin. In one way or another, love is showing a sorry tendency to become mere violation.

Anticipating the broad design of justice in which men are punished with their own vices, but using it now merely to perfect the "harvest of his desires" (p. 175), the eager Musidorus quickly helps each person in Dametas' family to seduce himself with his own leading passion. The "muddy mind" of old Dametas can be stirred by avarice; the heart of Miso, by jealousy; and Mopsa's eyes, by ravenous curiosity. In quick Chaucerian touches, Dametas is sent to find "golden acorns" at an ancient oak, Miso to the Odyssean "Oudemain" (*nowhere*) street in Mantinea, where she supposedly will find Dametas making love to one Charita, and Mopsa to Apollo's ash, where all her wishes will be granted.

As always, the materialistic louts parody the royal family. Such a parody can become double-edged. Royal greed in love is not necessarily better than Dametas' avarice, under which "many times he . . . wished himself the back of an ass to help carry away his new-sought riches" (p. 177) or Mopsa's ambition, under which she hopes to become "the greatest lady in the world . . . never after to feed on worse than furmenty" (p. 184). And when Musidorus hoists Miso on Medean "wings of anger" (p. 181) first with a lovely song from the supposed Charita ("My true love hath my heart, and I have his/ By just exchange one for the other given"— p. 179), and then with a ludicrous response attributed to Dametas ("Gay hair, more gay than straw when harvest lies/ . . . Eyes fair and great, like fair great Oxes' eyes"—p. 180), he may forget that both the songs are *his;* and each mocks the other. It ill behooves him to deride the louts, in any case. He will shortly follow a sensual Dametan blazon almost into rape, and will wrap Pamela in a concealing scarf like that in which Mopsa even now roosts, up in Apollo's tree. He even plans to truss up Mopsa violently, until he is stopped by Pamela.

Later, the elder prince's "harvest" makes him very nearly a Lovelace to Pamela, even though she tries to return them from seductive rhetoric to judgment and reason. Seeing herself "in her self," she has objectively judged "with what wings she flew out of her native country and upon what ground [Musidorus] built her determination" (p. 185). However, his present "determinations [in] restless desire" (p. 163) make him resemble Ulysses not in Ithaca but in the rape of the Palladium from Troy. Although he tries to assure her that he is of no base mind or estate, he had attracted her love as a shepherd. Their "right harmony of affection" (p. 186) suffers from that original deceit.

Although a just exchange of hearts cannot truly be said to have taken place between them, they do exchange names, becoming doubly united as "Pamedorus" and "Musimela."

Yet their love remains unequal. While she poetically vows that her love will be with "virtue clad" so that their "private forms" may join in "one sight of Beauty," he all the while is employing a "baser hand" toward a "downward fall" (pp. 187–188). His songs soon became "ravishing," lulling her to sleep. Rapt in dreams, her innocent inward breath or soul is the life of her outward "picture [made by some] excellent artificer" (p. 190); but the lustful Musidorus sees only her sleeping body. Like Porphyrio, he is on the point of stealing his way from dream to reality:

> Let no strange dream make her fair body start:
> But yet, O dream, if thou wilt not depart
>
> . . . . .
>
> Then take my shape and play a lover's part.
>   Kiss her from me, and say unto her sprite,
>   Till her eyes shine, I live in darkest light [p. 189].

After moving through a physical blazon that all but makes him a "stranger to his [own] counsel," he is "overmastered with the fury of delight . . . having all his senses partial against himself" (p. 190). Only the counter-violence of rebels breaking in upon them saves Pamela (and Musidorus) from his lust; and even then, the furious Musidorus—he who had saved her from a she-bear in Act I—wheels on the mob "with the look of a she-tiger, when her whelps are stolen away" (p. 190).

Because his aspiring love and even his shepherd's attire and lyrics had been degraded by deceit, a most reasonable prince and his most spiritual princess have come at last only to a bower of desire. A pattern of judgment must now arrest the wrongdoing and, if possible, restore the lovers to their rightful selves. Then "justest love [might still] vanquish Cupid's powers,/ And war of thoughts [be] swallowed up in peace" (Third Eclogues, p. 229).

"I invoke [the Almighty powers] to be the tryers of my innocency": Pyrocles *versus* Basilius' lodge, for Philoclea

When Kenneth Thorpe Rowe compared the *Arcadia* with similar romances,[21] he was impressed with its almost single-minded propriety in love. Within the *Old Arcadia,* however, desire can be as lubricious as even an Aretino might wish. Whenever Pyrocles takes the early stage, at least, love is not only released, but offers to rise to a full rainbow of polymorphous perversities. Nevertheless, Sidney handles the threatened loves of Basilius for a man, of Philoclea for a woman, and of Gynecia for her daughter's lover with tact and comic seriousness. It is to his credit, and the credit of his two warm and attractive youngest lovers, that the consummation of their love seems natural and laudable. They seem morally superior to the more exalted, but also more secretive and constrained, Pamela and Musidorus. But then, physical rather than spiritual love is more nearly their only element. It is well that they should seem especially handsome in it.

And yet the practice of deceit endangers Pyrocles' heroism more than did that of his cousin. Whereas Musidorus' "comic" assurance leads him only to gull the lodge of Dametas, Pyrocles pretends to love each member of the other lodge. A centripetal deceit may seem more generous than a centrifugal plot, yet even it causes Pyrocles to welcome war against Basilius, to lure the king and queen into a dangerous double assignation, and finally to heavily compromise Philoclea.

The proceeding under which Arcadian love will plummet

[21] Kenneth Thorpe Rowe, "Romantic Love and Parental Authority in Sidney's *Arcadia*," Univ. of Mich. Contrib. in Mod. Phil., #4 (April, 1947), p. 44.

toward death, in close parallel with the onrushing Arcadian political disintegration, is initiated by Pyrocles. By keeping the king on tenterhooks of doubt and desire, he goads Basilius into worshiping Pyrocles, not Apollo. The dazzled old man sings, "Phoebus, farewell, a sweeter saint I serve/ Thou art far off . . ./ She heaven on earth . . ./ She doth possess, thy Image is defaced." The king pointedly announces that this worship is in no way ancestral; it was "begun in myself" (p. 167). When Basilius finally tries to offer his Amazon a palace, Pyrocles is alarmed. To avoid the prospect of return to "any public place," he quickly hints a private assignation. In a backhanded rebuke to two present unheroic princes, Basilius, tingling with the wish for sexual if not political heroism, cries, "O Hercules!" (p. 168).

Because of the promised assignation, Pyrocles significantly misses a last meeting with Musidorus. He goes instead to the hidden cavern [22] that indicates absolute selfhood. (Musidorus has sought out a similar bower for Pamela.) Although darkness cannot hide him from himself, desire will not let him leave the labyrinth. His song therefore speaks for all men who are torn between wit and will:

> Since that the stormy rage of passions dark
> (Of passions dark made dark by beauty's light),
> With rebel force hath closed in dungeon dark
> My mind ere now led forth by reason's light,
>
> · · · · ·
>
> I like this place, where at the least the dark
> May keep my thoughts from thought of wonted light [p. 169]

As if taking up the burden of those alternating rhymes "dark" and "light," a shadowy *alter* figure answers from the

[22] See Porphyry, "The Homeric Cave of the Nymphs," tr. Thomas Taylor (London, 1823), p. 176, and Walter R. Davis, "Actaeon in Arcadia," *SEL*, 2 (1962), 109.

furthermost reaches of the cavern. It is Gynecia; and she forces the argument of light and dark to a conclusion, the tomb. She has reversed the pattern in which she had discovered Pyrocles in Act II. Because clear self-inspection reveals unbearable shame, she explicitly associates the secret self and its hidden love with death:

> The heavens conspired to make my vital spark
> A wretched wrack, a glass of ruin's end.
>
> . . . . .
>
> Come cave, become my grave; come death, and lend
> Receit to me within thy bosom dark [p. 170].

Although Pyrocles appropriately recoils in death's "cold sweat" as if she were a "stinging adder," he still associates himself with all Gynecia's "mangled mind . . . with sense possessed" (p. 171). Whereas the cave had been a refuge for Pamela in Act I, it now is only a "picture of . . . inward darkness" or of a "soul abandoned" (p. 172). If its terrible love is rejected, the lover directly threatens homicide. When Pyrocles thus acts the "hard-hearted tiger" in refusing her, Gynecia vows, "I will not be the only actor of this tragedy; since I must fall, I will press down some others with my ruins." Her "rage of love" (p. 173) explicitly threatens her daughter, but in the upshot it will have seemed to kill a king.

At this point the author, in one of his rare direct intrusions, offers rueful judgment upon all such erotic obsession. It always must involve double self-deceit: "In such a mold are we cast, that with too much love we bear ourselves: being first our own flatterers, we are easily hooked with others' flattery, [and] easily persuaded with others' love" (p. 195). His fiction at once enacts the idea. The scene returns to Basilius' troubled lodge. When Philoclea (more in the mood of a Gynecia than a Juliet) urges night forward, time being the "father of occasion dear" (p. 196), she makes Pyrocles more bold and careless, and her mother more competitive. Speaking of the two women, the acute strategist Sidney notes, "Enemies [are] no small cause of the town's strength." Even recognition of such self-love does nothing to prevent it. Despite Gynecia's having carved a judicial poem on her lute, she continues in disruptive passion:

> The world doth yield such ill-consorted shows
>
> . . . . .
>
> [That] noble gold down to the bottom goes,
> When worthless cork aloft doth floating lie.
>   Thus in thyself, last strings are loudest found
>   And lowest stops do yield the highest sound [p. 199].

The ill-consorting effects of passion become most marked in Philoclea. Her competitive love gradually brings her to exalt Pyrocles into a "mirror of mankind" (p. 198), far above even the rational soul. His attraction thus seems at once infinitely desirable and yet safely remote and spiritual. Like Pamela with Musidorus, she decides to defer all political and ethical judgment to her paragon—only to realize, not long afterward, that his cause is unjust. His "mirror" had been daubed over with an "enchanting mask of . . . painted passions" (p. 198). She can now fly neither to cruel parents nor an apparently faithless lover. She has no strength of her own; as she says, "I have given away myself." Isolated and almost tragic in her grief, "neither thinking of revenge nor studying of remedy" (p. 199), Philoclea here approaches the patient dignity of the princesses in the *New Arcadia*. Although her mood does not last, it may further explain Sidney's preference for her over all the other characters in the *Old Arcadia*.

Meanwhile, for a moment Pyrocles again justifies her trust. His pitying "reason [having given] an outward blow to [his] passions," he renews her image as queen of his "inward part" (p. 200). It is not long, however, before he sybaritically rejects the mere "acorns" of Gynecia for her daughter's ravishing "garden of most delightful fruits." Imagination so ignites his "vehement desire" that even the parents notice his change. Following him, all inhabitants of the lodge are once more "full fraught with diversely working fancies" (p. 202). Later that night, under a deceitful moon now become Venus' candle, Basilius fancies that his Amazon's eyes have banished both Apollo and Arcadia. In his song, both the hint of hallucination and the ironic portent of loss are full of meaning:

> When two suns do appear,
> Some say it doth betoken wonders near,
> As princes' loss, or change [p. 201].

The more hesitant Pyrocles, in doubt how he may "join obtaining with preventing" (p. 202), instead invokes Aurora, as if dawn's "blushing light" might yet prevent the erotic collisions. Although he wishes to avoid the night's dilemma, knowing that he is "fain for love to hurt her I love, and because I detest the others, to please them I detest," a hasty "confused conceit" (p. 203) leads him to speed the proceeding. He remembers the cavern of self and erotic fancy. Up to the cavern goes a bed. Pyrocles announces that he will live religiously in the cave and be a very warm friend to the king and queen. In effect, he makes himself, and it, the physical oracle to every wandering desire. Assignations are soon made with both the king and the queen.

In the *Old Arcadia,* it is the nature of eroticism to seek a fatal assurance, even as Basilius sought sure foreknowledge. Much as the two princes have made plans that did not stop at rape and invasion, so Gynecia, who after exchanges of clothing and of presence in Basilius' bed beats Basilius to the cave, tries to guarantee desire with chemistry. The asso-

ciation of love with death will convert her drink from a
Circe's posset into a Borgia's poison, however. The gold that
has already been devalued from Apollo's light into an object
of greed also slides farther down the scale; it now becomes
both the payment and an ingredient in the poison of love.
Similarly, the Gynecia who had resisted exile now wishes her
life "much more solitary" (p. 212), freed from any restraint
by her family.

Under the secret workings of providence, fortune casts
down all such attempted assurances. Time brings the queen
not a young hero but only her old Basilius, "groping and
scambling" and celebrating his own "cunning gladness . . ./
Instead of thought, true pleasure" (pp. 213–214).[23] He is
the foolish harbinger of the two young princes in this night's
unthinking loves. The deflated Gynecia can only think upon
"her unquenched desire [and] the doubt that [Pyrocles] had
betrayed her to her husband, besides the renewed sting of
jealousy, what in the meantime might befall her daughter."
Just at this point, the author turns for an instant from the
fictional Gynecia to his own fair pupils, asking, with charming relevance, "[Is it not] better to know by imagination than
experience?" (p. 214).

Whether or not providence had designed the original
oracle, folly has brought it to pass. That is the ironic extension of Basilius' vow, "Instead of thought, true pleasure."
Almost miraculously, however, Sidney closes the Act upon
a more straightforward and natural act of providence: the
unsullied love which Pyrocles and Philoclea attain, if only
for a moment. In a situation that might have evoked Ovidian
erotics from most writers, Sidney works with grave lyricism.
Thus, in the midst of darkness and ironic imbroglios, the
golden light of the conclusion can be briefly glimpsed.

[23] Deceit has restored a marriage, and Pyrocles has acted unintentionally as Puck; cf. Dipple, "Harmony and Pastoral," p. 325.

Having led the parents away from the lodge (repeating Musidorus' action with the family of Dametas), Pyrocles comes to Philoclea's chamber heroically bearing a sword to ward off danger. He is also "rapt from himself with . . . excessive forefeeling," as if illustrating one aspect of Bruno's heroic fury. Yet even in this rapture, he continues to resemble Basilius; he would abdicate even the "great estate of his father" for this pleasure (p. 216). Philoclea, too, determines that "none should be judge of her passion but her own conscience" (p. 216). (Because of her passion, she may perhaps be forgiven a poem in which the Sidneian triad turns into a maddened troika, triplicating every part of speech in its path, as Philoclea wishes that the time and place might "loose, quench, ease" her "knot, fire, disease.")

For a time, the ecstatic lovers sense a harmony far above that of the spheres. On such a night, silver light dances almost religiously upon Philoclea's body. Only when Pyrocles pleads the "perfecting [of] mutual love" before "the Almighty powers, whom I invoke to be the tryers of my innocency" is the spell broken. Innocence suits poorly with his several deceits. Reminded of his past "imposthumed heart's" disguises, Philoclea judges them both severely, promising that in her turn her "only defence shall be belief of nothing" (p. 221).

The unanticipated trial of his innocence depresses Pyrocles into fainting. Sidney asks us to believe that the swoon is quite real, a mark of the young hero's Troilan depth of emotion. Coming at almost the same moment that Basilius is seeming to die from a love potion and crying out, "O Gynecia, I die, have care," Pyrocles' seeming death also points the way to heroic sacrifice. He pleads only, "Oh, whom dost thou kill, Philoclea?" (p. 222). His seeming death serves to transfigure their love. Instantly become fully a loving woman, "like Venus rising from her mother the sea," the merciful and repentant Philoclea is "the morning sun" to Pyrocles as he recovers. He once more sees her as a complete "image" of beauty. Thus death or the threat of death has acted against the drivel Cupid's association of death with love.

If Sidney's account does not wholly suppress the suspicion that the two have been playing rather elegant erotic games with each other, he nevertheless steadily maintains their honor and his own tact. A blazon of Philoclea's beauty, for instance, is removed into a song recalled from Philisides; and it praises most highly not the body's "fair inn" but the "fairer guest which dwells therein" (p. 226). However, lest the immediate audience should fear Pyrocles' being Platonic overmuch, Sidney then shows him to be heroically Argus-eyed and Brierius-handed in physical love.

As the night wanes, the author gently wishes his lovers the best effects of their brief bliss, "whose loyalty had but small respite of their fiery agonies" (p. 227). The Arcadian love-bower, so shameful in its deceits but so warmly Edenic in its own limited truth, thus becomes a place of quiet repose at the end of Act III. Although the attack of rebels upon Musidorus and the seeming death of Basilius already toll it back to the general Arcadian context, the bower shows how love might be peace, that had been rage. The ensuing Third Eclogues will discover, at a celestial level, the true pattern of such love.

"Coupled joys": The celebration of love's harmony

A royal marriage can graciously join the spheres of politics and ethics. The *Old Arcadia* was initiated in the "coupled joys" of Basilius with his kingdom and with his family. The two princes also had been "coupled" both to their nations and to their mutual friendship. Although imagery of warfare and degradation arose with the proceedings of desire, it frequently was tempered by images of love as intellectual and spiritual elevation. Thus, the pastoral celebrations of love, which might otherwise seem ironic in the context of Act III, reflect both the foreconceit of the entire work and the end toward which it will move: the golden world, both ethical and political, of a "right" Arcadia.

In the Third Eclogues, which loosely imitate the *Old Arcadia*'s general structure, three central tales of discord are framed within two great embracing images of concord: an opening epithalamion, and a closing Golden Anniversary tribute by Geron to his old wife, "worthy to be a queen" (p. 245). These Eclogues as a unit also resolve the former pastoral antagonisms into harmony.

In recollection of the first high Platonic adoration of the princes, and in implied judgment upon their present seductions,[24] the marital Third Eclogues begin with the golden affection of the shepherd Lalus for the typically "good" bride, Kala. Lalus had celebrated their love in the first poem of the First Eclogues. His love has nothing to do with princely disguises or "painted words [and] false-hearted promises"; it is only "a true and simple making her know he loved" (p. 228). A good governor, he cares for her family's sheep along with his own. In turn, she is as devoted in church-going as she is zestful at the maypole. Unlike the affairs of the princes, their coming marriage is blessed with the permission of both families. From the lovers' openly celebrative "bower of boughs," love irradiates all their "beloved" community (p. 229); the marriage is thus both an image and a center of more general union. The shepherds

24 In "The 'Fore Conceit' of Sidney's Eclogues," p. 47, Miss Dipple contends that the final Eclogues envision a harmony lost to the royal characters. It is not so much lost as deferred—to the marriages of the final Act.

celebrating the marriage, who make up a cross-section of the ages of mankind, gradually devote all their thoughts to the "holiness of marriage." In prospect, Dicus sings a form of epithalamion:

> Let Mother Earth now deck herself in flowers,
>   To see her offspring seek a good increase,
> Where justest love doth vanquish Cupid's powers,
>   And war of thoughts is swallowed up in peace . . . :
>   . . . . .
> O Hymen, long their coupled joys maintain [p. 229].

Having invoked the blessings of marriage, Dicus then exorcises its curses—churlish words, "peacock's pride" (p. 231), and jealousy. His touching estimate of a just marriage ends in a *collector*, which brings back all of its elements for a curtain-call:

> The Earth is decked with flowers, the heavens displayed,
>   Muses grant gifts, nymphs long and joined life,
> Pan, store of babes, virtue, their thoughts well staid;
>   Cupid's lust gone, and gone is bitter strife.
>   Happy Man, happy Wife [p. 232].

The boisterous second set, which immediately picks up Dicus' reference to jealousy, is expressively introduced in the bantering competition of Nico and Pas. Although the "holiness of marriage" actually has elevated their thoughts, too, they are youthfully reluctant to admit to any such wisdom. Instead, Sidney's spirited young Tweedledum and Tweedledee burlesque their own deep seriousness: "Sentences, sentences (cried Pas), Alas, how ripe-witted these young folks be nowadays!" (p. 232). After that, the company has to coax Nico before he is willing to sprint away upon his tale of a jealous neighbor. That somewhat Basilian "foul, unhandsome groom," fearing that a courtly stranger would dazzle his young wife, forces her to move from mere imagination to reality. His suspicions give her "fuel to seek, and not to quench the fire" (pp. 233–234); and his example recalls Philanax' early advice to Basilius. Intrigue in which the husband was the unwitting pander to his wife's seduction brings the song to a somewhat raffish echo of Dicus' "coupled joys": "Sure, no jealousy can that prevent,/ Whereto two parties once be full content" (p. 236).

In a swaggering prose rejoinder, Pas promises "wise words" to match those of Nico: and then seriously delivers them. Working forward from his friend's tale, he insists that a husband should be true to himself, trusting the effect to form a correspondent fidelity in his wife: "This done, thou hast no more, but leave the rest,/ To Virtue, Fortune, Time, and woman's breast." Such realistic trust will resemble that within a state, in which governor and people also should be "as far from want, as far from vain expense" (p. 237). With good government once more imaged as a bond between the political and the ethical, the melancholy Philisides is asked to extend such implications still further.

In the fourth song, Philisides at last offers some few quasi-autobiographical references to Philip Sidney, the man. He speaks far more generally for Sidney the maker, however, as imitative fiction and conceiving author cooperate in the one pattern. The double consideration of marriage also proceeds.

Philisides begins with his having battened his flock against the shades of night—shadows like those that have afflicted the Arcadians in Book III. As a character in the Eclogues, he himself has matured from an impatient youth into a sad mythologist for all mankind. He sings a song supposedly taught him by "Languette," who had helped him "to have a feeling taste of him that sits,/ Beyond the Heaven, far more beyond our wits" (p. 238). The older shepherd had tried to harmonize the younger man's "wit and will." In order to lend a Christlike staff to his friend's "slippery years" (p. 238), Languette told his pupil how animals in a golden age had turned their peaceable kingdom into an Animal Farm.

The animals, unwilling to leave well enough alone, had demanded a king. Reluctantly, Jove gave them man. Man shares all their capacities for evil, and adds to them the human attributes of speech and reason. Although he had at first said "we," not "I," to the "guiltless earth," he soon guts earth's ore, induces factions among the animals, enslaves the horse and dog, and becomes a meat-eater. Man is, indeed, a fit figure for the Arcadian night against which Philisides would protect his sheep.

The audience of shepherds receives the myth as allegory, wondering "what he should mean by it" (p. 242). Not so the implicated reader. In this painful alteration of the Genesis story, man is seen to be the worst of all possible governors. The contract imposed upon nature by man guarantees arrogant passions in the governor and slavery for the governed. These are extensions from the passions that even now rend Arcadia.

So far, the central sets of the Third Eclogues have shown a fall, both general and Arcadian. The initial "coupled joys" have degenerated to the uncoupling pictured in Philisides' grim Orwellian parable. It remains for the final set to find intimations of pastoral reintegration and Christian restoration.

Although the final poems cannot wholly regain paradise, they can at least restore the person and community to possibilities of love. Because the fall is general, such restoration is no mean feat. Geron, the new speaker, has been impelled to song by "fallen" jealousy of Philisides, grumbling that young men "think . . . they speak wiseliest when they cannot understand themselves"; his fellow, Histor, condemns marriage because he had failed to win Kala for himself. Even among the shepherds, then, age and a generalizing mind are not immune from weak judgment. These two men anticipate the errors of Philanax and Evarchus in Act V. Despite their brazen infirmities, however, Geron leads the discussion upward toward the permanent place of true reason.

Although Geron's defense of marriage—"this sweet doubling of our single life"—may lack the ardor of a young man, it has its own serene harmony. Again, marriage is seen to join the ethical and the political and, what's more, to resolve the seeming conflict of friendship with love. Such concord opposes mutability and fortune; it governs lust. Within its mellow "state," a wife provides a "friend without change, playfellow without strife,/ Food without fullness, counsel without strife" (p. 242).

Disappointed in his love for Kala, Histor opposes Geron. Few men, he says, ever find such ideal phoenixes or "golden fields"; most get crows and shrews. Reflecting Philisides' parable of a fall, his sour idea of marriage expects wives to produce "dull silence or eternal chat," either of which causes Histor to condemn "what spite they spit" (p. 243).

The judicious Geron concedes such a possibility. He nevertheless urges the cause of man in this difficult world. The peaceable generation and care of human children contributes to the general "commonwealth." In their polity, husband and wife can both "command, and yet obey," bearing their "double yoke with [that] consent" (p. 245). Such a marriage would deliver the princes and princesses from blind Cupid to their future children and governments. It would thus convert anarchic passion into harmonious private and public service: "Marry therefore, for marriage will destroy/ Those passions which to youthful head do climb,/ Mothers and nurses of all vain annoy" (p. 245). Most men in Sidney's age, welcoming the echo of Paul, would have considered the advice to be neither a joke nor a damning with faint praise.

Within the Eclogues, the idea of marriage is at once therapeutic. The jilted Histor at last pays tribute to the bride, and the community is restored. A night of festive rejoicing in marriage couples the public joy of the community with the private joy of Lalus and Kala.

Such a world makes golden noon of every night. In the world of the princes, however, a discordant image of darkness now closes the Act: Gynecia is discovered "making doleful lamentation" over a seemingly dead Basilius. Dirge interrupts the marriage celebration. A long course of judgment must now precede the restoration of "coupled joys" to the actual conditions of Arcadia.

"Our theater public": The Fourth Book or Act

As a "stage play of love," the *Old Arcadia* is of course a five-act heroic comedy. In Act IV, however, its character alters decisively from the Terentian to something approaching the Dantean. The setting removes from private caverns and bowers to a tragic "theater public" and a law court; the proceeding again becomes public and political. Although the leading characters suffer under justice as they had never truly suffered under desire, they increasingly act as princes, not as mere bodies that enclose calculating fancies. And the debates, which had subsided within the privacies of Act III, also resume, greatly magnified in subject. Their argument now must deal with questions concerning the great universal triad.

Act IV opens from the immense perspective of Everlasting Justice, which makes men "the punishers of [their own] faults" (p. 247). Private error or crime, which had been thought secret and isolated, becomes publicly known. The infected will and its deeds may be purged and restored within that great revelation. As error recedes before increasing light, only "that which hath the good foundation of goodness" can remain (p. 247). It is as if a self-concealing Adam, once again discovered in a great corrective Arcadia, were to be led to restore himself and his polity.

With Arcadia generally becoming the punisher of its own faults, even Dametas can be an agent as well as an object of justice. He therefore serves as a preliminary case study. As object, he had grubbed for gold only to find Musidorus' jibing note: "Earth thou dost seek and store of earth thou hast" (p. 247). When he trudged back to the lodge, he found a similar "solitary darkness." His charge, Pamela, had vanished. And because of his supposed love-affair, his bawling Miso has given him a painful "wooden salutation" (p. 251). But as agent, this "right pattern of a wretch dejected," hastening like "a man that would have run from himself" (p. 248), first brings Mopsa crashing down from her tree in a great comic fall, then parts the mother and daughter when they fly at each other's throats, and finally idiotically demands of his hands, "O hands, why want you a heart to kill this villain?" (p. 254). So far, he has blundered about only in his own mere "comedy of . . . tragical fancies" (p. 251). A justitial "constellation [greater] than his own" (p. 254) next guides him straight to Basilius' lodge, where the two youngest lovers lie sleeping. He hopes, of course, that "the revealing of this fault [would] make his own the less" (p. 255). Serviceable though he may be to justice, he himself is only an informer, not a judge.

Upon his outcry, scandalized shepherds rush the lodge. They are interrupted by the still more grievous word of Basilius' death. Over all the "following tragedies" (p. 255), daylight slowly increases, like a searchlight of justice. And Dametas has already supplied a model of the sinner under correction! Despite himself, he may have been right in singing at the close of Act II, "Who hath saved all? It is even I" (p. 126).

"The true shapes of all the forepast mischiefs": Gynecia with Basilius; and with Philanax

Lest the tragedies of Act IV be taken with unwarranted somberness, Sidney precedes the account of Gynecia's self-flagellating grief for a Basilius seemingly dead with a flashback in which he still is comically alive. The purpose of the flashback is serious enough, however. It anticipates the serene comedy of the close, by restoring a chastened Basilius to his wife. That reunion is a token of his coming restoration to Arcadia. Like Dametas, Basilius will never again be merely silly. Justice has other uses for them both.

In that earlier darkness, while making not very satisfactory love to his "misconceived bedfellow" the king had praised not Apollo but Pan, his own exile, and delicious night—that "first begotten child of time":

> Be victor still of Phoebus' golden treasure,
> Who hath our sight, with too much sight, infected,
> Whose light is cause we have our lives neglected [p. 256].

With mad invention, he also insisted that save for this fantasy all his life has been a dream. In the *Old Arcadia*, it turns out to be the Oberon who is the most deluded.

After the queen hears with no great pleasure that he "did prefer herself to herself" (thinking her to be Pyrocles in disguise), justice illumines all the intrigue to her. Like a judge, "she saw in him how much fancy doth [not] only darken reason, but beguile sense" (p. 257). Resuming the disclosures begun by Dametas, she reveals the truth of their assignations to the king. Although she does not judge herself yet, she nevertheless speaks for the general restorative justice: "Well, well, my Lord . . . it shall well become you so to govern yourself, as you may be fit rather to direct me, than to be judged of me. . . . It is high season for us both to let reason enjoy his due sovereignty" (pp. 258–259). In a swift debate, he wholly agrees; although still trying to divert blame to destiny, he vows to return to his home and his state. He believes that all the exiles should now feel "like far travellers [who by distance] were taught to love their own country." He half senses Everlasting Justice in all this movement. No longer fascinated with furious women, he believes that guiding "destinies . . . had wrought her honor out of his shame, and . . . made his own finding to go amiss, . . . the best mean[s] ever after to hold him in the right path" (p. 259).

And so the *Old Arcadia* might have ended, could the time have been set right by one man's partial recovery. But it has not been. Gynecia and all the young lovers must still be conducted to the theater of justice. That proceeding begins when Basilius drinks off the love potion intended for Pyrocles. Partly because of his comic "long disaccustomed pains" of the night (p. 259), the effect is one of death, not love. Although his seizure actually is only a trance, it images the charmed love-death and passion-exile from which all the Arcadians, not merely the king, must now be returned.

In her ensuing remorse and despair, the abject Gynecia becomes almost a type of the admittedly guilty sinner. When the seeming crime is revealed, she at first rushes to the woods to hide her face, as if she were a sinner at the Last Judgment. No longer does she ask for pity, or even want it. She insists that the people of Arcadia recall the divinity that should have hedged a good governor, and then spare nothing in judging her:

Continue, continue, my friends; your doing is better than your excusing. . . . Remember, remember you have lost Basilius, a Prince to defend you, a father to care for you, a companion in your joys, a friend in your wants . . . if you loved him, show you hate the author of his loss . . . what stay ye shepherds, whose great Shepherd is gone? [p. 263]

Partly because their guide is gone, his stricken people are reluctant to rush to the extreme judgment of an execution. Therefore, Gynecia, like the great wreck Oedipus, drives herself forward in profound misery, alone.

In an elegiac public processional "after the ancient great manner" (p. 264), utterly unlike the erotic secrecy in which Basilius had come to the cave, the troupe winds its sorrowful way back from the cave with his body. Along with Gynecia, Arcadia now recalls the true character of a prince. Despite his lapse into folly, Basilius had deserved the "sacred titles of good, just, merciful, the Father of the people, the life of his country" (pp. 264–265). He is not quite Immanuel, but he has been stamped upon his people's inmost conceits and affections—"a more lively monument, than Mausolus' tomb" (p. 265).

Come to grief's "theater public," the Arcadians cry out against the greatest public damage—the loss of a governor to nature and "filthy fortune." Even the elegy's sestina form expresses the whirling hazards which they assign to fortune. Its end words—*sorrow, fortune, public damage, nature,* and *wailing*—circle as if in an endless pattern of loss.

The sound of their lament reaches Philanax, who has been governing Arcadia with a modified martial law because of the rebellion. He swells into a vessel of wrath, a Spenserian Talus who rages that the tomb of Basilius must bear the blood of the murderers. His debate with the accused Gynecia therefore opens up a horrible agreement between them. Her terrible self-hatred has found an all-too-willing advocate in the counsellor, who in a latter-day transformation alters from governor into a fury of "unjust justice." Thus love of the state, like love of a person, can be perverted, even as immortal grief can change to "mortal hate." To Philanax, repentance is only self-accusation, not the sorrowful restoration of a sinner to his righteousness. His is not the way of the prince. Far less is it that of Everlasting Justice. Until that way is found, public Arcadia must follow her private rulers toward death.

"Prisoners for love, as . . . prisoners to love": Pyrocles with Philoclea

As debates of love in the first Acts had pitted reason against base desire, so the darker but more universal contests of Acts IV and V pit providence against despair, and "higher" laws against retribution. In these debates, the princesses, with their greater spiritual strength, now save the political princes from despair or suicide. And as the way down had begun with Pyrocles in Act I, so the present way up begins with him.

As the early Eclogues had shown, young lovers may irritate older men when they claim all for love, with the world well lost. If the lovers also precipitate a crisis of state, the ire of their judges may exceed all bounds. When the accusing Philanax moves from Gynecia to Pyrocles and Philoclea, he smells absolute perjury and conspiracy. For them to be young and loving as well as guilty somehow makes their errors seem even the more unbearable.

All the pleasantly mournful earlier talk about love's being a prison now becomes hard reality. The young prince's magnanimity is powerless against the Arcadian death penalty for adultery. With some of Gynecia's recent unblinking judgment, he has a "perfect vision" of the death that must come to him. He also realizes that men will judge Philoclea's love to be "a death-deserving vice . . . , which had in truth never broken the bands of a true living virtue." He further knows that his face may then become for her only an image of "the accursed author of her dreadful end" (p. 271). He therefore considers suicide. Like Book IV as a whole, he believes that a criminal may be his own executioner. And he hopes, incidentally, to receive his death at the hands of a hero—himself—rather than a hangman. That mortal paradox, born of his mortal mixture, leads him to a noble prayer. Although it seems to do so, however, it does not really submit his will to that of Jupiter:

O great maker and great ruler of the world . . . to thee do I sacrifice this blood of mine, and suffer (O Jove) the errors of my youth to pass away therein. . . : Neither be offended that I do abandon this body, to the government of which thou hadst placed me, without thy leave [p. 272].

Thus, he is more like the abdicating Basilius, at this point, than an Isaac or Jesus. He asks a confirming sign from Jove, but no oracle other than his own reason is given him. He therefore symbolically strikes "his heart side" (p. 273) with a prison bar, hoping with one blow to undo life, passion, and the charge against Philoclea.

Upon overhearing Pyrocles' attempt on his life, Philoclea rushes to him—much as she had done earlier, when he swooned. She is in a way the very sign he had asked from Jove. She now sees through all the obscurities of their infected wills to the perfection they had once envisioned. In light of that renewal, she assures him that his death would seem a ruin of the original idea of mankind. To give up all hope now would be to concede fear; to surrender the "fort" of the body would be treason both to heroic selfhood and to God. She asks instead for a perfecting union of their virtues. To his heroic "unshaked magnanimity" and "judicial habit of virtue" will be added her almost Christian "innocent guiltlessness" and "simple voidness of evil" (p. 274). Such "coupled joys" would make up a restored humanity.

In trying to answer her, Pyrocles gropes forward from private to public issues. He considers with grave reason, not affectation, whether his Roman suicide would not deliver her; he asks if hope, too, may not be a passion to be overcome. Admirable as the spirit of his argument may be, Pyrocles is still acting the merely valorous hero in it. He has not yet approached Milton's "better fortitude/ Of Patience and Heroic martyrdom" (*Paradise Lost,* IX, 31–32). Philoclea therefore leads him toward that higher argument. With Arcadian exile and hasty judgment behind her, she insists that man must not "prejudicate [his] own determination"; to rush upon a fate is to reveal "a doubt of goodness in Him, who is nothing but goodness." She quickly frames an imperative: let all evil be removed from an action, so that it will be "allowable before the ever living Rightfulness." Unless men's reasons are stayed in that "assured virtue," they are certain to come from a "disguised passion" (p. 278). Such is the case with Pyrocles' argument for suicide. Pyrocles is convinced. He asks only that he tell the world that he had forced her into the sexual consummation, and that his own heroic name remain concealed in order that he bring no shame to his family. By gesture, Philoclea assents, just as Philanax bursts in upon them.

Again becoming the third member in a swiftly transformed debate, the regent is at first moved by their beauty and valor. However, his vengefulness converts all possibility of "compassion . . . into hateful passion" (p. 281). He tells himself that evil often is thus garnished with beauty. When Pyrocles unwisely launches into a swift defense of Philoclea's chastity, as yet knowing nothing of Basilius' "death," Philanax interprets his ignorance as cold cunning. And when Philoclea then defends the "virtuous marriage whereunto our innocencies were the solemnities, and the gods themselves the witnesses" (pp. 283–284), he takes it to be only a confession of her adultery, and Pyrocles' perjury. Cynically assuring himself that any rape must have been mutual—that "the violence the gentleman spoke of is now turned to marriage; he alleged Mars, but she spoke of Venus"—he dismisses the daughter as a "fair devil," like her mother. He coldly warns her that because the royal family murdered its good king, it must now look only to "dead pitiless laws."

Although Philanax is secretly convinced of the princess' innocence of murder, he only whips up his wrath. Vengeance, a "disguised passion" but an open poison, has begun to run as virulently throughout Arcadia as the earlier seeming poison of love.

"Chastisers of Musidorus' broken vow": Musidorus with Pamela

The debate by means of which the human triad's uppermost prince and princess regain their proper selves is relatively brief. Intellectually, at least, they have the least distance to ascend. Pamela's serene wisdom soon triumphs over Musidorus' fear that chance commands the universe, much as Philoclea had argued down the claims of prejudicated fate. Once again, however, Philanax rejects the lovers' stands. As a result of their secret fault and his public wrath, Arcadia now hurtles through the steps of political disintegration plotted in the *Republic*. At the close of the Act, and in the final Eclogues, universal darkness threatens all.

But "Everlasting Justice" (p. 286) all the while makes its way through secret inlets. It had preserved the sleeping Pamela; "the coming of her enemies [had] defended her from the violence of a friend." Justice uses even such

"scummy remnant" as the rebels and Dametas as base matter
for its eventually well-wrought image. Immediately, it helps
Musidorus to become once more the hero (even though he
has a rebel in his own breast). Putting Pamela in a place of
safety as he had also done in Book I, he disperses the rebels
with comic slaughter, until one at last traps Pamela. Like
Pyrocles earlier, Musidorus at once offers his life in exchange.
It is of no use. The hope of a reward causes the remaining
rebels to spare their lives, and to conduct them by stages of
travel back to the lodges.

When darkness falls, it offers the lovers a reflective "kind of
desolation" (p. 290) for their debate. Not quite sincerely,
yet, Musidorus makes "unmerciful judgments" upon himself. He feels guilty of treason to Pamela, and thus no longer
able to offer even "counsel." Speaking through the agency of
Pamela, the "universal and only wisdom" (p. 290) brings
him safely to a more just judgment of himself and human
life. She offers him a first kiss as a token of trust before
declaring, "Chance is only to trouble them that stand upon
chance." Her love also reveals a Christlike willingness "to
descend in most favor when . . . lowest in affliction" (p.
291). She is assured of two things past change: her own
virtue, and the honor attributed to her by her lover.

Her calm wisdom, in which she seems almost a second
Beatrice, elicits from Musidorus a great prayer which balances
that of Pyrocles. It is ultimately addressed to divine wisdom:

O mind of minds . . . the living power of all things which dost
with all those eyes [the heavens] behold our ever-varying actions
. . . grant me ability to deserve at this lady's hands the grace
she hath showed unto me [p. 291].

In refusing the double sorrow of Musidorus' death in her
service, Pamela speaks partly as a Stoic, partly as a Christian,
and almost as a Hamlet: "What is prepared for us we know

not, but what with sorrow we can prevent it, we know" (p. 292). When sleep comes to Pamela and Musidorus, their "inward intelligences" return to absolute power (p. 293). As they rest in one another's arms, it is almost as if death had kindly taken their souls, as sleep has released their minds from the burdened flesh.

Just as Musidorus is trying, next morning, to persuade the rebels to take the couple to Thessaly, Arcadian troops sweep down and kill the mob. Sidney considers the slaughter to be a recoiling form of justice, that "unlooked-for end [which] the life of justice [worked] for the naughty wretches, by subjects to be executed that would have executed princes" (p. 296). With that, all the members of the accused royal family are gathered in custody.

Tribulation begins to work some good effects almost at once. Friendship, which had suffered during the princes' careers in selfish love, is restored. The heroes are now to be tried not in arms nor in the unfairness of secret love, but in the "higher" patience. They determine to show that "in adversity [they] can triumph over adversity." Trouble also helps them to triumph over appetite. Musidorus now can say, "I well know there is nothing evil but within us, the rest is either natural or accidental" (p. 297). He resolutely turns to face the vengeful ire that is within Philanax.

The major contest between Musidorus and Philanax awaits Act V, however. To close this Act, Sidney quickly draws up seemingly irreconcilable "dissentanies"—Pamela's princely love, against Philanax' cynical sense that such love is murderous lust; and the opportunistic cruelty of one Tymantus, against the soft permissiveness of Kerxenus (reappearing from Act I). Private obscurities have so confused the public mind that Arcadia increasingly swings rudderless, the prey of rumor and factions. Having never thought about government, the people are helpless in "public matters"; they waver between finding each new thing "vehemently desireful, or extremely terrible." Under the sway of polar public passions, not so much divided as divorced in mind, among the Arcadians there can be only "[infinite] disagreeing."

The full horror of regicide, together with Philanax' unprincely hatred, now descends upon the state. The province disintegrates, like a "falling steeple" (p. 299) or Plato's crumbling state. Its gentlemen strive privately for aristocratic rule, its soldiers for war, its merchants for money. When a body of wise men tries to quiet the tumult by appointing Philanax life-regent, a faction of shrewd enemies opposes him utterly.

Into the chaos steps a model of malicious opportunism, Tymantus; Sidney translates his name as "extreme ambition" (p. 300). He should have been a warning against extremes. In a pattern already familiar to private Arcadia, he makes his wit "servant to unbridled desires" (p. 301). He would replace the heroes through his marrying one of the princesses, and Philanax the other. He then would topple Philanax at his leisure. Although the regent peremptorily refuses, he may have been correctly judged by Tymantus; that climber predicts that Philanax will either master or murder Pamela.

For a moment, Philanax is shocked out of his murderous excess of righteousness. It is good that the accuser has become, for a moment, the accused. He quietly urges the listening Arcadians to be more than mere "private judges in so common a necessity . . . since his [own] end was to bring all things to an upright judgment, it should evil fit him to flee the judgment." The doctrine looks hopefully to the end of the *Old Arcadia*, but Philanax has not yet accepted it. Only he, in attempting to recommend an Aristotelian mean opposing the extreme violence of Tymantus, could still imagine that cruelty was a trifling "severity." In his own defense, he pleads: "Consider that all well doing stands so in the middle betwixt his two contrary evils that it is a ready matter to cast a slanderous shade . . . [and] call severity, cruelty, and faithful diligence, diligent ambition (p. 303)."

Although the regent obviously will not do as a mean, an excess opposing Tymantus does appear. No reasonable debate arrives with Kerxenus, however, who now speaks as an almost mindless hero-worshiper. Repeating the permissiveness of Act I, he holds that the princes are "demi-gods," Pamela a fit queen, and Arcadia a wholly untainted garden of "perpetual flourishing" (pp. 304–305). In disintegrative Arcadia, the only political truth is thus the violent swinging of political opinion.

Caught between such excessive, opposing factions, Arcadia all but dies along with her king. Even the sun, weary of "tumult upon tumult" (p. 305), exiles himself in the west. The private passion of the night before is now extended into the community and state. Partly to express that darkness, but also to counter it, the lyrical shepherds complete Act IV. If they are called "poor" (p. 305) as they sing eclogues that have turned wholly to elegy, it is only because of the great Arcadian darkness that they must witness.

"Cries instead of music": The lament for man

A demand for perfect symmetry might have produced five Eclogues to correspond not only to the *Old Arcadia*'s five Acts but also to the internal tendency of the Eclogues to form miniature five-act patterns. A rather obvious reply would argue, after pointing to the primacy of Arcadian narrative, that a truer sense of symmetry would ask that the work end as it began: in Arcadian prose. A still better answer would suggest that the Eclogues are absent at the close of Act V because there is no spiritual necessity for them; by then, the restored

Arcadians have risen to the level of the shepherds. The virtual resurrection of the king in Act V, together with the happy marriages of the lovers, firmly replaces Arcadia in the golden world and makes active Arcadia its own best "speaking picture."

But those happy events await the leading of providence. In the present, there is only image after image of loss or abandonment. The five segments in this final chorus are all laments—three for an ideal that is absent yet ecstatically adored, two for a bereaved state. Because the private and the public are so intimately correspondent in the *Old Arcadia*, the shepherds who mourn for Arcadia mourn also for themselves, and for mankind. Ultimately, the eclogues lament the loss man apparently was born for, including that of Eden and Christ. Even the setting and condition for the Fourth Eclogues are eloquent of that lot:

The shepherds, finding no place for them in these garboils, to which their quiet hearts (whose highest ambition was in keeping themselves up in goodness) had at all no aptness, retired themselves from among the clamorous multitude: and . . . went up together to the western side of a hill whose prospect extended so far, as they might well discern many of Arcadia's beauties. And there looking upon the sun's . . . declining race, the poor men sat pensive . . . [p. 306].

The nearest literary parallel in English for the set of five elegies that follows is *Lycidas*. Because of their position in the *Old Arcadia*, however, Sidney's lyrics can do no more than intimate an Easter. Nevertheless, these last Eclogues in the *Old Arcadia* supply the initial mood for the *New*. If that change indicates a quicker movement to loss in the *New*, it also suggests the quicker pressure toward patience and recovery. Light, it appears, may also enter from the western windows of seeming loss.

The first poem in the final Eclogues is so splendid that it later is used to introduce the entire *New Arcadia*. Thanks to equally splendid commentary,[25] it has gained such fame that it is probably better known than either of the parent *Arcadias*. It remains to be pointed out, however, that its two speakers, Strephon (*writhe*) and Klaius (*weep*), have fairly distinct characters, roughly corresponding to those of Musidorus and Pyrocles. As they cry out against the absence or loss of the celestial (Urania), Strephon speaks more for the natural level, Klaius for the spiritual. Like the two princes on their first appearance, the shepherds share friendship "of so high a quality . . . that they never so much as broke company one from the other" (p. 307). Although the loss of Arcadia has a part in their grief, it centers upon the absence of heavenly thought and its expressive poetry. "The general complaints of all men" having raised the question of "their particular griefs" (p. 307), the two shepherds sing a lament significant for all mankind.

In fixed grief endlessly reiterated by the doubling counters of the sestina form, Strephon pleads with nature to attend his grief, which now darkens the day; looking higher, Klaius sees the evening planets, fallen silent before earth's stricken music. Following the same general division, Strephon then considers himself to be an exile among monstrous mountains, his cry having become that of a "screech owl" each morning (p. 307); Klaius too observes music degenerate into cries of pain. Strephon describes a history of his personal falls, including that of his "state thrown down"; Klaius's history in-

25 William Empson, *Seven Types of Ambiguity*, 3rd ed. (New York: New Directions, 1966), pp. 34–38. See also John Crowe Ransom, *The New Criticism* (Norfolk, Conn.: New Directions, 1941), pp. 112–113; Theodore Spencer, "The Poetry of Sir Philip Sidney," *ELH*, 12 (1945), 251–278; Kalstone, *Sidney's Poetry*, pp. 71–83; and Jean Robertson, "Sir Philip Sidney and His Poetry," in *Elizabethan Poetry*, ed. John R. Brown and Bernard Harris (New York: St. Martin's Press, 1960), p. 125.

cludes fear and hatred on the part of a populace, along with thoughts that now pursue *him* "like beasts in forests" (p. 308). To Strephon, transformation and metamorphosis collapse the stately mountains into valleys and replace nightingales with owls, while for Klaius, filth, noise, and the cries of murdered men displace sun, scent, and music. Each violently hates such transformed "show and mind"—Strephon by loathing night, evening, day, and morning, Klaius by detesting himself and by stopping his ears against such cacaphony, "lest I grow mad with music."

The reason: the loss of Urania has cast Strephon into night and has deprived Klaius of her "whose least word brings from the spheres their music." Hymns of praise, standing at least for all lyric poetry and possibly for the golden world lost to an infected will, have therefore turned into a tormented, unchanging "morning hymn . . . and song at evening" (p. 309).

Their double sestina leads Strephon and Klaius at once into a related "debate" (a duet, in effect). In a complex dizaine, Strephon rejects all joys as parodic, even as Klaius asks to breathe only the "infectious grave" (p. 310); Strephon abstracts himself into Sorrow itself, Klaius into a wreck or wrack; Strephon finds that reason, hope, and fancy are whipped by storm from any congruency, and Klaius moves that implication forward into images of shipwreck upon the "rock despair" (p. 311); in a reflection of Acts IV and III, Strephon finds that desire brings on its own punition, while Klaius sees that even love may incorporate "sweet poisons" (p. 311); Strephon would have his too solid flesh melt, except that his spirit, already in hell, can expect no release, while Klaius, inviting the Last Judgment as Gynecia might, wishes that both earth and heaven would disintegrate. Both believe that even their expression is as hurtful as the killing breath of dragons—or, in a more familiar image, as the canker to the rose. The torment of an ideal love "unsatisfied" or grown festered closely resembles Arcadia's flamy torment of love, as it had recently swept to illusory satisfaction among the princes.

The burden of the Fourth Eclogues is next assumed by Philisides. He casts himself in a role like that of the two princes. Born in "Samothea," he relates, he had been neither "so great that I was a mark for envy, nor so base that I was subject to contempt . . . [education and experience] offered learning unto me, especially that kind that teacheth what in truth, and not in opinion, is to be embraced and what to be eschewed (p. 312)." In due course, his own Cyropaedia had directed him, also, to a heroic Grand Tour, after which he had begun public life with a "quiet mind"—until love created in him an Arcadia-like change, partly "in state, but more in mind" (p. 313). His song describes the event as a dream, but it clearly is more an emblem than a dream vision.

His impressive tale reflects both Genesis and the present Arcadia. It begins as light is extinguished and "Mother earth" (p. 313) reduced to a sleep that resembles death. His higher intelligence, however, like that of Musidorus or Pamela during the preceding night, is not clouded. "Made of heavenly stuff," it is suitable to the Eden that had been Samothea:

> . . . a land which whilom stood,
> An honor to the world, while honor was their end
>
> . . . . .
>
> . . . there my calmy thoughts I fed,
> On nature's sweet repast, as healthful senses led.
> Her gifts my study was, her beauties were my sport,
> My work her words to know, her dwelling my resort.
> Those lamps of heavenly fire to fixed motion bound,
> For ever-turning spheres the never-moving ground;

What essence destiny hath, if fortune be or no,
Whence our immortal souls, to mortal earth do flow

. . . .

[I thought] the depths of things to find [p. 314].

This Edenic life is broken by thunder and a recollection of
the Arcadian falling tower. The moon, severed like Leda's
egg, releases a chariot for descent. In it are Diana and Venus,
representing love in its familiar dilemma as ice or fire. Like
the young princes in Arcadia, Philisides is forced to judge
and act within that tormenting problem. He must serve as
a new Paris in a contest that seems to lack a Minerva. However, there is a third figure, Mira; she is servant to Diana. Although the fretful Diana and Venus try to patch up some
form of concord, aware that both their temples have fallen
into decay much as the worship of Saturn has ended, neither
can agree which should rule. Reflecting the "garboils" of the
present Arcadian tumult (p. 306) and the past division of the
princes' minds, they can only exchange guarded insults while
trying to shout one another down.

Philisides duly judges them. He begins by saying, "How ill
both you can rule, well hath your discord taught" (p. 317).
The judgment obviously can embrace the present public
factions in Arcadia as well as the past private factions in the
princes, princesses, and royal couple. When he chooses
Mira over either Diana or Venus as the proper governor in
love, he is rewarded by the goddesses with love's torments—
fire for his "foolish mind" (p. 317) from Venus, the cold
ashes of a chaste despair from Diana. The catastrophe resembles that in the double sestina. When he awakens, he
finds that while he was asleep, unarmed, the treacherous
Cupid had overpowered him.

His farewell to Mira had again distantly suggested the
earlier image of a falling steeple. After struggling with the
despair attendant on such a fall—a recapitulative love that

must try to "shine from a dark cave," a sun that blinds, and a passion that proceeds toward rage and a "hasty revenge"—his subsequent long poem finds in memory the temporary recovery of Eden and of aspiring ideal love: "Shall I not—oh, may I not—thus yet refresh the remembrance?/ What sweet joys I had once . . . ? / . . . Did not a rosed breath, from lips more rosy proceeding,/ Say, that I well should find in what a care I was had?" (p. 320). Yet he must end with, "Farewell, long farewell, all my woe; all my delight." The foreconceit is still a possibility; the present loss, a relinquishing of any misplaced hope.

In the fourth set in the Eclogues, Dicus takes up the burden of lament from Philisides. Because he, too, assumes the fall of Arcadia to have universal meaning, intimations of the loss of Eden and of Christ enter into his sorrow at "this general loss" (p. 320):

> Since that to death is gone the Shepherd high
>
> . . . . .
>
> And you (O trees) if any life there lies
> In trees . . . if among yourselves some one Tree grow
> That aptest is to figure misery,
> Let it, embraced, bear your griefs to show [p. 321].

He invokes the weeping myrrh, flowers such as the hyacinth that once were men, the rudely forced Philomela, and finally the heavens to witness that virtue is dead. What is almost worse, vice thrives. The poem's angry reaction anticipates the central section of *Lycidas:*

> And ask the reason of that special grace
>   That they which have no lives should live so long,
> And virtuous souls should so soon leave their place.
>   Ask if in great men, good men so do throng,
> That he for want of elbow room must die,
>   Or if that they be scant; if this be wrong,
> Did wisdom this our wretched time espy? [p. 322]

Combining the *Old Arcadia*'s frequent concern with mutability and fortune into two embracing images, Dicus finds
that man, unlike nature, is both caught in the circle of time
and yet expelled by it. He has no part in a garden of Adonis.
Whereas the old snake sloughs its skin as its "time ever old and
young is still revolved," man, being to "nought resolved," is
sent only to death. He who helps nature to "revolve" life and
is nature's best work thus becomes her prey. Within time,
he seems to be trapped either in the private contraries of
biological love and hatred or in the public "contention" (p.
323) of elements.

Dicus' cry has been that of a Job or a Hamlet. Anticipating
Act V, he mourns, "Justice, justice is now . . . oppressed."
The only verity is that "death is our home, life . . . but a
delusion." Because the "Shepherd of [good] Shepherds"
(Basilius; but also Urania, or even Christ) is gone, in whom
"private with wealth, public with quiet garnished" so that
"far was home strife . . . / His life a law, his look a full
correction" (p. 324), the judicial shepherd believes that
the prince's death is also that of the shepherds. In that terrible void, the only Muse also is Death. Like mankind, poetry
seems to be "to nought resolved."

That the circle of time and lamentation, mirrored over and
over in the sestina, can at least be broken by death has been
indicated by Dicus. The final poem, delivered by Agelastus
(*unmirthful*), accordingly makes a departure from the hated
circle. He bids farewell to the sun, "Arcadia's clearest light"
(p. 324), along with the clear light of Arcadian governance.
The people have become orphans, "left void of all public
might/ . . . Father's might." Now "wandering from all
good direction," they can only bend "unto death . . . our
thoughts' direction." Like Oedipus, they are able to stop
the whirl of guilty or vacant time only by the "putting out
of eyes [in order to seek] our light." Then, in a reprise of

Philisides' valedictory, they murmur, "Farewell direction, farewell all affection" (p. 325).

And so the Fourth Eclogues end. Like the elder lovers earlier, the heavyhearted shepherds try to forget themselves in sleep. They are interrupted, however, by a troop of twenty horsemen seeking Basilius. Is the high shepherd, then, not absolutely or eternally gone? Can a prince yet be sought out, as if by contemporary Magi?

Even the shepherds' somber Good Friday lamentations have been shot through now and again by rays of dawn, confirming an Arcadia in both recollection and aspiration. If Book IV has witnessed the descent of deep political shadows upon Arcadia, reflecting in a dark mirror the earlier ethical obscurity of her leaders, it thus also anticipates the comic illumination that is to come.

"Wisdom . . . an essential and not an opinious thing": The Fifth Book or Act

Two errors had brought on Arcadia's disintegration: private desire, coupled with public irresponsibility. Those which dog her painful reintegration are overscrupulous private rage (seen also in political ambitions), and inflexible public legalism. In Robert Frost's terms, the earlier fire has been exchanged for ice; and it is a question which more "suffices" to destroy Arcadia. Fortunately, providence in its character of Eternal Justice contrives a renewal of the temperate, humane Arcadia. To do so, it has to raise the nation along with its seemingly fallen governor from death.

No matter how comically it may have been engendered, a resurrection is to be treated no more lightly than a true judgment. In weighing the "miraculous" conclusion of the *Old Arcadia,* some past readers (perhaps expecting gritty realism, not romance) brought in very adverse judgments indeed. They accused Sidney of fashioning an incongruous and perhaps an impatient ending, one especially ill-advised in view of the impressive debates of justice that immediately precede it. An advocate for the author might explain swiftly that Basilius' trance, fully explained in Act IV, was a highly useful image of private blindness and public darkness; that the conclusion was bound to be comic, in both the Terentian and the Dantean veins; and that the originating oracle had prophesied an end to enchantment within that "fatal year." A more defensible complaint might be made on grounds of decorum. The gravity of the rest of Book V, which sees all the accused lovers purified and finds their judges very needful of judgment and mercy, may appear to be negated by the conclusion. Also, the work may seem to end almost in a sub-plot when it turns from the young princes, who have risen to such a dominant place, in order to bring back Basilius. And yet both complaints may be equally wrongheaded. Neither of the two young princes, no matter how noble, can restore Arcadia. Not only have they engaged in crimes against it, but also they are pledged mainly to Thessaly and Macedonia. Nor would the judges be adequately benevolent rulers. The ending therefore demands Basilius. As his emblematic exile had begun the train of disintegration, so only his return can finally reverse it. Although he has appeared on occasion as a ridiculous *senex,* in the end he must again be the father, the political governor, and the vessel of restoration—not in himself, necessarily, but in that which he embodies. With him, the household and the state also can rise from the passional grave. His resurrection is not so much the lame retirement of a fiction, then, as an emblematic demonstration that the circle of time, which may be broken by death, can also be severed by a return to the eternal pattern of life.[26]

[26] In *The Virtues Reconciled: An Iconographic Study* (Toronto: Univ. of Toronto Press, 1947), p. 87, Samuel Chew reported finding no

Throughout the Act, issues of fallible human judgment are paired with themes of providential rebirth. They appear in Philanax' simultaneous pull toward "desire of revenge," on the one hand, and "care of the state's establishment" (p. 327) on the other. They proceed in the elevation of Evarchus of Macedonia to be both judge and Protector. They are emphasized in the wish of each of the defendants to sacrifice himself, in his guilt, in order to save others in their virtue. They move into close harmony when love and friendship are joined to duty and valor, and when harsh judgment adapts itself to concord. Ultimately, they are joined in the justice of heaven, which was doubly demanded—first, in order that human crimes be set right; and second, in order that human justice create no new crimes. Only the greater government higher than humanity could so penetrate lies that are half-truths and judicial truth that is half in error.

"The excellent trials of his equity": Evarchus in justness

The first of several justitial "miracles" in Act V is the timely appearance in Arcadia of another prince—Evarchus, king of Macedonia. Arcadia lies wretchedly near death because of the "dangerous division of men's minds" and the "ruinous rending of all estates." Somewhat as the young princes had gone to Asia Minor in order to restore public equity in its states, so Evarchus comes to Arcadia as a Solomon. He alone seems capable of acting against the twin threats of "barbarous violence or unnatural folly" (p. 329). Philanax, urging Arcadia to make Evarchus judge, succeeds; the people, thoroughly "tired . . . with their divisions" and

---

English poetry in which "Time does not discover and release truth but cooperates with her in the exposure of iniquity," thus confirming the motto *Veritas filias temporas.* However, time serves truth as well as fortune in both the *Old Arcadia* and *Twelfth Night.*

"manifold partialities," are eager to return to "attentive judgment [instead of] forejudging passion" (pp. 329, 330).

Evarchus, so resolved in love of virtue that "never was it
dissolved into other desires" (p. 331), is the long-neglected
model of a prince and shepherd. Unlike Basilius, who had
"put himself from the world" and all but orphaned his
people, the line of action by Evarchus has always been
"straight, and . . . like itself, no worldly thing being able
to shake the constancy of it" (p. 331). Moderate and tractable
internationally, even though he knows that Greece (like
medieval Byzantium) is pressed by "Asiatics of the one side
[and] Latins of the other" (p. 332), he agrees to serve the
single province of Arcadia by enacting all princes. He will
be a monarch who can "as a man take compassion of mankind, as a virtuous man chastise most abominable vice, and as
a prince protect a people" (p. 334).

His long and virtuous life permits Evarchus, now the
"Elected Protector," to ignore charges of ambition, such as
had been leveled at Philanax. Assured that "wisdom [is] an
essential and not an opinious thing," [27] and wanting to "help
. . . them of like creation" (p. 335), he resembles the poet of
Sidney's *Defence* in believing that wisdom can be propagative. Thus, in contrast with the many-headed people and
their fortunal "circles of imaginations," in Evarchus' "one
man's sufficiency" is the power that can counteract "ten
thousands' multitude" and bring order to "the present dis-
orders" (pp. 336–338). Beyond even that height, in which
reason still may be "darkened with error," stands the tempering constant of true reason and providence. In its action, the
coincidences of romance need not make us "abashed with
[their] strangeness" but grateful for their "jump" accord.

[27] Cf. Justus Lipsius, *Two Books of Constancy*, tr. Sir John Stradling,
ed. Rudolf Kirk (New Brunswick, N.J.: Rutgers Univ. Press, 1939),
p. 82.

As a complement and sign of Arcadia's renewal after the dark night, Apollo's light opens the new day: "Lo, the night, thoroughly spent in these mixed matters, was for that time banished the face of the earth" (p. 339). Thus it is night, the emblem of exile and passion, that receives the first in a series of corrective judgments.

"The dawn of coming day": The princes in patience

Although the two young princes had been led forward ethically by their princesses in Act IV, in the final Act they first move heroically to Stoic endurance and then to an almost Christian patience. In a return to the proper balance of masculine and feminine virtues, it is now they who supply strength.

The need for their strength is established in a preliminary flashback to Gynecia. While night had still lain like a shroud over Arcadia, the guilty queen "did crucify her own soul" in self-loathing. She also murmured against the heavenly powers "not like a child but like an enemy." With Job and the Jesus of Gethsemane, she had demanded, "Why did you make me, to destruction?"; and with Milton's Samson, "If you loved goodness, why did you not give me a good mind?" (p. 340). The drifting furies of her fancy cause her to think that she sees her husband leading her not to a human trial but to the implacable "magistrates of [the] infernal region" (p. 341). Yet even in her lurid despair, she never reduces her infatuation. Desire remains a "high authority" even when "her own knowing of good [would] enflame anew the rage of despair" (p. 341). She is the type of all those who would have their crime and rue it, too. And her daughters, also, can only weep that the counsellors who once helped them now stand to injure them. Neither yet quite realizes "that an eagle when she is in a cage must not think to do like an eagle" (p. 343).

Opposite all such fear for life and fortune stand the two young heroes. By exercising themselves in endurance and patience, they again become fit "governors of necessity [rather] than servants to fortune." Having been schooled by the firmer Pamela of Act IV, Musidorus holds that "human chance" cannot overthrow "him that stands upon virtue"; and having thanked nature for her fine gifts, this new Socrates will not execrate her for other "chances we like not" (p. 344). He knows that, taking their careers on balance, the two of them "have achieved the causes of their hither coming, [for] they have known and honored with knowledge the cause of their creation." Men will have seen that it was "behoveful" that they had lived (p. 345). They exactly qualify for Sidney's definition of the propagative hero.

Like a musing Hamlet or Lear, the elder cousin disdains all currents except those of eternity: "When [death] is once come, all that is past, is nothing; and by the protracting, nothing gotten but labor and care." Musidorus' firmness even now helps the wavering Pyrocles. "Soberly smiling" in a philosophical agreement that seems to project their friendship into eternity, their intellectual victory over mortality leads them to consider immortality. In a Tennysonian mood, Pyrocles wonders if the happy dead will even recognize one another; and, if they do, whether ties based partly on earthly passions and grief might not disturb heaven.

Although Musidorus begins the answer with his assurance that senses and memory will be purged in death and then, by means of "contemplative virtue," will be absorbed into "the omnipotent good, the soul of souls, and universal life" (p. 346), it is Pyrocles who joyfully completes it. He has become sure that the purged human soul, if possessed of absolute knowledge, will know, without pain, of the time it spent in the body. He believes that the human mind on earth can no more imagine the pure light of that knowledge than the human foetus can imagine the light of the living world.

But as the human being can know of that pre-natal time, so the soul will know of its time in the world—by clear reason, not dim or painful memory. Like their love for the princesses, the friendship felt by the princes will suffer a change only into "that high and heavenly love of the unquenchable light" (p. 346).

In many ways, the recovery of the two princes is not only the first but the most important of the regenerations in Act V. It is sealed in a hymn sung by Musidorus to heavenly love and beauty. This is the final poem of the book, the last lyrical assurance that such love and beauty may be "known," even on earth, within the kingdom of the mind:

> Our . . . eyes, which dimmed with passions be
> And scarce discern the dawn of coming day,
> Let them be cleared, and now begin to see
> Our life is but a step in dusty way.
>   Then let us hold the bliss of peaceful mind;
>   Since this we feel, great loss we cannot find [p. 347].

Following these consenting swan songs that constitute "their own obsequies," the princes are called forth to trial. Although they conceal their true names, they put on their royal garments and march forth as princes. Their minds are now resolved "against all extremities" (p. 347). They will make some human errors during the trial, but they will not again mistake their high origins and end.

"Truth doth make thee deal untruly": Philanax and the defendants in trial by passion

The judicial theater to which all Arcadia now comes is magnificently set, but the display is also a "showing forth" of the state and its conditions. Dawn backlights the "throne of judgment" in which human wisdom will try to imitate the divine. Evarchus, acting the prince in his capacity as judge, is mantled in black. All about him stand Arcadians in mourning. Before them lies the body of Basilius, similarly shrouded. So far, Evarchus, who knows that emblems can comprise both "armor [and] ornament" for a state and that in "pompous ceremony . . . a secret of government much [consists]" (p. 348), has been stage designer and chief actor. Unkown to him, a higher design in a greater theater has opened out beyond him. By the "order of the heavens" (p. 349), he will be revealed as uncle and father as well as judge to the two heroic defendants. By his response to that terrific revelation, the human judge will be judged; and thus coincidence can be divinest sense, to heaven's discerning eye.

Bold ceremony has also been commanded by the defendants. Although Gynecia wears a long russet cloak, she covers her head with a grotesque "poor felt hat," which pictures how greatly she has been "deformed by fortune and her own desert." Clothed in "the Greek manner," Pyrocles strides forward in a white velvet coat, sandals, and a white ribbon as diadem. Behind him, the more regal Musidorus appears in a purple "Apostle's mantle" and an Asian tiara. They no doubt hope to overpower their accuser with regal "violence of magnanimity" (pp. 349–350), even as their defense frequently will claim royal immunity from prosecution.[28] However, their dress also marks their return to the composite best of man—Musidorus, more "severe . . . much given to thinking," and Pyrocles, more courageous and "lovely" (p. 351).

The trial merits lengthy study in its own right. Here, it can be described only in its most general proceeding. It moves through a quick sentencing of Philoclea and Gynecia before

[28] See Irving Ribner, "Sir Philip Sidney on Civil Insurrection," *JHI*, 13 (1952), 263, and D. M. Anderson, "The Trial of the Princes in the *Arcadia*, Book V," *RES*, n. s. 8 (1957), 409–412.

coming to the major charges by Philanax, the counterstatements by the princes, and then Evarchus' judgment upon them. Because no explicit charge has been made against Pamela, and because she is heir-apparent, no direct trial is made of her. Indirectly, however, she stands accused of the general crimes.

The action begins with Musidorus' attempt to claim royal immunity for Pamela, the prospective ruler. It is a wrong tack. Although if all questions of guilt were put aside Sidney himself would have found much to recommend the point, it is here groundless. Because a princely Protector has been selected, the trial represents no ultimate threat against monarchy. In much the same way, Pyrocles also asks that Philoclea be excused, with him assuming all the penalty for both of them. More winningly eloquent than Musidorus, he is also, prophetically, more a "suppliant" (p. 352) to Evarchus.

His plea does not sway the judge in the slightest. Evarchus consigns the supposedly adulterous Philoclea to a nunnery. With sinking hearts, the princes know that cold legalism has replaced princely ardor. The audience in turn knows that a merely human justice now threatens to add judicial severity to the original crime. A more universal judgment must thus arise to be "judge of [the] judge" (p. 339), as well as judge of strict laws that cannot be repealed. They are a sad parody of the knowledgeable constancy of God. If they in any way break the circle of passion, fortune, and death, it is only with a similar iron "law."

Now that it is clear that Evarchus will be a severe judge, the trial is increasingly commanded by Philanax, whose counsel has been perverted into prosecution. Encouraged by the law's haste, he attacks each of the princely characters with deadly, malicious fury. He moves first against Gynecia. Although she again wearily accepts all his accusations, she rightly decides that judges such as Philanax "deal untruly, and [with] love of justice [frame] injustice" (p. 354). As for herself, she is already her own "judge [and] executioner," within the hell of a "self-condemning mind" (p. 355). In his sentence, Evarchus takes note of the private and public destructiveness of her crime. In the one sphere she had destroyed the family, that root of society, and in the other, the government. She is therefore to be locked in Basilius' tomb (as if Arcadia were Ephesus) so that "his murderer might be a murderer to herself" and "death [thereby] redress their disjoined conjunction of marriage" (p. 356).

If Gynecia's too-willing confession had temporarily thwarted Philanax's vengeful rhetoric, the princes' ensuing pleas of justification give him full rein. They also offer him rope with which to hang them, first by supplying erroneous names, then by claiming immunity from trial, as "absolute princes." Arcadian laws, to say nothing of their affected roles as private persons, dispose of the claim. In all this proceeding of the trial, dog seems to be fighting cat. It is well to recall that justice is something other than a Philanax lunging at the throats of the defendants while they respond with partial truth, passionately pleaded. Sidney therefore reminds the audience that in all this trial its participants see only in a "shadow or . . . pit of darkness," like that of the cavern. Foreknowledge is possessed by unseen, but active, "higher powers" (p. 358).

The case against Pyrocles is parodically exalted by Philanax into a "tragedy invented of the extremity of wickedness." He plays upon the anonymous arrival and subsequent disguises of this "what you will" (p. 359); and he is positive that the intruder had intended to seize the "regiment of this mighty province." The counsellor's fairly substantial case becomes inane, however, when he announces that the condemned queen could not have conspired "without somebody to conspire with" (p. 361). But one section of his charge tells strongly with the Arcadians: that of Pyrocles' changefulness. Such alterations in a prince, rages Philanax (as the author winks), are more than a "quiet poet could . . . fill a poem with." A negatively polytropic hero must resemble malevolent fortune, or "a great actor perchance to an evil end" (p. 362); he is "the dishonor of both sexes," a "mankind courtesan," and—in a runaway parade of invective—"a strumpet in luxuriousness, the cunningest forger in falsehood, a player in disguising, a tiger in cruelty, a dragon in ungratefulness" (pp. 362, 363).

When Pyrocles is allowed to answer, he indulges a largely histrionic rage in objecting to the too-democratic "tongue liberty" (p. 364) allowed to Philanax. Passingly inane in his own right, he says that Basilius' exile provoked his own disguise; that the princess Pamela had been reduced to "thralldom" from which she had to be released (p. 365); that the plot at the cave virtuously restored Gynecia to her husband; and that Philanax's charges are only the rebel-associated "scum of base malice," not a necessary "proof clearer than the sun" (p. 366). He does his case no good by arguing that if he seemed to ravish Philoclea, it was only because he had first been ravished by love. Thus, although he speaks with "resolute patience" and advises the judge of the difficulty of administering justice—whether "correction is necessary," or if "grace doth more avail"—his final words remain largely a manifesto for passion: "I cannot nor ever will deny the love of Philoclea, whose violence wrought violent effects in me" (p. 367).

Relation of the case against Musidorus is delayed for a moment by letters to the court from the two princesses, which Philanax basely conceals. Although the women are not directly on trial, Philoclea's letter pleads the private aspect of the defense and Pamela's the public. The younger princess reminds the counsellors that Arcadia owes its salvation to Pyrocles (as if he were a second Oedipus), and warns that executing him will be equivalent to forcing "Philoclea to use her own hand to kill one of [the] Duke's children" (p. 369). The much more haughty Pamela reminds the court that it has made its prince into its prisoner. With some of the fine fury of a Mary or Elizabeth, she meaningfully palpates the word treason, adding, "If you let me live, the murderers of [Musidorus] shall smart as traitors" (p. 370). The letters of the princesses, composed with careful rhetoric, are impressive attempts to force the court either to free the princes or also condemn the princesses. If they are not quite the "naked truth" they are claimed to be, they nevertheless are so important that Philanax's suppression of them renders any judgment by Evarchus suspect.

Before listening to Philanax's case against Musidorus, Evarchus brusquely rules out the trial by combat that Pyrocles had offered the counsellor. Echoing Musidorus' earlier judgment upon the senses and fancy, Evarchus refuses to have "force . . . be made judge over reason" (p. 371). He apparently has not reckoned with the violence of words. Philanax now hisses that Musidorus is both a bond-slave, fit for whip and halter, and also "the knot of all this tragedy" (p. 371). At best, he is a "wolfish shepherd" and "counterfeit prince"; at worst, he is the type to all mankind of "disguisers, falsifiers, adulterers, ravishers, murderers, and traitors" (pp. 372, 373).

Like his cousin, Musidorus replies to the charge with a partly affected rage. He denounces the system that will permit such "drivel." Turning the attack, he urges that Arcadia be freed from the "partial jangling" of such a counsellor (p. 373). He contends that his taking Pamela to be duchess of Thessaly could not be treasonable to Arcadia. Finally, in a reversal of the pity once demanded of him by Pyrocles, he states that law should be a lighthouse, not a limetwig, and that judges should be like wise fathers, who turn "even the fault of . . . children" (p. 375) into fair action.

The jangling ceases. Evarchus now must judge the princes, disregarding the wonderful effect of their speeches upon the Arcadians. His long, painstaking decision rests upon a few central points: that in Arcadia the princes acted as private persons under private laws; that Greek and Arcadian law, not "free discourse of reason and skill of philosophy" (p. 377), must determine the case; that the princes must have been accessories, if not principals, in the murder; and that their past services to Arcadia are not relevant. As for the argument of love, it could have been met, very simply, by marriage. On the other hand, marriage under the immediate circumstances would set a disastrous public precedent for royal marriages. Unwittingly subjecting himself to the same implied judgment, Evarchus holds that law must be obeyed, lest mankind grow "monstrous" (p. 377).

The Protector's judgment attempts to suit punishment to the crimes. Because the body of Pyrocles had brought down the Arcadian body politic like the falling tower of the Fourth Eclogues, Pyrocles will be destroyed by being thrown from a tower. Because Musidorus would have taken away the "head" of the nation (p. 378), he must be beheaded. Such an example, the judge stresses, will deter rapes such as these, or even those of Helen and Europa. Finally, Dametas, who was "beastly [in] forgetting the careful duty owed to his charge" (p. 380), must become the permanent executioner!

With hope gone, the two princes react in one kind, although differing according to their characters: "Pyrocles was something nearer to bashfulness, and Musidorus to anger," but both emotions are heroically "over-ruled by reason and resolution" (p. 380).

"So uncertain are mortal judgments":
  Everlasting Justice

More than a suspicion of over-righteousness had invaded even the careful judgment of Evarchus, somewhat as the early judgments of Musidorus had been faintly priggish. The young Oedipus had been similarly over-certain about his solving of a human riddle. Almost as if *Oedipus Tyrannos* were being transferred into a Terentian framework, at this instant a messenger from a shepherd arrives. He is Musidorus' man Kalodulus (*good servant*), a balance with Kalander in Book I. In a swift, harrowing recognition scene, he reveals to the judge that he has just condemned to death "his own son and nephew, the one the comfort of Macedon, the other the stay of Thessaly" (p. 382).

It must have seemed that immortal and "sacred rightfulness" (p. 383) had somehow been blindingly revealed. Even Philanax is "mollified" by the revelation. However, it does not move Evarchus to a reversal. Despite a rising agony like that of Job, which wrings from him the cry, "Let my gray hairs be laid in the dust with sorrow," he will not change, lest "justice halt" (p. 383). He could not love the young men so much, he thinks, did he not love justice more. And even he can descend into partiality. He groans that because their vices made the young men not themselves, they have "forced a father to rob himself of his children" (p. 383). His over-severity has become as questionable as was Basilius' permissiveness; either one threatens to destroy the children in its care. It is not only Dametas who may be both criminal and executioner.

As ultimate lessons begin to be driven home for each of the characters, Musidorus savagely seizes the role of judge.

In this final passion, he recapitulates the *Old Arcadia*'s frequent rebellions against age and law. If the sentence is carried out, he grates, Evarchus will have destroyed Thessaly, exactly as he accuses the princes of having destroyed Arcadia. Musidorus can only hope that his own province will war on Macedonia in revenge. He cannot pity the grieving father; he instead imagines the whole earth crying out, "See how the gods have made the tyrant tear his own bowels!" (p. 384). It seems to him that justice, like crime, has insisted upon rending itself.

Like the previous judges, Musidorus has created an error even in making right judgment. He in turn is rebuked by the more faithful Pyrocles. Once an image for the most scatter-brained and passional part of man, he now is the better, or best, judge, prince, and son. He will have no more of rebellion and threatened regicide. He instructs Musidorus "not to do him the wrong to give his father ill words before him" (p. 384). He quietly reminds his cousin that it is their crime, not his father's administration of justice, that is on trial. Finally, he turns to his father. If need be, he says steadily, he will act the Isaac to Evarchus' hard sense of justice. Yet how much better if he were to be a life-serving "comfort to your mind, [rather than] an example of your justice; rather a preserver of your memory by my life, than a monument of your judgment by my death"! (p. 385). And he makes one last plea for the life of Musidorus, the only possible heir to Thessaly—a life surely of more worth than a "too precise . . . course of justice" that can only bring "many just execrations" upon the judge (pp. 385, 386).

However, because the conditions of the crime remain, the laws also stand. Evarchus enacts a Cato, loving "goodness more than himself." As the cavern of love had become a tomb, so his legal chair has "been his grave" (p. 386); nevertheless, he persists. Human justice cannot bear within its limited, yet "absolute," laws the possibility of relativism and mercy. In Arcadia, only the arrest of the crime, not justice itself, can supply a reversal. No number of merely human recognitions can alter the iron chain that binds crime with punishment.

It is therefore the part of divine justice to bring about a "miraculous," comic reversal, even as it had moved the serious recognition.[29] Replacing the terrible lamentations of the Fourth Eclogues, comical groans arise from the royal corpse. Because of Gynecia's mistake and a divinity that has shaped such accidents, the love potion has been only a midsummer's sleeping draught. Blind love, like blind justice, was a trance from which all Arcadia can now awaken.[30]

To the great joy of Evarchus, the resurrection of the king relieves him of the fiery shirt of magistracy. The king, restored to his governing, suddenly realizes that the oracle has been fulfilled, although certainly "not as before he had imagined" (p. 388). He judges that among the guilty his fault was greatest; he was not only the original cause but also a type for all the later exiles and disguises. Because Basilius is once again the model of a prince, Musidorus can even imitate him by acknowledging his recent faultiness with Evarchus. Basilius humbly asks his wife's pardon. Somewhat sardonically, Sidney notes that the recently reviled queen will later pass into a fame as great as her disgrace, "and neither justly." But then, as the entire work has demonstrated, justice is no plant that

[29] In this, I differ with Richard A. Lanham, *Old Arcadia* (New Haven and London: Yale Univ. Press, 1965), n. 5, p. 236.

[30] I do not find that the ending is pessimistic, but see Franco Marenco, "Per una nuova interpretazione dell' 'Arcadia' di Sidney," *EM*, 17 (1966), 48, along with Miss Dipple, "Harmony and Pastoral," pp. 313–318. I find that the whole work intends not so much to concede as to convert "flawed character and action." Although it demonstrates the infected will, the *Old Arcadia* is fundamentally "about" the erected wit and its golden world.

grows on mortal soil, even though its transplanted seedlings may flourish there.

A round of happy marriages of the heroes and princesses completes the proceeding and reasserts the great pattern. The marriages are not more or less "miraculous" than the resurrection, being the normal course of things which now displaces the recent abnormalities and aberrations of Arcadia. They are also the basis and type of all stable society. With them appear public reunions of counsellors with princes— Philanax with Basilius (and later with Musidorus, inheritor of Arcadia), Kalodulus with Musidorus, the useful balance Sympathus with Evarchus, and Kerxenus with Pyrocles.

And so the *Old Arcadia* [31] comes to a conclusion as mar-

[31] A full-length study of the *Old Arcadia* by Richard A. Lanham bears that title (New Haven and London: Yale Univ. Press, 1965). Among other important studies, many of which bear upon both of the *Arcadias,* are these: D. M. Anderson, "The Trial of the Princes in the *Arcadia,* Book V," RES, n. s. 8 (1957), 409–412; John Buxton, *Elizabethan Taste* (London: Macmillan, 1963), pp. 246–248; Lorna Challis, "The Use of Oratory in Sidney's *Arcadia,*" SP, 62 (1965), 561–576; Clifford Davidson, "Nature and Judgment in the *Old Arcadia,*" PLL, 6 (1970), 348–365; Elizabeth Dipple, "The 'Fore Conceit' of Sidney's Eclogues," *Literary Monographs,* 1 (1967), 3–47, "Harmony and Pastoral in the *Old Arcadia,*" ELH, 35 (1968), 309–328, "Metamorphosis in Sidney's *Arcadias,*" PQ, 50 (1971), 47–62, and " 'Unjust Justice' in the *Old Arcadia,*" SEL, 10 (1970), 83–101; P. Albert Duhamel, "Sidney's *Arcadia* and Elizabethan Rhetoric," SP, 65 (1948), 134–150; J. H. Hanford and S. R. Watson, "Personal Allegory in the *Arcadia,*" MP, 32 (1934), 1–10; Virgil B. Heltzel, "The Arcadian Hero," PQ, 61 (1962), 173–180; Alan D. Isler, "The Allegory of the Hero and Sidney's Two *Arcadias,*" SP, 65 (1968), 171–191, and "Heroic Poetry and Sidney's Two *Arcadias,*" PMLA, 83 (1968), 368–379; Franco Marenco, "Double Plot in Sidney's 'Old Arcadia,' " MLR, 64 (1969), 248–263, and *Arcadia Puritana* (Bari: Adriatica, 1968); Irving Ribner, "Machiavelli and Sidney: The *Arcadia* of 1590," SP, 47 (1950), 152–172; Mark Rose, "Sidney's Womanish Man," RES, 15 (1964), 353–363, and *Heroic Love* (Cambridge, Mass.: Harvard Univ. Press, 1968), pp. 37–73; and

riage bells ring back in a golden age of concord: a conclusion, but not quite an end. The fiction remains open. It leaves some characters of Asia Minor and the recent complaints of the shepherds in suspense. Teasingly, Sidney lets those loose threads from the heroic past, the again idealized present, and the adventurous future drift up and away from an otherwise well-made play. At the brisk end of a period, he says that either his spirit or his pen is too dulled to continue the story. He makes as if to pass the torch to "some other spirit." That spirit, of course, turns out to be the author of the *New Arcadia.*

But then, the leading intimations in a speaking picture cannot be terminated. A marriage of true minds between maker and fiction, and fiction and audience, may be celebrated but cannot be completed. Its source and end, however, are "known." If a romance teaches that there is no end to the "strange story" and "wonderful chances" of human action (p. 389), its heroic foreconceit is equally insistent that there is no end to the pattern of everlasting reason. Fiction can embrace both. By means of its imitative harmonizing of proceedings with pattern, and of restored will with erected wit, mankind may see, beyond the "ever-turning spheres, the never-moving ground" (p. 314).

Kenneth Thorpe Rowe, "Romantic Love and Parental Authority in Sidney's *Arcadia,*" Univ. of Mich. Contrib. in Mod. Phil., #4 (April, 1947).

Chapter 2

The *New Arcadia:*
A "room full of
delightful pictures"

When a *New Arcadia* [1] rose from the completion of the *Old,* Sidney had transformed his work much in outward show but even more in mind. In the process, he had surrendered a comely, simple structure and many delightful effects related to it. Dramatic "speaking" had been largely replaced by emblematic pictures; dialogue, often built upon Ramistic twinning patterns, was displaced into very numerous exemplary stories; the shepherds' eclogues, already redisposed, were all but overshadowed by pageant-like tourneys; and a simple, direct action moved by a few characters had seemed to disappear into manifold actions and multiplied characters. During the period before revision, the Aristotelian distinction between drama and epic evidently had been taken very seriously indeed. Whereas the *Old* had stressed heroism largely by showing a simple, "fatal," comic distraction into error, the *New* celebrates heroism in its successes against vice. [2] In changing the general mode of perception from the ear to the eye, both for characters within the work as well as readers without, Sidney also shifted from discussion within a falling, or

[1] Quotations from the *New Arcadia* are accompanied by parenthetical page numbers in the text.

[2] See Gerald F. Else, *Aristotle's Poetics: The Argument* (Cambridge, Mass.: Harvard Univ. Press, 1957), p. 596.

fallen, world to the meditation which could prevent a fall. This change makes Arcadia much more constant to its original golden idea, for most principles of error now are lodged in foreign states or alien factions. It converts Musidorus and Pyrocles into princes who are older, far more noble, and more sensitive, even as it maintains Basilius as Arcadian captain during most of the erotic folly. Correspondingly, Pamela and Philoclea become almost saintly under torture. Heroic chivalry itself, which at first appears to be essential to the *New Arcadia,* gradually gives way to an almost Miltonic "new heroism" of patience.

These alterations in the direct action and characters assist in the most far-ranging alteration in the *New Arcadia:* the expansion of the past heroic exploits of the princes from a moment's passing exposition into the body of the work, as it now stands. The princes' triumphs over masculine and feminine vices are now used not only to celebrate martial and political governing in the past, but also to provide contemplative, emblematic, tutelary examples to the princes (and auditors) in present trial. "External" heroism from the past is made to be the explicit guide to inward virtue in the present, and active accomplishment in the future.

In radically simple terms, the long body of reflexive narratives about Asia Minor resembles the section of the *Odyssey* known as the Wandering (or the Adventures) of Odysseus. In it the hero tells of his own past adventures in "foreign" places. In the *New Arcadia,* however, the princes (and other narrators) tell the tales not as a chart of former moral progress but as present moral guard, one that will *prevent* such an Odyssean decline and reascent. Furthermore, the simple telling of one story has radiated into a complex narration of many stories, unified now not by the hero or his action but by their being parts in an emblematic moral spectrum. Not only has Sidney made the shift to narrative his major alteration upon the *Old Arcadia,* then, but he has also worked extremely imaginative—if often distracting—changes upon the boundaries of narrative, itself.

The multiplication of narratives and narrators clearly has much to recommend it, even though in the last two centuries it has produced much distress and disaffection among Sidney's readers. He no doubt wanted to maintain a sense of present action by the use of Arcadian narrators even during the times when extra-Arcadian tales were being told, somewhat as Chaucer's links maintain the Canterburian action around and within the tales told by his travelers. He probably was equally interested in the possibility of the doubled "speaking picture" that could be achieved if a narrator were simultaneously to tell a tale and, in himself, to figure forth its meaning. A still greater attraction in the interior narrative, however, lay in its capacity to replace the usual descriptive analysis of a character's moral situation with an icastic, fictive presentation. If the narrative technique of the *Old Arcadia* might have offered a version of Hamlet who debated, soliloquized, and spoke daggers of rhetorical instruction, the *New* would have its hero invite characters and readers alike to listen to several narrators and to look upon both the picturing stories and the picturing narrators for a doubled "this picture, and . . . this." Narrating characters, as well as the listening audience both within and without the fiction, therefore gaze back and forth from the "picturing" narrative to the present condition in Arcadia, and from both of them to what "may be" and "should be" in the future.

Because of the radical changes that Sidney worked upon narrative itself, pattern and proceeding in the *New Arcadia* are more intimately interconnected than they were in the *Old Arcadia*. Pictures tend to inform the action, on the one hand, and narratives tend to recede into a collection of instructive tableaus, on the other. Nevertheless, in broad terms the general *pattern* is icastic, or emblematically pictorial; the *proceeding,* a processional accumulation of pictures from the past which will guide characters in the present as they shape the future.

An icastic pattern is predicted at the outset of the *New Arcadia* when two shepherds bid farewell to Urania. If the pure poetic idea is to be absent from this Arcadia, that is all the more reason why its material representatives should appear. In an extended preparation, picture after picture is revealed to the two exploring northern princes—especially in the gallery of Kalander, the *New Arcadia*'s definitive "good man." In the work's three Books, three great pageant-like tourneys incorporate character and action in picture. Most importantly of all, Book II, which becomes the major part of the revised *Arcadia,* consists of one quick verbal "picture" after another, showing the rulers (feminine as well as masculine) whom the young princes had encountered earlier in Asia Minor. Most of these pictures present negative examples. By having looked "on this picture, and on this" from the past, the heroes can steer safely through present storms of passion and fortune. In that way, they can guarantee the future. However, the use of the past for a pictorial instruction of the present and a guide to the future not only greatly increases the number of episodes in the *New Arcadia* but also fashions a far broader, if less driving, literary action than that of the *Old Arcadia.*

It may seem anomalous that a larger action should take place among the *New Arcadia*'s "pictures" than in the twinned, dramatic "speaking" of the *Old.* Although proverbial wisdom would have it that a picture is worth a thousand words, most people expect pictures to be essentially static. Elizabethans of Sidney's stamp would scarcely have understood what the proverb implies, of course—that is, that a picture somehow offers information and perhaps a visceral "knowledge" that words alone cannot give. The cultural difference cannot be circumscribed in a paragraph, but it is obvious that where we expect to find reproductions from "nature" (including the reproduction of an artist's state of mind, or of his state of vision, or of the possibilities of paint), they asked for creation or re-creation from idea. The lesser painter, Sidney said, can "counterfeit only such faces as are set before [him]"; the "more excellent," when he uses his colors to create a Lucrece, paints not a living woman but "the constant, though lamenting look" that is the "outward beauty of [her] virtue" (*Defence,* p. 10). At its worst, poetic "speaking," too, may display nothing better than the mechanical stuff of the lesser painter.

Perhaps for that reason, Sidney concedes at one point in the *Defence* (p. 43) that he must "deserve to be pounded, for straying from poetry, to oratory," despite their affinity in "wordish consideration." The difficulty with words as used in orations is distantly like that with precepts as used in philosophy; they may set one at a remove from truth by using "figurative speeches, or cunning insinuations" rather than revealing it utterly in a directly imitative "homely and familiar [tale]" (*Defence,* p. 21). Finally, because poetry usually brings to speech some of the delights of music, which is the "most divine striker of the senses," the poetic use of words will directly impress affective meaning upon the ear and the mind. And that will be tantamount to stamping meaning upon the will. The "pictures" thus created for senses, mind, and will should share many of the qualities of the visual "places" used in arts of memory (*Defence,* p. 27), including those of coherence and retentiveness.

Because of the penetration required from the viewer if he is to "strike through the mask" of the icastic sign and reach its meaning, even the icastic pattern of the *New Arcadia* can hardly be called static. Extremely interesting recent studies, such as those of Frances Yates, have unfolded the possibilities of meaning, and quest for meaning, in emblems and allegorical pictures, including those used in arts of memory. A great deal of activity, both intellectual and moral, is implied in the viewer's gradual penetration to the full significance of the picture, together with that of its sometimes accompanying motto or "word." Although the viewer may not be exactly a co-creator of meaning with the artist, he is nevertheless a co-aspirant in reaching from the visible to the invisible and from the material to the spiritual.[3] In such pictures, the value does not inhere in the design, even though a superior design is "better" than a poor one because it will be more moving; it inheres instead in the idea that the design indicates, figures forth, or illuminates. Similarly, actual places and persons appearing in masques and *tableaux vivants,* like the correspondent settings and characters in fiction, were understood to be emblematic. Place could become precept, and a living person no less than a fictive character could be "conceived" by means of his clothing, armor, mottoes, and physiognomy. Any single emblematic picture could lead to conception, thus moving the heart as well as the mind of the viewer while at the same moment "incarnating" the idea toward which the mind and heart should move. This somewhat Neoplatonic "descent" of divine idea into a representative matter, which then supplies the motive for a viewer's related "ascent" or aspiration beyond that matter, is eikonic in the Eastern Orthodox meaning of the word.[4] At its best, the icastic stimulus can confirm the erected wit by converting the infected will.

However, the major principle of movement in the *New*

---

[3] See Frances Yates, "The Emblematic Conceit in Giordano Bruno's *De Gli Eroici furori* and in Elizabethan Sonnet Sequences," *JWCI,* 6 (1943), 101–121, and *Theatre of the World* (Chicago: Univ. of Chicago Press, 1969), p. 168; also, see André Chastel, *The Age of Humanism* (New York: McGraw-Hill, 1963), pp. 80–95.

[4] See Ernst Benz, *The Eastern Orthodox Church,* tr. Richard and Clara Winston (Garden City, N.Y.: Doubleday, 1963), p. 6.

Arcadia is not limited to penetration of the single picture. Characteristically, the proceeding conducts a character or a group of characters through whole galleries of pictures, or long anthologies of pictural narratives. This active principle in the work is perhaps best described as "processional." The word suggests the movement of an audience from one fixed "stage" to another as it accumulates a total meaning. Although in stage history it might also be used to indicate the passage of moveable "stages" before a fixed audience, it is the former meaning that best applies in the *New Arcadia*.

If a single picture produced an effect somewhat like that which Sidney assigned to the lyric poem, a more complex system of inspection, contemplation, and movement would be demanded from a setting in which several related works were arranged, and in which several interinvolved characters, with differing accesses of blindness or illumination, then moved and responded to the pictures as well as to each other, both in their "pictured" character and in their inventive "speaking." Among all the arts, perhaps epical fiction alone could present the latter kind of movement. It leads almost inevitably to forms of recognition and reversal like those described by Aristotle and is therefore indeed an "action," not a mere gallery-hop.

The general setting for a processional movement was common to Elizabethans, awaiting them on almost every side. Many of their homes and public buildings, as well as their pageants and masques, were galleries of a sort. They would have viewed the collection of separate "pictures" not as a modern catch-all but as a generalization—a picture composed of pictures; a macrocosm made up of smaller units. Each of the units, however, would reveal a principle that predicted or reflected the total unity and therefore acted in full cooperation with it. Such a structured collection might have merited Sidney's laudatory word *architektonike* (*Defence*, p. 11), especially if the theatron or chamber is a collective image of the church or the cosmos, and if the end of the audience's proceeding is the gathering-together of knowledge.

Although we are not accustomed to thinking of a processional principle in fiction, it appears regularly in Renaissance allegory and the Renaissance heroic poem. Because the general principle is of direct help in reading the *New Arcadia,* it may be useful to recall some of its many appearances outside fiction. Men of Sidney's time would have encountered the processional movement in the Byzantine church, in which the moving spectator could join a great congregation of pictured divine, allegorical, and historical personages; in emblem books, in which a particular device offered its own meaning but also joined in a general collection to compose a mirror or theatron of human significances; in chronicles, wherein a series of narratives might compose a kind of universal mirror; and in commonplace collections. What is more, Walter J. Ong has identified something like this same proceeding in the essential book itself, which, significantly, used "types" and "fonts" and "impressions." [5]

***

[5] See Samuel C. Chew, *The Virtues Reconciled: An Iconographic Study* (Toronto: Univ. of Toronto Press, 1947); Robert J. Clements, *Picta Poesis* (Rome: Edizioni di Storia e litteratura, 1960); John V. Fleming, *The Roman de la Rose: A Study in Allegory and Iconography* (Princeton: Princeton Univ. Press, 1969), pp. 10–11; Allan H. Gilbert, "The Function of the Masques in *Cynthia's Revels,*" *PQ,* 22 (1943), 211–230; E. H. Gombrich, "Icones Symbolicae," *JWCI,* 9 (1948), 163–192; Sister Joan Marie Lechner, O.S.U., *Renaissance Concepts of the Commonplaces* (New York: Pageant, 1962), pp. 1–4; the introductions to the several masques in *A Book of Masques, in Honor of Allardyce Nicoll* (Cambridge: Cambridge Univ. Press, 1967); Dieter Mehl, "Emblems in Renaissance Drama," *Ren. Drama,* n. s. 2, ed. S. Schoenbaum (Evanston, Ill.: Northwestern Univ. Press, 1969), p. 47; Alice S. Venezky, *Pageantry on the Shakespearean Stage* (New York: Twayne, 1951); Glynne Wickham, *Early English Stages: 1300 to 1600* (London:

In any of these examples of the processional, the spatial, visual, diagrammatic, and contemplative tend to displace the more familiar modern expectations—temporal, aural, exploratory, and discursive. Much as a reader then perceived great pictured meanings page by page, even in the letters of an illuminated book or manuscript, so the present reader of the *New Arcadia* is asked to look within individual pictures (in "outward" setting, dress, armor, or fixed tale) to see their inward significance, and then to move processionally with them and among them. Although the proceeding is emblematic, it is seldom allegorical. Because Sidney asks that his reader comprehend meaning as it accumulates, processionally, the general significance is discovered or realized, not allegorically "translated." Similarly, characters are representatives of ideas, not signs for them. If within the *New Arcadia* the processional technique offers a display *of* meaning in eikonic pictures, within the audience it offers a display *for* meaning and effect. Individually and in sum, the many pictures, along with the characters who proceed among them, serve Sidney almost in the same way that religious symbols served George Herbert: the end was "something understood."

Sidney was convinced that "poetical imitation" consists in "the right description of wisdom, value, and justice" (*Defence*, p. 20). He must have believed that the *New Arcadia*'s proliferation of exemplary narratives would contribute to that "right description." Although Tillyard was correct in stating that Sidney's "heraldic mind" was more interested in the "plastic or pictorial [than the] literary and progressive," it is quite wrong to think of either of the *Arcadias* as great

Routledge, 1959), I, 15–71; Frances Yates, "Elizabethan Chivalry: The Romance of the Accession Day Tilts," *JWCI*, 20 (1957), 22–25; and Walter J. Ong, *Ramus: Method and the Decay of Dialogue* (Cambridge, Mass.: Harvard Univ. Press, 1958), pp. 307–314.

friezes—or as great cobwebs.[6] In Sidney's universe of heroic "simple tales," narrative moves within itself and, in so doing, moves the reader back to the originating concepts of the erected wit and forward to the actions of a reformed will. In the *New Arcadia* even more than the *Old,* the golden pattern and a judicial proceeding (now occupied with comparisons between past and present and between tale and teller) are continuously held up to our consideration. Although a modern reader may find the technique of processional internal narratives "digressive" and diversionary in practice, he may well envy Sidney the amplitude of its range in theory. The machinery is not perfect, but it offers an author the valuable cross-reference of internal example with internal auditor; of tale and teller; of Castiglione's courtier and Chaucer's courtly instruction; and even a hint of Browning's multiple monologuists and Joyce's present-tense parade of narrators in their unions with remembered or associated event.

The processional principle of action in the *New Arcadia* suggests that the structure of the work is complex and intricately interrelated, yet fundamentally simple and unified. Our discussion of the proceeding will close upon a swift overview of that structure.

As Walter Davis has recently shown, narratives as well as direct action move out from the Arcadian center in two increasing circles—first, including Corinth, and then including Asia Minor.[7] Those circles are seen to be interrelated in

---

[6] See E. M. W. Tillyard, *The English Epic and Its Background* (New York: Oxford Univ. Press, 1954), p. 316. The cobweb metaphor, borrowed from Sidney, is Hazlitt's.

[7] Walter R. Davis, *A Map of Arcadia,* in *Sidney's Arcadia* (New Haven and London: Yale Univ. Press, 1965), pp. 52–54. See also the brief structural comment in E. M. W. Tillyard, *Shakespeare's Last Plays* (London: Chatto and Windus, 1951), pp. 71–72.

action (in heroic idea, they have always been one, not three) as the revised portion of the *Arcadia* ends.

Book I aligns Arcadian action with a "procession" of Corinthian models of heroic love. They scale down in a triad from the perfect love but dangerously "perfect" honor of Argalus and Parthenia (*troublous; virginal*), through a middle relationship between Amphialus and Helen (*at sea; torch*) that is wracked by misunderstanding but in the end seems destined to flourish, to the completely negative example of two unloving egoists, Phalantus and Artesia (*line of battle; hanger-on*).[8] These "pictures" and the internal or direct narratives that speak for them inform and guide the young Arcadian princes and princesses as they fall in love. In terms of narrative time, those emblematic narratives gradually converge in the present, thereby involving the princes directly as well as icastically. The resulting double action for the princes is framed on the one side by a Basilian oracle and a fortune-induced shipwreck,[9] both of which stand against order and harmony, and on the other by a related attack of savage beasts. Much the same framing service is provided by a tourney in which heroic love is about evenly matched with unheroic vanity, and by eclogues which restore a vision of the ideal.

The much more complicated Book II, commencing with an earlier shipwreck, supplies "pictures" from the outer circle of time and distance. These examples seem farther from the direct action than those in Book I, but are actually nearer to it. They supply present instruction for the princes and prin-

[8] See Friedrich Brie, *Sidneys Arcadia: Eine Studie zur Englischen Renaissance* (Strassburg, 1918), pp. 151–159.

[9] See John F. Danby, *Poets on Fortune's Hill* (London: Faber and Faber, 1952), p. 86, and Moses Hadas, tr., Heliodorus, *An Ethiopian Romance* (Ann Arbor: Univ. of Michigan Press, 1957), p. viii.

cesses, who alternate as narrators and auditors according to Sidney's subtle sense of their greatest needs and interests. As mnemonics become monition, they see, think, and know the images for a spectrum of male tyrannies; for another spectrum of feminine misdirections in love and politics; and for a combining third, in which are ranged both male and female strength, lust, and miserliness. Around these are placed other, related pictures. In general, the princes are shown to have put down "masculine" tyranny and "feminine" lust in Asia Minor while exalting fair government and love. Double consequences of their good government live on. Although an assembly of kings honored them when they left Asia Minor, they were pursued from Asia by Armenian enmity. It caused the second shipwreck and continues to threaten both the princes and the state of Lycia. Similarly, the present tyrannous lusts of Basilius and Gynecia reflect the past Asian tyrannies, and are in turn reflected in a second attack—that of Arcadian "mutineers." Again, eclogues recall Arcadia to a better pattern.

Book III is given over to active present warfare and trial, as the ambitious, Argive Cecropia wars with Basilius' inviting slackness. In a third major attack, the Arcadian princesses are abducted. Although narrative has returned to the "present" and profound debates reminiscent of the *Old Arcadia* move much of the action, the general mode remains emblematic. Not only are the two sides (the "Basilian" and the opposing Argian, or "Amphialan") made to be almost absolute emblems of opportunistic vice and enduring, patient, sometimes sacrificial virtue, but also external armed attacks on the castle where the princesses are imprisoned correspond closely with the moral and religious attacks that they endure within. "Pictured" executions are staged in the hope of breaking the captives' wills. And a general turning point is reached by means of several combats or tourneys, which present the opponents as living images—pictures that figure forth their own characters, desires, and beliefs.

Not long before he stopped writing, Sidney had brought both Musidorus and his complicated rival, Amphialus, almost to death. He apparently intended that such suffering should lead them toward rebirth into heroic harmony. He had also arranged that Pyrocles, like the returned Odysseus, should triumph over a remaining evil faction by wit as well as by courage. Most significantly, he had given Basilius a second oracle, which placed the first in a light very different from that in the *Old Arcadia*. Near that point, the *New Arcadia* was broken off.[10] I, for one, do not think that it was abandoned. The general direction in which it would have moved seems clear, although details of the probable execution must remain entirely speculative.

The total effect achieved by this serious, all but tragic, principal action and its large body of almost icastic narratives is that of heroic and redemptive justice striving against a world of infected wills. Love, however, which had been comic rage in the *Old Arcadia,* is now an harmonious adjunct to heroism. Like epic and pastoral when combined in a heroic poem, the brave and the fair can now envision and inhabit one world. Interest therefore shifts from the "siege of contraries" in reason and passion to the somewhat more modern concern with the psychology of international discord, on the one hand, and with heroic patience, on the other. If Sidney has laid aside his Terence and his Achilles furious in skirts, he has taken up his Plato, Paul, and a hero striving toward

---

[10] Among those who have doubted if the *New Arcadia* could have been finished are Tucker Brooke, "Sidney and the Sonneteers," in *A Literary History of England,* ed. A. C. Baugh (New York: Appleton-Century-Crofts, 1948), p. 476, and Robert Kimbrough, ed., *Sir Philip Sidney: Selected Prose and Poetry* (New York: Rinehart, 1969), p. 244.

holiness. The action of the *New Arcadia* will be the definition and trial of virtue, especially when under cynical trial by
men who worship only fortune and expediency.

"A reason in passion": The First Book

In the *Old Arcadia,* marriage and other reintegrative
unions had resolved the work, at almost the last possible
moment. In the *New,* marriage, within a vastly enlarged idea
and implication, is placed "in the beginning." Before man
appears on the scene or the single province of Arcadia is isolated as a setting, the whole earth puts on "her new apparel
against the approach of her lover," the sun (p. 5). Sidney's
fiction begins "in [that nuptial] time." Marriage is therefore
both foreconceit and emblem, the ideal beginning and the
wished-for end, to all of the *New Arcadia.*

Yet the great physical union of earth with governing sun
can provide no more than a setting and emblem for man. His
political and ethical world must be of his own making. The
New Arcadia therefore looks past nature to man—first, in
his melancholy separation from his own idea of perfection,
and then, in his direct physical danger from outrageous history and fortune. With nature having proved to be "other"
and the ideal to be "known" but absent, the human condition may seem to be defined only by loss, shipwreck, piracy,
and blank seas. However, the work at once moves to construct
images of human virtue, including human marriage, which
man may first envision and then realize within his own life.
With the cosmic marriage as a sign and the absent ideal as a
guide or goal, man in the world of nature may "create"
within actual persons and deeds a manifestation of the ideal,
a human duplicate of the golden cosmic sign.

In this emblematic synthesis, the former phases of integration/ disintegration/ reintegration merge into one field of awareness. If nature and the ideal are in themselves separate from man, then mediatorial man (who in some measure participates in both) can join the two, emblematically, and make a golden world. The range of his moral and philosophical actions and meanings may then be seen at a glance, and he can proceed to simple, emulative enactment. Elements from nature will become "pictures" for meaning, and elements from idea, the moral guides for physical action. In particular, the cosmic wedding supplies a sustaining image for the two princes when they welter in fortune's perilous flood. Later, a real marriage, together with graphic images of perfection in a real household of a real state, heals and guides them. They thus avoid the two shepherds' opening grief because the ideal, though known and loved, now lay absent from their direct experience.

In the first large sweep of meaning, then, the *New Arcadia* proceeds from natural emblem, through the loss of its spiritual equivalent, toward a Piconian middle ground of realization and re-attainment.

Within the splendid nuptial time, the first human characters who appear are the shepherds Klaius and Strephon, brought forward all the way from the *Old Arcadia*'s Fourth Eclogues. Images of union and of separation thus stand together at the portals of the work. The shepherds introduce a vast sense of loss and alienation. Although they are natives of Arcadia, they are discovered near the blank sea in barren, hostile Laconia. They recall a past Arcadia as idyllic as earth and sun in love, for then their lover Urania [11] had been phys-

---

[11] See Katherine Duncan-Jones, "Sidney's Urania," *RES*, 17 (1966), 123–132; Kenneth O. Myrick, *Sir Philip Sidney as a Literary Craftsman* (Cambridge, Mass.; Harvard Univ. Press, 1935), p. 115; Clements, *Picta*

ically present. But she has since debarked for Cythera; if Venus or Urania comes to men from the turbulent sea, she may depart in the same way. Similarly, Arcadia can seem to degenerate into Laconia. At once, the seas and shipwrecks of Hellenistic romance take on emblematic qualities. They intimate the physical threat of fortune, on the one hand, and of static distance between man and the ideal, on the other.

Like love, therefore, memory now brings the two shepherds as much of torment as delight:

Did . . . not [remembrance] cry within us, 'Ah, you base-minded wretches, are your thoughts so deeply bemired in the trade of ordinary worldlings . . . to let so much time pass without knowing perfectly her estate . . . to leave that shore unsaluted, from whence you may see to the island where she dwelleth?' [p. 6].

There is then no choice for lovers of the purely ideal. They will not love at lesser rate, but the object of love is "away." In the meantime, most physical objects are only pictures, to them; phenomena merely "call to memory more excellent matters," much as the supposed physical beauty of Urania was a "fold" that contained her "flock of unspeakable virtues." The mutual dedication of the shepherds to their love has at least one present benefit: it propagates in them a "love-fellowship" that makes them cooperative apostles, not ordinary rival lovers.

Unlike the contemplative shepherds, the two young princes will have to actualize love and make it an active virtue—one that can redeem themselves and Arcadia. Redemptive patience will grow from their pathos of loss. If to them Urania is too bright to hit the sense of human realization, they must

---

Poesis, p. 34; and Richard Cody, *The Landscape of the Mind* (Oxford: Oxford Univ. Press, 1969), pp. 11, 46–49.

turn to "her works [within] some meaner subject"—such as the princesses and themselves, within the state of Arcadia. They can all be representative "shadows" [12] of Urania and of the celestial Arcadia of pure idea. They will discover then that the ideal can cast "reason upon our desires, and, as it were, [give] eyes unto Cupid" (pp. 7–8). In that way, a foolish blind boy may become a timeless seer or saint.

In the immediate present, however, the loss of the ideal is at once matched with physical loss, although the direction of movement is significantly reversed. The empty sea sends a young man ashore on a board that seems "a bier to carry him . . . to his sepulchre." Although it will turn out that this flat sea has been "kind in love" (*Twelfth Night,* III, iv, 18), it seems only to have undone a "young man of so goodly shape, and well-pleasing favor, that one would think death had, in him, a lovely countenance" (p. 8). When the solicitous shepherds restore him, he, like them, greets existence with a groan.

This model for every young man, now being reborn within the unlikely womb of fortune and loss, is Musidorus. Having seen his cousin Pyrocles apparently swept to death at sea, Musidorus would destroy himself in it. Even though he consents to live, he must recall that icy waters of fortune had been joined by a fire aboard ship, which testified to "human inhumanity." Its wreck, which the three can now see to be still burning on the seas, forecasts the wrecks of persons and states that are to come. As is the case in *Lycidas,* it is man,

[12] See Elizabeth Dipple, "The 'Fore Conceit' of Sidney's Eclogues," *Literary Monographs,* 1 (1967), 46; Davis, *A Map of Arcadia,* pp. 84–86; John Charles Nelson, *Renaissance Theory of Love* (New York: Columbia Univ. Press, 1958), pp. 57, 178, 202; and François Bucher, "Medieval Landscape Painting: An Introduction," in *Medieval and Renaissance Studies* (Chapel Hill: Univ. of North Carolina Press, 1968), p. 120.

not nature, who produces such a mystifying "shipwreck without storm or ill footing . . . and a waste of fire in the midst of water" (p. 10).

Within the same fortunal context, another young man then appears in the water. He is clothed in Apollonian blue and gold,[13] rides the mast like Shakespeare's Sebastian, and brandishes a sword against the whole threatening universe. It is Pyrocles, of course. But even as the two princes greet each other within their apparent change of fortune, man's inhumanity again strikes. Pirates on watch for booty race to the scene and enslave Pyrocles. The twice-bereft elder cousin is convinced that death would have been better for them both. However, he is comforted by his "true friends," the shepherds. In a statement of general faith, they liken his situation to that of a shepherd who cannot find his flock. Man's lost sheep are not necessarily dead or nonexistent. In time, the shepherd shall "know they were but strayed . . . though readily he knew not where to find them" (p. 12).

Recovery from loss begins for the young prince when he again sees images of living perfection. Conveyed to Arcadia and her representative "good man," Kalander, Musidorus runs a suggestive three-day course of grief. At its end, nature's rose and violet dawn (recapitulating the opening marriage of sun with earth) blots out harsh Laconia. Similarly, Arcadia opens out before him as a kind of national Penshurst, a living emblem of the orderly, harmonious state:

There were hills which garnished their proud heights with stately trees; humble valleys, whose base estate seemed comforted with refreshing of silver rivers; meadows, enamelled with all sort of eye-pleasing flowers; thickets, which . . . were witnessed so to by the cheerful disposition of many well-tuned birds; each pas-

[13] Pyrocles also resembles Sidney, as described in Thomas Zouch, *Memoirs of the Life and Writings of Sir Philip Sidney* (New York: Wilson and Son, 1808), p. 181.

ture stored with sheep feeding with sober security . . . ; here a shepherd's boy piping, as though he should never be old; there a young shepherdess knitting, and withal singing, and it seemed that her voice comforted her hands to work, and her hands kept time to her voice's music [p. 13].

Such a condition is largely the golden work of man's creation. As such, it marks a way between nature and the absolutely ideal. This province forms a total contrast with the fruitless soil and the civil wars of Laconia. Arcadia's people want "little, because they desire not much"; they live in "accompanable solitariness" in a state "decked with peace and . . . good husbandry" (p. 14).

More immediately, as if in a reduction from the public to the private, such a golden world is manifested also in Kalander's own house. It does not affect

so much any extraordinary kind of fineness, as an honorable . . . firm stateliness. The lights, doors, and stairs, rather directed to the use of the guest, than to the eye of the artificer . . . each place handsome without curiosity, and homely without loathsomeness; not so dainty as not to be trod on, nor yet slubbered up with good fellowship; all more lasting than beautiful, but that the consideration . . . made the eye believe it was exceeding beautiful [p. 15].

As such polities may be golden, so may the microcosmos, man. Musidorus increasingly returns to exactly that proper human self, showing "high-erected thoughts seated in a heart of courtesy [and] a behavior so noble, as gave a majesty to adversity" (p. 16). In man, then, Urania's fold of virtues may appear, incarnate.

Finally, this procession of physical images that emblematize man's possible golden state arrives at real galleries. In Kalander's garden, in the approach to the pictures, even a small pond is a kind of image—"a perfect mirror to all the other beauties, so that it bore show of two gardens; one in deed, the other in shadows" (p. 17). Statues of Venus and Aeneas at the base of a fountain similarly enfigure a related heroic "deed." In the gallery proper, Musidorus comes upon a group of paintings that image a cross-section of possible deeds—Diana with Actaeon [14] (anticipating Pyrocles' spying on Philoclea), Helen, Omphale, Iole. Among them, in an interesting trans-fictional reference, he sees Philoclea. He assumes that she must be beyond "the reach of invention"— feeling either that she is completely an ideal or, more hopefully at this point, that the human manifestation of beauty is better than mere fancy could produce. Like Urania, the elder princess is absent from the scene, although she "may be found" with Dametas, humbled into shepherd's attire.

Up to this point, the difference of *Old* and *New Arcadias* has been marked in the change from fixed definition and rhetorical trial, to ideal form and lesser manifestation. It now extends to a related, but more striking, alteration. In place of the traditional movement by epic between narrative and dramatic modes, the *New* seeks an internal narrative, delivered by one of the characters. This device not only allows the present to move within a context of the past and vice versa, but also draws both past and present act into a sense of permanent deed or being. The first use of the device is given to Kalander.

After "looking on the picture" of the royal family in his gallery, Kalander reunites image with history and with moral analysis. Event becomes a kind of mirroring image—so much so that the Plutarchan epithet "speaking picture" can almost be changed into "picturing speech." Such speech from history can supply the listener with a definition or a parallel for his own life.

[14] See John Buxton, *Elizabethan Taste* (London: Macmillan, 1963), p. 107.

Kalander's picture of the Arcadian family therefore speaks of Basilius' model kingship and manhood. He creatively joins "the virtues which get admiration . . . as depth of wisdom, height of courage, and largeness of magnificence [with] those which stir affection, as truth of word, meekness, courtesy, mercifulness, and liberality" (p. 19); he thus combines the present virtues of Musidorus and Pyrocles. The queen had been a model for women, in her turn, and the princesses are "over-excellent" in their pairing of attractive grace with intellectual and moral virtue. But Kalander's narrative "speech" now has to relate the loss of that golden ideal or achievement, as a result of Basilius' fortunal fancy. The human triad is reversed as government is abdicated and the princesses are subjected to the anti-models of Dametas' family. To all this, Kalander steadily offers judgment of the past that can instruct Musidorus in the present and thereby guide the future.

This radical displacement of narrative is extended further when Kalander employs a letter—a narrative in its own right—to tell Musidorus of the debate between Philanax and Basilius. It may be useful to remark just here that when Sidney displaces narrative to a concerned character who will offer judgment within the tale but often also receive judgment from its meaning, and when he then has that narrating character introduce still other related stories that bear on his concerns, as author he has allowed a dangerous diffusion of the principal account. The risk is offset by major advantages, however: the implications of the account can catch up many more people within the work's effective cast of characters, as the persons of the several fictions interrelate; the effective number of narrative "times," together with their interrelationships, can also be multiplied; and all the while, the fundamental unity of "internal" narrating character with an auditor can reflect that same unity in the "external" situation of author and reader. The partial sacrifice of drama and direct authorial control, then, is countered by the gain in persons involved in judicial reason as well as in representative persons concerned in the interrelating actions.

An immediate example is offered in Kalander's handling of the debate of Philanax with Basilius. It is of course removed into Kalander's judicial narration, and, as we have seen, makes use of its own internal narrative, the letter. It includes a present concern, however, for Kalander's son, Clitophon (*summoned*), who had copied the very letter that Kalander now reports. The letter, which nearly duplicates Philanax' first speech in the *Old Arcadia,* makes two significant additions: first, it warns that love, which can never be wrong if it follows the "God of nature" who cannot "teach unnaturalness," may nevertheless follow passion into "strange loves" (p. 25); second, it emphasizes the ambitious men who welcome Basilius' abdication, in order to show the danger of a power vacuum.

By joining narrator and auditor in attention to a fiction, this story has helped to form Kalander and Musidorus into an almost Homeric polity, in which their difference of age is of no importance. In another graceful parallel with the *Odyssey,* the apologetic host recalls that in Homer long speeches (such as his story of Philanax) were deferred until after a meal, but the guest assures him "that he had already been more fed to his liking than he could be by the skilfullest trencher-men of Media" (p. 29). They also agree that Klaius and Strephon are such shepherds "as Homer speaks of, that be governors of peoples" (p. 27). Thus past story and judgment again move into present applicability. When Kalander goes on to champion poetry itself, which has been encouraged by "example and emulation" in Arcadia (p. 28), the fictional union reaches out also to embrace Sidney and his reader. If the golden world is receding in Basilius, it remains constant in Kalander, Musidorus, and the more general "host" and "guest."

But the real world with its threats and losses also continues, despite the model community in Kalander's house. News comes that Kalander's son, Clitophon, has been seized by rebels in neighboring brazen Laconia. Because the rebels "hate all gentlemen," the young Arcadian is almost certain to be killed. Still the good Homeric host, Kalander muffles his grief; and still acting the true hero, Musidorus decides to go help Clitophon, or else avenge him. He also hopes to learn something of Pyrocles, who may be in similar trouble somewhere. He will need more than historical speaking about the past, however, as he moves into strange new seas of ethical demand. He must be guided by a timeless model that can instruct his present and lead his future. He is therefore given the first of Book I's major "icastic" narratives. It is a picture of a love and marriage that are perfected even within the currents of actuality and loss. Not only does it translate the cosmic image of earth and sun into human terms, then, but it also shows that the ideal Urania or Adonis can be made flesh, to dwell among men. Perfect picture is to proceed to lively knowledge.

"Inward worthiness shining through foulest mists": Argalus and Parthenia

The image of the perfect nuptial union has been approached by proceedings of loss—the embarkation of the ideal Urania, the reverse tossing to the Laconian shore of Musidorus and the piratical abduction of Pyrocles, and the seizure of Kalander's son. The action had been preceded or opposed by a pattern of natural or ideational union. The two strands now join.

The first great internal narrative is delivered by a messenger. It establishes Laconia even more firmly as the enemy (but also as the condition to which Arcadia may slide if she indulges her own rebellious passions). But more importantly, it shows two politico-ethical people who triumph over fortune and loss. They are Argalus, a cousin to Gynecia, and Parthenia, who had been expected to marry a Laconian, Demagoras.

Each is originally a pattern of conduct. Argalus manifests such "a virtuous mind in all his actions" (p. 31) that he propagates virtues in other men—notably in Kalander's son Clitophon. As Argalus is a mirror for princes, so Parthenia is an image of the princess. Her outward beauty is the "fair ambassador of a most fair mind . . . and a wit which [delights] more to judge itself, than to show itself" (p. 32). When they fall in love, however, Laconian loss is thrust across their course. Her mother, anticipating the tyrannical matriarchies to come, would marry Parthenia to the Laconian Demagoras, or have Argalus killed. Her efforts prove fruitless. Even as their tyrannical aunt will fail to crush the Arcadian princesses, so Laconian trial serves only to make the love of Argalus and Parthenia "more pure" (p. 33). They thus offer a pattern that is proof against the worst proceeding of loss. Not even the abominable disfiguring of Parthenia by Demagoras' poison alters their "constancy of affection" (p. 33). However, as has been seen with the shepherds and the two princes, such loss of beauty serves to try constancy on a radical new front. The image of the two lovers' handling of the new trial indicates a clear danger to all concerned, but it also shows the way to victory. That victory in turn produces an even "more perfect union."

Under the trial of loss of beauty, Argalus stands firm. He maintains that the truth of love was "the first face" of the disfigured Parthenia, thus providing a splendid example of a "virtuous constancy . . . and inward worthiness shining through the foulest mists." (Again, Sidney almost duplicates the language of the *Defence* in his fiction.) Much more questionably, Parthenia, also swearing by the name of love, wanders far afield in "a strange encounter of love's affects, and effects" (p. 35). In a perverse sense of constancy, she is sure that her ugliness is unworthy of Argalus. Therefore, conceding the defeat she had not allowed to her mother and Demagoras, she builds up a resolve "never to have him"; she will not "match Argalus to such a Parthenia" (p. 36). When she steals away like Urania from the shepherds, he all but throws away his life (as Musidorus was tempted to do) by attacking Demagoras and the helots. Only the intervention of a noble new captain, supposedly Laconian, has saved him, and the Arcadian lad Clitophon with him, from being killed. Both, however, are now kept "in a close and hard prison" (p. 37): and with that placement, narrative of the past and action in the present converge. Image at once encourages emulation.

The principle of heroic imitation having impelled Musidorus from "[passionate] delight" in hearing of Argalus into a present "noble emulation in him, towards him" (in which the transdevelopment of Cyruses celebrated in the *Defence* is again directly figured), he himself sets off for Laconia, leaving assurance of his victory etched propagatively in the "face and gesture" of Kalander (p. 38).

At the border, Musidorus learns in another internal narrative that the Laconian helots, once free, had been enslaved by Lacadaemonians.[15] Oppression having become unbearable, the underlings had revolted with "beastly fury," sparing no one of whatever age or weakness. Their success had forced the aristocrats to sue for peace. Musidorus realizes instantly that in such a state of turmoil, the delivery of

[15] See W. D. Briggs, "Political Ideas in Sidney's *Arcadia*," *SP*, 28 (1931), 137–161. The rebellion in Laconia is not condemned by Sidney, because it arises among a people formerly free. Otherwise, he carefully restricts the "right of rebellion."

Kalander's son demands more "discretion than valor" (p. 39). Saddled with brave but undisciplined troops, he must act the Odysseus, not the Achilles.

Profiting from the histories he has read (and suggesting that Cyruses may be propagated from history as well as poetry), he disguises most of the Arcadians as helots, reserving two hundred of the best to act as if they were chained "gentlemen" held by those rebels. Similarly, an Arcadian messenger to the helots carefully uses a deceptive plainness, in a highly artificial rhetoric that has carefully (and "rebelliously") "weeded out all flowers of rhetoric" (p. 40). By such imitations of rebellion are the rebellious deceived. Like so many Trojan horses, therefore, the Arcadians are granted leave to "harbor under the walls" (p. 41). When Musidorus thereafter casts off his chains, he staggers the helots much as the revealed Odysseus had amazed the Ithacan suitors. Only the sudden return of their captain, "the first mover of all the other hands" (p. 42), prevents a general helot surrender.

In heroic acceptance of the whole battle into their own persons, Musidorus and the new Laconian captain, both of them heroic in "delightful terribleness," engage in single combat. After much equal battle reveals that "their courage [is] guided with skill, and their skill . . . armed with courage," the helot captain in desperation strikes a blow that knocks away Musidorus' helmet—upon which the captain reveals himself to be the lost Pyrocles.

At once, in token of recovery from loss into union, a retreat is ordered for both sides. In a gesture that may show the course the entire book might have taken had it been completed, the cousins lead the two factions to successful parley; it resembles the concordant assembly of Asian kings with which the Asian adventures will close. The parley results in the release of Kalander's son, Clitophon. The prophetic and significant reunion of father and son (perhaps projecting a future complete reunion of Evarchus with Pyrocles) follows that of the two princes. The services of a Pyrocles or a Musidorus have become almost Christ-like for, as Clitophon says of Pyrocles, "Here is he, who (as a father) hath new-begotten me, and (as a God) hath saved me from many deaths" (p. 45). Heroism begins to be defined in terms of salvation. Clitophon is justified in such praise by Pyrocles' magnanimous decision to return again to Laconia in order to free Argalus.

If by entering Laconia in disguise Musidorus had imitated Odysseus, in addressing the rebellious helots' assembly (but subduing it) Pyrocles recalls Telemachus. His speech, anticipating the great arguments to come in Book III, is a careful defense of moderation. He tells the helots that, having gained a right to retain the land they have captured and having been set free, they are now as one with the other Laconians. Peace must confirm that the two sides are one. The emulative helots protest when he says that he himself must leave Laconia, but they receive his promise that if need should arise he would return. They treat him as if he were Urania or a "demi-God," "thinking it beyond the degree of humanity [that he should] have a wit so far overgoing his age, and such dreadful terror [proceeding] from so excellent beauty" (p. 47). Such reason and valor, in a concord of the brave with the fair, forms this Pyrocles in an image radically different from the over-hasty transvestite of the *Old Arcadia*. Not only has he repeated the heroic services he had once performed in Asia, but also he has almost combined the imaged virtues of Argalus and Parthenia.

Later, after having freed Argalus, Pyrocles too is brought to the house of Kalander. It is now his turn to encounter the gallery of images and be introduced to his direct proceeding in love. His heroism in arms and government in Laconia may turn dangerously to its opposite in love, for in the private sphere his youth and bashfulness may prove seductively "effeminate." [16] It sometimes seems that "nature [might have] mistaken her work to have a Mars's heart in a Cupid's body." Relatedly, many people who had formerly admired Musidorus now give the "moist and fickle impression of eyesight" (p. 48) to the newcomer. It is a threatening indication not only of the temptation Pyrocles will offer to Gynecia and Basilius, but also of the dangers into which his own eyesight will lead him. But as the image of Argalus and Parthenia had helped Musidorus, so now it will offer a saving foreconceit to Pyrocles. In a way, however, he will be more closely associable with the second pair of lovers, Helen and Amphialus; they tend to share his "mixed" central position in a triad.

In the present, peace having been restored to Arcadia and Laconia, the emblematic lovers Argalus and Parthenia arrive in Kalander's house in the flesh, offering lively knowledge to the princes directly "within the limits of Arcadia" (p. 45). Somewhat as Philoclea will do much later with Pyrocles, the recovered and therefore unrecognized Parthenia tells Argalus that in dying "Parthenia" had wished him to marry the present speaker. His constancy is unshaken. He assures her that if beauty were all that mattered he might do so, but that it "was Parthenia's self [he] loved . . . ; which no likeness can make one, no commandment dissolve . . . no death finish" (p. 50). With that, they are united. She reveals that she has been healed by a physician to Helen of Corinth. When they marry, the ceremony itself is less complete than the marriage of love and beauty in the temple of the bride's eyes.

Pyrocles is ecstatically impressed by this model of love, murmuring, "O Jupiter . . . how happens it, that beauty

[16] For a justly famous analysis of the masculine and feminine components in the young lovers, see Danby, *Poets on Fortune's Hill,* pp. 56–60.

is only confined to Arcadia?" (p. 54). Somewhat like Klaius
and Strephon, he becomes a constant lover before ever becoming the lover of a particular woman, or even of her
portrait. When Musidorus argues their duty to leave Arcadia and continue north, therefore, Pyrocles cannot agree.
He is only too well aware of the claims of a newer constancy,
even as he is sure that his mind has been drawn to matters
higher than the eye can see.

Sidney breaks off their debate, familiar from the *Old
Arcadia,* at about the halfway mark. In its place, Kalander
recalls a political constancy and its loss. It is a rebuke to
Basilius and the princes, any one of whom might now betray
one another or the nation. Arcadia, says Kalander, agreeing
at a lower level with the lamenting shepherds, has changed
since his boyhood: "activity and good fellowship being nothing in the price it was then held in, but according to the nature of the old-growing world, still worse and worse" (p. 60).
In a recollection of that older melody, he takes the young
men hunting for deer,[17] camouflaged in green "as though
they were children of summer." It is not yet a Chaucerian
heart-hunting, however. Even while the deer emblematically
sheds tears at man's unkindness, Musidorus looks about and
finds that Pyrocles has once more vanished, seemingly having
abandoned friendship as Basilius has abandoned Arcadia.
Between them, the prince and the ruler seem to have justified Kalander's complaint.

When a letter from Pyrocles at last turns up, bidding Musidorus return to Thessaly without him, Musidorus properly
berates him for this second, willed, fortune-imitating loss:

[17] See Hallett Smith, *Elizabethan Poetry: A Study in Conventions,
Meanings, and Expression* (Cambridge, Mass.: Harvard Univ. Press,
1964), pp. 323–324, and André Grabar, *Byzantium from the Death of
Theodosius to the Rise of Islam,* tr. Stuart Gilbert and James Emmons
(London: Thames and Hudson, 1966), pp. 102–103.

". . . now thyself is the sea, which drowns my comfort, thyself is the pirate that robs thyself of me" (p. 61). Nevertheless, he begins to restore the Arcadia that once had manifested a pattern of fellowship. He determines to follow Pyrocles in whatever quest his younger cousin has chosen. Breaking away from Kalander's importunities, which suggest those of Nestor with Telemachus, Musidorus with Clitophon swiftly scouts all the regions of Arcadia until they reach a Happy Valley, girdled with high hills and watered by cheerful brooks. Although it may seem to suggest an Arcadia regained, it actually serves to introduce the second couple in the first book's descending scale of love.

"Now weigh my case, if [the] least you know what love is": Amphialus and Helen

Of the three sets of emblematic Corinthian lovers introduced in Act I, only three persons are alive when Act III is over. Two of those—Amphialus, nephew to Basilius, and Helen of Corinth—are introduced at this juncture. In a triad scaling down from "pure" love to love *à la mode,* they occupy the restless, mixed central position. It evidently has one major virtue: survival, directly in the face of turmoil and loss. Whereas those at the top, loving honor more than life, will lose both, and those at the bottom are so inconstant that one of them leaves and the other is executed as a traitor, the star-crossed lovers of the middle endure. Perhaps for that reason their image seems most directly associable with Pyrocles, even though the image is also general in applicability and the story is experienced by Musidorus, not his cousin.

The intra-Arcadian Arcadia of the second tale seems to promise a Bower of Bliss, much as a defile which Pyrocles enters in Book II will suggest a feminine topography. The lovers about whom Musidorus now learns, however, are no hedonists. They are almost foes, wrenched by fortune, cross-purposes, and misunderstandings. The misunderstandings bedevil not only them but many people around them, imperilling friendship as well as love.

Traveling in company with Clitophon, Musidorus comes upon the discarded armor of Amphialus. It was on this shield that Sidney had intended to display the *New Arcadia*'s first major armorial device—that quintessential Renaissance "speaking picture." In a sudden but symbolic decision to seek Amphialus as well as Pyrocles, Musidorus puts on the armor. The gesture indicates an association between the two men reaching through sympathy to possible identity. Although Musidorus is not a Red Cross Knight and Amphialus no Paul, the possible transformative identification of the one man with the other is filled with meaning. Not only may Musidorus now become just such an unfortunate anti-Cyrus, but, at the end of the *New Arcadia,* it seems possible that Amphialus will grow into a Musidorus. What is more, the disguise temporarily leads Musidorus directly into that hero's actions. He and Clitophon are attacked by a troop guarding the carriage of Helen of Corinth. Musidorus beats away the soldiers to find the lady and her attendants musing upon a portrait—the second one to appear directly in the work. The lady, taking him by his armor to be Amphialus, upbraids him, even as she presents to him much the same ideal of beauty that Pyrocles had seen in Parthenia: hers is such "a beauty, as showed forth the beams both of wisdom and good nature, but all as much darkened as might be with sorrow" (p. 64). For the young princes, Helen with Amphialus thus will constitute a median image of love. It is lower than that of Argalus and Parthenia yet capable of ascent, for the persons involved are basically valorous and constant. Love now produces yet another internal narrative, this one delivered by Helen herself.

She is queen of a nation that was once as contented as Basilius' Arcadia. At her father's death, however, Corinth had been overrun with suitors, like a latter-day Ithaca. She had leaned slightly toward the prince Philoxenus until the day when he introduced his friend Amphialus, the nephew and once the heir-apparent to Basilius. Like Argalus before him, Amphialus is overtly celebrated as a general pattern for princes: "What ear is so barbarous but hath heard of Amphialus? who follows deeds of arms, but everywhere finds monuments of Amphialus? who is courteous, noble, liberal, but he that hath the example before his eyes of Amphialus? where are all heroical parts, but in Amphialus?" (p. 67).

The object of this Ophelia-like tribute resembled Musidorus, even in his youth; although reared in exile, Amphialus too always had the company of his best friend. During his adolescence, he had gained the enviable epithet, "courteous." As he entered early manhood, however, all his personal relationships had turned treacherously upon themselves. In pleading his friend's cause with Helen he unintentionally had attracted her himself. Her queenly pride, "not ashamed" to declare her passion, anticipated the overt avowals of passion to come from Pyrocles and Gynecia. However, its revelation to Amphialus produced much the effect of Phaedra's revelation of love to Hippolytus. His blush "taught [her] shame" (p. 69), as with mixed courtesy and contempt he had refused her. In a quest exactly opposite that of Pyrocles, he had abruptly left his friend and Corinth. His friend, believing himself betrayed, had pursued Amphialus. In defending himself, the triply unfortunate Amphialus had killed his friend and had been discovered in that horror by his friend's father—who is also, of course, his own foster-father.

Grieving that her heart is "nothing but a stage for tragedies," Helen can hardly bear to relate the episode. For Sidney's readers, it indeed combines some elements from the stories of both Theseus and Priam. In agony, Amphialus—wishing that mountains like those of Klaius and of the last judgment "had lain upon him" (p. 71)—had thrust away his heroic armor. Later he will all but throw away chivalry along with life, for almost the same reasons. For now, the distracted Helen, speaking for herself as well as for Amphialus (who attributes the catastrophe to her), charges Musidorus, and the *New Arcadia* as a whole, "Now weigh my case, if [the] least you know what love is" (p. 72). When she hears from a page that Amphialus tortures himself by keeping the fawning dog of his slain friend always by him and by hiding out in solitary places, she again traces her seemingly fated tragedy: "I see the end, I see my end" (p. 74).

With this second general model as strongly impressed upon him as that of Argalus and Parthenia, Musidorus turns aside to seek Pyrocles. Reflecting the agonized, solitary quest of Amphialus, he finds even the Olympic games a "tedious loneliness" without his friend (p. 74). His search takes him through Achaia and Sicyonia before circling back to Arcadia. There he recovers Pyrocles, at last; and their debate of love, long interrupted by internal narratives, resumes.

When Pyrocles announces his bondage to Philoclea, the models of the Corinthian lovers make the debate far more somber than it had been in the *Old Arcadia*. This time, Pyrocles associates himself openly, and somewhat defiantly, with Hercules bearing the distaff. He wears a jewel with that device, which bears the motto "Never more valiant." [18] His song, however, still tells of being overthrown "with outward force, and inward treason" (p. 76). Drawing at once upon the pattern recently supplied by Helen and Amphialus as well

[18] For contrasting viewpoints of Pyrocles' imitation of Hercules, see Mark Rose, "Sidney's Womanish Man," *RES*, 15 (1964), 360–362, and Elizabeth Dipple, "Metamorphosis in Sidney's *Arcadias*," *PQ*, 50 (1971), 60.

as that of the political disasters in Laconia, Musidorus now even more forcefully lists the attendants of love: "unquietness, longings, fond comforts, faint discomforts, hopes, jealousies, ungrounded rages, causeless yieldings" (p. 78). As had happened with Philoxenus and Amphialus in Helen's narrative, wrath rises between the cousins. Musidorus is led almost to the point of forsaking Pyrocles from anger, as Pyrocles had earlier abandoned him from love. Their friendship, renewed at almost the last possible moment despite the Parthenian fear that Pyrocles' "unperfectness [is] unworthy of . . . friendship" (p. 83), asks instead that Pyrocles lay bare the story of his love. Internal narrative therefore again occupies the full attention of the men. This time, the story is offered not for its general or timeless pattern but as a case for present judgment.

In the *New Arcadia,* Pyrocles' movement into love is far more Platonic than in the earlier work. Not only has he been impressed in the near present by the beauty of Parthenia, but in the past, far more somberly, he had witnessed the love and beauty of "the lady Zelmane, whom too well [he had] loved" (p. 84). Love of beauty and of the ideal of love, including that which was a "lecture" in Parthenia's "fair face," has preceded his attraction to Philoclea's picture. For a time, love of virtue and reason had even strongly opposed his new will, but eventually reason had assured him "that all eyes did degenerate from their creation, which did not honor such beauty" (p. 85). Resembling Amphialus in having tried to escape from both love and his friend's accusatory reason, he had fled to Messenia before returning to Arcadia and the Amazon disguise that is his love's invention. In the *New Arcadia,* he assumes the name "Zelmane" rather than Cleophila. Instead of playing at union with a presently desired love, that is, he honors a girl from the past who had sacrificially loved him. Anticipating the effect of stories in

Book II, the definitive example of a person truly in love works in him at least as strongly as present passion.

Relatedly, the *New Arcadia*'s device of having a character narrate his past encounter rather than having him enact it in the present causes the narrating character to be much more judicial and ironic. What may be lost in drama is made up for in broad self-awareness. A self-historian must be less partial than a self-advocate, by the very nature of narrative. He cannot hold the contextual world well lost; if his story is to make sense, that world has to be acknowledged. Similarly, he must be somewhat detached and objective about himself. If in direct action a character might ignore a counsellor, in narrative he must not only identify the concern but also give it a portion of his own voice. Kalander had introduced the technique in passing, but it is Pyrocles who now brings it to a full, and extremely profitable, employment. In Book II, each of the other young Arcadian lovers will take it up in turn. Thus the emblematic tales of Greece and Asia are not alone in providing detached reflections, instructions, and guides to the young lovers. Pyrocles' narrative, which gradually moves out to include his encounters with Dametas and Basilius, will have converted him in part from an experiencing Amazon into a reflective satirist. For example, he reports telling Basilius that he himself is "niece to Senicia" (p. 89), thereby glancing at Basilius' temporary role as *senex*. Such meditative wit also leads him to praise Philoclea in ideal terms which resemble those of the two shepherds for Urania. However, transfixed like "a well-wrought image," he also ardently blazons her physical beauty (p. 90). Perhaps for that reason, Sidney now describes the two elevated lodges of exile as being one a star, the other a satellite. If the form of the lodges suggests a stellar love, it also suggests a fort which can be held against helot passions.

Something of the same emblematic use of setting appears

in arrangements for dining al fresco. Waters that feed the splendid lodge garden imitate the play of distance and fortune (and suggest the interrelating narratives of the *New Arcadia*), as gears move all the tables in complex orbits. They frequently carry "Philoclea [to an] equal distance" from Pyrocles, so that only his eyes can "overtake her" (p. 92). The two lovers perhaps also picture the parting of Urania and the shepherds, despite their mutual attraction.

Such separation is only an increased lure to them, however. It does little good to tell Pyrocles "that he should more moderately use his delight"; like Basilius with Philanax, the passion that has overcome a prince is not likely to concede to reason "the place of a counsellor" (p. 93). Comically, the infection he feels for her has so spread into a love by her parents for him that after eight weeks he has never yet had a "privy conference" with Philoclea.

Laying satire aside, Pyrocles at last recognizes that the solitude of all the principals has served to make their passions more violent. They now make up "a notable dumb show of Cupid's kingdom," all but replacing the former kingdom of Arcadia. Love is so productive of anarchy that it transverses even the Aristotelian order of fiction: whenever Gynecia interrupts Pyrocles' approach to Philoclea, "her unwished presence gave [his] tale a conclusion, before it had a beginning" (p. 94). Although the several loves might promise to serve passion and assist disguise, they instead produce mainly a "foolish fortune, or unfortunate folly" that seems to shape a reflective destiny. Pyrocles ends his account judicially and prophetically, saying, "And thus . . . you have my tragedy played unto you by my self, which I pray the gods may not in deed prove a tragedy" (p. 94).

So much self-analytical, satiric, and almost tragic awareness on the part of the *New Arcadia*'s Pyrocles nearly relieves Musidorus of his former role as judge. The elder cousin finds that the gods must have somehow secretly mixed in "this humor of love" among his friend's heroic excellencies. If in itself love is not excellent, however, it nevertheless has directed Pyrocles to "so rare a woman" that his passion can by no means be called hostile to virtue. Friendship, too, asks that Musidorus remain nearby for aid, rather than rejecting a friend who has become "Zelmane" (*zealous imitation*) for the sake of love.

So thoroughly has reflective telling replaced direct doing that Sidney now manages the present narrative of love's labyrinth with almost Baconian dispatch:

Zelmane returned to the lodge, where (inflamed by Philoclea, watched by Gynecia, and tired by Basilius) she was like a horse, desirous to run, and miserably spurred, but so short-reined, as he cannot stir forward: Zelmane sought occasion to speak with Philoclea; Basilius with Zelmane; and Gynecia hindered them all [p. 95].

Having only an oblique present interest in this action as such, the author instead offers a series of emblems within the narrative—for example, the princesses catch fishes, that are like the hearts of princes; Pyrocles points out a seeled dove that, like Cupid, strives the higher, the more he is blinded. Sidney then swings to the entrance and history of Phalantus of Corinth. He and his unloving Artesia, the third couple in a procession that included Argalus with Parthenia and Amphialus with Helen, will be speaking pictures (or parodies) for the sophisticated, egoistical nadir of love. A negative model, it is associable directly with its narrator, Basilius. It is also entirely useful for Pyrocles, if he is to avoid being the Lovelace he had all but become in the *Old Arcadia.*

"No wisdom but in including heaven and earth in oneself":
Phalantus and Artesia

The fond and foolish Basilius appropriately narrates the
third and lowest internal story of love. It tends to identify
his level of passion. He notes that Phalantus, who has
brought a present challenge to the knights of Arcadia, is the
bastard brother of Helen. Although Phalantus too had served
as a hero in the Laconian civil war, he is much better known
for being "lovely" and having a "cunning cheerfulness" (p.
97). He had moved with the currents natural to such a brittle
and popular character, somewhat as the present Pyrocles
might once have done. Eventually, after the way of the light
world, he had come to imagine that he was in love. He is a
clear warning to the princes and princesses that honesty will
be as difficult as it is necessary to love, especially when love
appears to be at once a popular pastime and an ideal quest.

Aping romantic fictions, then, Phalantus had become a
"servant" to Artesia, but more "for want of other business"
than from actual love. He is soon repaid with "his own
money." Disdaining him, Artesia calls such treatment "chastity"; besides, she wants a lover who will be "all worthiness."
Such enormous pride had been taught her by her foster-
mother, Basilius' wicked sister-in-law, Cecropia. For teacher
as for pupil, "there is no wisdom but in including heaven
and earth in one's self; . . . love, courtesy, gratefulness,
friendship, and all other virtues are rather to be taken on,
than taken in oneself." Both women "peacock themselves" in
all their affections (p. 98). Both also gravitate toward the
pride of political power.

If Artesia (like Helen of Corinth) has a fancy for Amphialus, Cecropia's son, it can represent only liking, not love,
for she loves and wants to please herself alone. Because

Amphialus is occupied in being Platonically in love with "nothing less than Love" (pp. 98–99), however, in the meantime Artesia does not mind demanding the full, if unmeant, "service" of poor Phalantus. Learning in a hard school that it is a "foolish wittiness, to speak more [of love] than one thinks" (p. 99), he has been forced to challenge all the heroes of Greece either to joust with him or to concede that Artesia is more beautiful than their mistresses. He is privately certain that Helen, the two Arcadian princesses, and Parthenia are all much fairer than Artesia. Nevertheless, having unwillingly championed her beauty in Laconia, Elis, Argos, and Corinth, he now has come to challenge Arcadia.

Old Basilius completes the narrative by reflecting its foolish lover, murmuring that "Zelmane's" eyes can so sharpen his blunt lance that he is as able as any Phalantus to "protect an undeniable verity" (p. 100).

Somewhat like Adam's dream in *Paradise Lost,* internal narrative in the *New Arcadia* almost always has a way of becoming real. Because most of the accounts of the past lead either toward Phalantus' folly or toward Pyrocles' witness, the entrance into Arcadia of Phalantus himself unites the direct action and its reflective, complementary plots. It also serves to introduce the first of three major congresses of armorial impresas, devices, and emblematic personages, which serve not only as galleries of "speaking pictures" that comment upon the principal action but also as limited actions in their own right. By its nature, it becomes also a congress of almost all the characters in the work—those from the Asian past as well as the Greek present.

Because a chivalric contest such as that initiated by Phalantus is at once a trial of the knight's heroism and his lady's beauty, Phalantus' shield, hung up as a challenge, both instigates the case and with its impresa also defines and judges it. His impresa, reminiscent of Urania but also indicative

of ambition, is of "a heaven full of stars"; its motto, ironically assigning merit to such beauty rather than to his might,
reads "The beauty which gave it the praise." A pageant of
pride, Artesia herself sweeps on to the field in a chariot of
carnation velvet. As if in a progress, she is preceded by foot-
men bearing pictures of all the mistresses recently defeated
by Phalantus. It is also a roll call which gathers together
characters from the three circles—Asian, Corinthian, and
Arcadian. It includes Andromana, who distantly like Elizabeth has "exceeding red hair with small eyes" (p. 101); the
princess of Elis, little better favored; Artaxia of Armenia, too
mannish to be attractive; Erona of Lycia, whose unsymmetri-
cal beauty but "pitiful look" unite to make "one find cause
to crave help himself" (p. 102); Baccha, far too free in her
sexuality and mirth, and her opposite, Leucippe, gentle and
demure; the Queen of Laconia, who has no recommendations to beauty except that (as Sidney says, daringly) "she was
a queen, and therefore beautiful" (p. 103); Helen, whose
beauty, combining the characteristics of the Arcadian princesses, was so great that if it did not strike with "admiration,
it ravished with delight" (p. 103); the Athena-resembling
Parthenia, whose gray eyes, "great-mindedness," and plain
dress might be a model of Puritanism at its best (Basilius
praises her also as a new Penelope, the "perfect picture of a
womanly virtue, and wifely faithfulness," who lets herself be
thus humiliated in show rather than cause her husband to
fight for her); a mainly emblematic speaking picture that
like the *New Arcadia* itself causes the "mouth [to] give place
to [the] eyes" (p. 104)—a "young maid, [who] sat pulling out
a thorn out of a Lamb's foot . . . the fair shepherdess,
Urania"; and finally, even Zelmane, the dead princess whom
Pyrocles now honors and imitates.

Artesia's pompous triumph and the challenge by Phalantus elicit no responses for a time. Then the Arcadian Nestor,

dressed wholly in black to challenge Phalantus in wavering white, accepts the dare. He loses, however, as do several more brave Arcadian knights who serve fair women. Not until an unexpected "ill-appointed knight" (p. 109), quixotic in appearance and lacking so much as an impresa, motto, or contemporary armor, is challenged by a Black Knight, and the two together are fought by Phalantus, does Basilius assume his significant role as tourney judge. In yet one more surprising turn, the three contestants are then joined by a fourth, who demands that the Black Knight surrender a stolen miniature of Pamela. His having let the picture timidly slip from him seems to be proof, however, that he is better fitted to serve the healer, Aesculapius, than the goddess, Venus.

Judging that in these confused challenges the ill-appareled knight had precedence, Basilius assigns him a turn with Phalantus; the latter loses. At once, Artesia spurns him, even as he turns from her in great relief. Such lovers greatly tickle Basilius, who prophetically notes that "young folks . . . that came in masked with so great pomp, go out with . . . little constancy" (p. 111). Opposing such inconstancy, the ill-appointed knight strips away his rags like an Odysseus, revealing that he is the "Amazonian" Pyrocles. His transformation to rags had briefly returned him to a humble heroism. He has desired the victory as a "secret passport" to Philoclea. He is again figuratively back at sea, not only as a "masked" hero but as a possible pirate, hoping for a similar victory over the princess. For both Pyrocles and the Arcadians, there is thus a clear need for the warning images of Asia and Corinth. Responding with the sensual manifestations of a purely physical "white and red" virtue, Philoclea blushes, while the jealous Gynecia turns pale.

Tourneys of arms having given way to tourneys of words, the Book will close upon the pastoral eclogues. Just before

they are staged, however, Pyrocles comes upon a man who is
ill-appareled as a shepherd (Musidorus, of course, in balance
with Pyrocles' recent appearance as a degraded knight). He
sings, "Come, shepherd's weeds." The elder prince, in a swift
narrative confession balancing the earlier one by Pyrocles,
recounts his falling in love with a "goddess, who in a definite
compass can set forth infinite beauty" (pp. 114–115); he adds
that because men can discern beauty, they must love it, for
"by love we are made, and to love we are made" (p. 113). Only
a sepulchre (which relates him to Argalus and Parthenia)
can shield him from her (p. 115). For that reason he had
entered the tourney as a Black Knight, using a color significant for all the *New Arcadia*—for if black can signify tragedy,
it can also suggest a Saturnian or Uranian melancholy and
the ideal, "too bright/ To hit the sense of human sight." If
because of love Musidorus is now to be a partly Uranian shepherd in Arcadia, Pyrocles humourously suggests that he himself will be a "good mistress" to him. Having already begun
to manipulate the king and queen, Pyrocles will also control
Dametas' acceptance of Musidorus, adding to flattery the
"golden eloquence" of bribery, if need be (p. 118). His over-
confident analysis of Dametas applies ironically to himself
and his cousin, however, insofar as they are disguised would-
be lechers: ". . . every . . . occasion will catch his senses,
and his senses are masters of his silly mind; . . . with that
bridle and saddle you shall well ride him" (p. 117). For a second, Musidorus—like the far more constant princesses, later—
draws back from such deceit and such applicable description,
condemning the princes' double departure from "the right
line of virtue [into] crooked shifts." He fears that a disguised
body warrants a disfigured mind. Yet he can still hope that
they are neither asses nor servants to the devil who may be
an ass; he trusts that "though the [present] ways be foul, the
journey's end [will be] most fair and honourable" (p. 117).

His hope is fair enough, unless the princes themselves become "foul" in trying to make foul means produce a fair end.

The site for the pastoral sports is again Sidney's unique combination of *locus amoenus* with theater. In the *New Arcadia,* however, the eclogues serve less as reflectors of the developing action, a function that has now been assumed by processional emblematic "pictures," than as thematic lines back to the lamenting adoration of Urania by the shepherds. They thus have far less to do with the action than did those in the *Old Arcadia;* for that very reason, however, they assert a somewhat greater lyric recapitulation of the primary lyric pattern. In that sense, they even more singlemindedly serve and celebrate the originating foreconceit.

The eclogues are preceded by the irruption of a lion and she-bear [19] into the gathering. They are at once emblematic of the present Arcadia and also directly instrumental in its action. (That was not quite the case in the *Old Arcadia.*) They are the first in three mounting attacks by the ambitious, jealous Cecropia. By association, they also immediately join and emblematize the love-pursuits already in process: "when the Lion's head was off, as Zelmane ran after Philoclea, so [Gynecia] could not . . . but run after Zelmane . . . each carried forward with an inward violence" (p. 120). After a throne for Basilius is set in place, somewhat resembling the seat of judgment in Act V of the *Old Arcadia,* he is informed that the two beasts had been set upon them by Cecropia's gamekeeper. In a warning to all governors of peoples or passions, the beasts' keeper had assumed that he could rule them easily, but had similarly been deceived. If the revelation tends to remove the princes from direct present association with the animals, it only increases the looming threat

[19] The lion and she-bear return in *The Merchant of Venice,* II, i, 29–30.

from Cecropia—a threat to which the distracted Basilius refuses to give proper thought.

The eclogues begin, exactly as they had in the *Old Arcadia,* with a dance and choric contest. Within the new context, however, the initial triumph of Musidorus over Lalus increases emphasis upon the ideality of the princes' love. So do the ensuing songs, including those of recounted advice by Languet to Philisides, which show a "mind . . . banished from the place [it] loved, to be in prison in his body" (p. 132), and which counsel man against all tyranny whatsoever; that of a general ethical and political serenity counselled by Geron to Histor; and that of hope, which Pyrocles opposes to the double sestina "Ye Goatherd gods." The reported lament of the absent Klaius and Strephon brings Book I full circle, helping to join the *New Arcadia*'s eclogues with its narrative. Even the giddy Basilius serves to form an exalted new context for the eclogues when he falls to earth, thanking the gods that he has heard "the very music they themselves used, in an earthly body" (p. 144). Although his teetering amour invites him principally toward a too, too solid earthly body, he is nevertheless within range of the Urania celebrated by Strephon—"she, whose least word brings from the spheres their music" (p. 143).

"Knowing Humanity": The Second Book

When the *Old Arcadia* came to be revised, it might have been easy to place much of its original material, virtually untouched, at the beginning of the new work, letting it serve the formula of beginning *in medias res.* New matter could then have been introduced in an equivalent of Odysseus' wanderings, after which the old matter remaining might have concluded the work. As we have seen, however, Sidney performs a transformation, not a revision, of the old matter. His work with the idea of a "past" section is even more radical. He causes tales of the princes' adventures in Asia Minor to master time, as they simultaneously make up a lasting general instruction for princes; guide as well as lead the present erotic and moral progress of the lovers ("She loved me for the dangers I had passed . . . "); and prepare them for trials as well as for good government in the future. Although Book II begins with the present loves of Gynecia and Basilius for the disguised Pyrocles and of the disguised Musidorus for Pamela, and although it maintains among the narrators a thread of Arcadian action in the present, it swiftly demands a return into the past: first, in "recent" internal narratives that continue the distancing technique introduced in Book I, in one of which Musidorus tells Pamela of his own history until they are brought amusingly into the present, and the narrator "Dorus" obviously has to stand revealed as the storied prince Musidorus, and in the other of which Pamela recounts the episode to Philoclea; and second, in the princes' histories in Asia Minor.

But then, the Asian past is so extremely illuminating, so general in its emblematic significance, and so full of matter for the present contemplation and the future guidance of princes and lovers, that the present almost becomes its prolegomenon, and the future, its predicate. The Asian past, that is, provides a moral end as well as an "historical" beginning. In the truncated *New Arcadia,* it comprises the moral and emblematic center. Its effects probably would have appeared in the end. Far from being digressive, then, the major internal narratives serve the functions that in Elizabethan plays have to be disposed variously among the chorus, subplot, exposition, dumbshow, and soliloquy; all of them can now be concentrated in one nuclear, but processional, system of awareness.

It would be idle to contend that the mix of internal narratives is uniformly successful. Among other difficulties produced in Book II, our sense of the past often overwhelms our awareness of the present. Nevertheless, Sidney's attempt is of great technical interest in itself as an exercise of narrative placement, and of extreme use ideationally in elevating the princes far beyond their status in the *Old Arcadia*. Sexual comedy as such now almost disappears. Its place is taken by a various and complex gallery of presently applicable models,[20] both negative and positive, for heroism and love. The heroic lovers thereby bring the political and ethical spheres into far closer connection than had been possible under the conditions of political exile in the *Old*. In the *New*, recent heroism in Laconia as well as past heroism in Asia Minor makes the Arcadian retreat more a seat for contemplation than a Bower of Bliss. The world remains almost too much with the young lovers, as Pyrocles had indicated when asking Musidorus' account of his love for Pamela; it would supply a "map of his little world . . . that [he] might see, whether it were troubled [like his own] with such unhabitable climes of cold despairs and hot rages" (p. 152).

If the resulting guide gives "light," it is like that which may come, prophetically, through "a small hole to a dungeon" or that which may appear to a Socratic scholar, "who

---

[20] See Hector Genouy, *L' 'Arcadia' de Sidney dans ses rapports avec l' 'Arcadia' de Sannazaro et la 'Diana' de Montemayor* (Paris, 1928), p. 79; Nancy R. Lindheim, "Sidney's *Arcadia*, Book II: Retrospective Narrative," *SP*, 44 (1967), 159–186; Angus Fletcher, *Allegory: The Theory of a Symbolic Mode* (Ithaca, N.Y.: Cornell Univ. Press, 1964), p. 36; André Chastel, "Le tableau dans le tableau," *Stil und Überlieferung des Abendlandes* (Berlin, 1967), I, 15–29; and Angel Rosenblat, intro. *Amadis de Gaula* (Buenos Aires: Editorial Losada, 1963), p. 12.

is only come to that degree of knowledge, to find himself utterly ignorant" (p. 153). Musidorus' ensuing thought corrects Dametas' too-quick, anti-intellectual agreement, that "they might talk of book-learning what they would; but for his part, he never saw more unfeatly fellows, than great clerks were" (p. 152). The princes and princesses must now become "great clerks" in virtue, using the past as their present school and future goal.

When Musidorus launches into the self-historical "map of his little world," which is parallel to that of Pyrocles in Book I, he begins upon that note of great seriousness. He describes Pamela as "majesty . . . sitting in the throne of beauty" (p. 153). His love is identified with the emblematic when he associates it with a nearby palm (pp. 152, 154). Both love and palm have connections with the immediate present, for he and Pyrocles walk under palm trees during the narration. Musidorus had echoed Philisides' recent eclogue by noting that young beasts, unlike men, approach love with "proud looks, and joyfulness" (p. 154). Confused by the seeming separation of love and honor, men

like bastards, are laid abroad, even as foundlings to be trained up by grief and sorrow. [The minds of animals] grudge not their bodies comfort, nor their senses are letted from enjoying their object; we have the impediments of honor, and the torments of conscience. . . . But [if] love . . . one time layeth burdens, another time [it] giveth wings [p. 154].

The hope of the entire work, of course, is that maintaining the ideal despite tides of loss will constitute a training-up "by grief and sorrow," thus giving wings to love. Musidorus sees at present largely the impediments, torments, and burdens which separate men from the simple beasts. If he looked upward, he might also see that his invention of disguises places a different kind of burden on love. Although torments may lead to just ethical and public policy, deceit will not even lead to a human "enjoying [of the] object."

Nevertheless, in the *New Arcadia* Musidorus' teasingly open story to Pamela and Mopsa about the prince Musidorus' fortunes receives multiple correspondences among ideal, actual and "fictional" existences. Whereas in the *Old* he had wittily remarked, when disguised as the shepherd Dorus, that he would like to "pattern" himself upon Musidorus (*Old Arcadia*, p. 99), in the *New* the same statement involves his consideration of his being as he tells "his own tale in a third person" (p. 177). It therefore raises the question not only of the relationship of a fictive to an actual Cyrus, but also of the relationship of both to the "essential" Musidorus. Nor is that all. He learns that Pamela, by means of recent interviews with the Asian Plangus, already knows something of the heroic Musidorus. She assures the somewhat discomfited prince that "Musidorus [together] with his cousin Pyrocles did both perish upon the coast of Laconia" (p. 162). Although it is true that Musidorus in a sense "died" there and was reborn from the sea, Musidorus turns her remark wittily by agreeing that her report is exactly like that of his story, "which that peerless princess did make unto him, when he sought to appear such as he was before her wisdom" (p. 162).

The two lovers thus melt in and out of fiction and reality like Penelope and Odysseus at the close of the *Odyssey*. Both preen themselves upon their princely wit in making such conceits—and in penetrating them. At the end, the question whether or not the fiction can be moved directly into the present is left to "astrology" and Pamela's "silent imaginations" (p. 163). The encounter was sealed in a jewel given by Musidorus to Pamela, which bore the motto "By force, not choice" (p. 165). Although the motto is faintly ironic in view not only of the lustful former Musidorus in the *Old Arcadia* but also of the prince who now envies the simple love of beasts, it here reflects his general sincerity and anticipates his later trials of love and patience.

If Musidorus had hoped that either conceits or passion would tumble Pamela from her governed serenity, however, he mistook her. In token of private governance and potentially tragic patience, she revealed to him only constant courtesy and a "keeping her course like the sun." Her control of love will be matched later by her control of fear and dread while under torture. Having associated her with Astraea, Urania, and Apollo rather than with Venus, Phaeton, or fortune, Musidorus with some justice calls her heavenly. As for himself, he acknowledges that he had once played "well the part of a king in a tragedy at Athens" (p. 165). He may now prove to have a prince's heart hid in a player's hide, even as, in repeating the role for Pamela, he had come almost to play himself while ostensibly playing a shepherd who was playing a prince.

Next among the Arcadian lovers to come to self-analysis is Philoclea. In its direct form, her experience is close to the isolated soliloquies in Book II of the *Old Arcadia*. She adds to that former method not only some new matter but also the "historical" detachment characteristic of the *New,* when she understands Pamela's confusion in light of her own.

She is led toward the encounter by having ridden in a carriage where she was joined from shoulder to foot with Pyrocles. Delight of the body is like wine with sugar added, but it causes Pyrocles to resemble both Musidorus' simple beast and Cecropia's ravenous lion; his heart is "like a lion new imprisoned . . . not panting, but striving violently" (p. 167). The goad of direct bodily delight, which Sidney has introduced into the *New Arcadia* to make self-control the more commendable, had appeared in the emblematic attack by a gyrfalcon upon a heron and by an accident which upset the coach, allowing Pyrocles to "bear the sweet burden of

Philoclea" (p. 168). These suggestions of physical union lead Philoclea toward a more profound sense of identification with Pyrocles.

In the *New Arcadia,* the former sense that Pyrocles has imitated Philoclea, effeminately, is almost erased. It is now she who accepts and adopts his character. The possibility of such identification has appeared earlier, as when a hero emulated another hero or when he read his own meaning in an emblem. It is of course essential to Sidney's *Defence,* in which imitation is a procedure of identification. When a lover identifies himself with the loved object at this point in the *New Arcadia,* the result can be either heroic aspiration or abject surrender and absorption. The whole process, as seen in Philoclea, helps to explain how a speaking picture becomes lively knowledge.

Like love itself, her identification with a loved object has moved in quick stages. Originally struck by his nature (as he had been struck by her picture in Kalander's house), Philoclea had given Pyrocles a "heedful attention . . . willingness of conversation . . . a liking and silent admiration . . . a most friendly affection . . . an unmeasurable liking of all that [he] did." Soon the physical representative defined the virtue, rather than the reverse: "[Pyrocles] was not prized for . . . demeanor, but the demeanor was prized because it was [his]" (p. 169). Then, as admiration swept on to imitation, his ways were taken "into herself, as a pattern of worthy proceeding." Become a mirror to Pyrocles, she threatens to assist in her own seduction; she imitates his melting looks, his sighs, his countenance, and, eventually, his "impatient desire." Not until she is in this sense a "second Zelmane" does she fully suspect that seeming arguments of reason have really been those of passion, fancy, and dream. That awareness can serve some of the "historical" purposes of reason, however. It permits love to rip away the mask, showing her how far she is beyond reason. She therefore suspects that the pattern of an anti-Cyrus may fashion anti-Cyruses, in perverse propagation.

In the *New Arcadia,* her sense of a context beyond her own experience also leads Philoclea to new matter, matter that will become increasingly important to the work: the argument of religion versus atheism. Having worked forward in theistic reasoning from the simple "sylvan" gods of pastoral past a Miltonic tribute to her own chastity, she gropes onward toward an understanding of the great gods of justice. She despairingly rejects the aid of Diana's moon and Urania's stars. Like a Penelope who had been given a beautiful natural sampler, she has been set "such a work for my desire to take out [that] is as much impossible" (p. 174). For the time being, as her easy logic continues to register the "impossible," she impatiently flings away all questions of "why and how." Looking no more to Pan and nature, and uncertain of any ideal other than desire, she embraces "the very ground whereon she lay," crying only, "O my Zelmane, govern and direct me; for I am wholly given over unto thee" (p. 175). It is almost a recapitulation of the *New Arcadia*'s steering between nature and the ideal, except that it now is threatened with obliteration by desire.

Philoclea thus has wandered among "divers sorts of discourses," not merely a complacent self-advocacy. Because of that experience, she helps to move Pamela into a more characteristic self-analytical internal narrative. Needless to say, it is colored by stories of the past, at least in context, and is relevant to those Asian tales that are soon to come.

Pamela is discovered by Philoclea with eyes red from crying. The elder sister thus betrays an internal Petrarchan fire, which Philoclea now understands quite thoroughly. Philoclea insists that her sister, who is a model far better than Gynecia—"a sister in nature, a mother in counsel, a princess by the law . . . a friend by my choice and your favor" (p. 176)—should open her thoughts, in narrative. Lying together with "dear though chaste embracements; with sweet, though cold kisses," in token of the possibility that love can appear without danger, the elder sister is drawn forward into stammering confessions while the younger sees penetratively, now, with the "blind eyes" of insight. Pamela is pleasingly half-Shakespearean, half-Congrevian, in her repetition of Philoclea's identification with a lover:

Ah . . . if you knew the cause: but no more do I, neither; and to say the truth: but Lord, how are we fallen to talk of this fellow? And yet indeed if you were sometimes with me . . . to see all the while with what a grace (which seems to set a crown upon his base estate) he can descend to those poor matters, certainly you would: but to what serves this? no doubt we were better sleep than talk of these idle matters [p. 177].

With a self-analytical wisdom that allows her to possess the role of Cupid, Philoclea says, "Ah, my Pamela . . . I have caught you." She ruefully knows of herself that the "shears" of warning "come too late to clip the bird's wings that already is flown away" (p. 177). The only question is whether love's pity and delight offer a third form between Aristotle and Horace that can free the bird to soar, or a snare for simple beasts.

Although Pamela had distrusted the persuasiveness of desire, well aware that "the nature of desire itself is no easier to receive belief, than it is hard to ground belief" (p. 178), and although she had shown Musidorus seemingly only cold courtesy, she was sure that his virtues really were almost Christ-like. Was not Musidorus "content so to abase himself, as to become Dametas' servant for [her] sake" (p. 178)? And did not his handling of a horse show the good governor (rather "[distilling] virtue, than [using] violence"), whereas

Dametas was "tossed from the saddle to the mane of the horse, and thence to the ground" (p. 179)? Did he not play Paris (thus involving himself in a triple fiction), in which role he courted Pamela as Oenone and chose Athene over Aphrodite, truly feeling "the part he played" (p. 180)? While Sidney was showing not only that nature's substance could be made gold but also that brazen myth might be reformed, Pamela had come to a final question: "Tell me . . . did you ever see such a shepherd? tell me, did you ever hear of such a Prince? and then tell me, if a small or unworthy assault have conquered me" (p. 180). And like the letter used earlier by Kalander, a letter from Musidorus is brought forward by Pamela to confirm his merit. In one last glancing allusion to Christian parallels, Musidorus had pleaded that the temple of his love be not merely razed, but instead, somehow, sustained or rebuilt.

Together, the princesses at this point figure sovereignty versus servitude in love, in part reversing the ostensible positions of Pyrocles and Musidorus. If the younger prince in disguise seems triumphant, in contrast to the suppliant Musidorus, the older Pamela shows a mastery rather than surrender in love. However, the elemental fire and ice of love have a way of producing instantaneous reversals, much as fortune does. It is high time that the princely lovers, caught between natural desire and the ideal of love even as they are suspended in self-knowledge between simple beast and soaring bird, be provided an equivalent of Kalander's house in Book I. The *New Arcadia* therefore moves into the great "gallery" of Asian tales.

In indication of her own cautious governing of love and in anticipation of the heroic justice to come in the Asian tales, Pamela asks her love, obliquely, to tell her of Pyrocles. Musidorus is now to speak not through the muddy medium of Mopsa but through that of the model prince—"of shape most lovely, and yet of mind more lovely; valiant, courteous, wise" (p. 184). But before turning to that prince (and himself) in his proceeding, Musidorus looks first to a larger pattern or emblem of the prince: Evarchus. Showing his magnanimity by releasing all the Greek states from subjection to Macedonia, Evarchus had given away kingdoms rather than seeking them. Taking him for all in all, he was

a prince, that indeed especially measured his greatness by his goodness. . . . A prince of a goodly aspect, and the more goodly by a grave majesty, wherewith his mind did deck his outward graces; strong of body, and so much the stronger, as he by a well-disciplined exercise taught it both to do, and suffer [p. 185].

His political doing and suffering, prophetic of two distinct stages of heroism in the *New Arcadia,* had recovered his land from a Platonic plunge into oligarchy and democracy. He had been a model to his people, "making his life the example of his laws" (p. 186). Such a Cyrus had soon propagated a nation of Cyruses, in one "politic body, whereof [Evarchus] was the head"; although "by force he took nothing, by their love he had all." A full "picture of his proceedings" would thus speak "the whole art of government" (p. 187). In a great symbol of union, he had arranged that his sister marry Dorilaus, prince of Thessaly—a prince described by Pamela as also being "valiant, wise, and just."

The encounter of the princes with Asia Minor had begun almost at their birth; it was never a mere "digression." Because the infant Musidorus, like a Christ-child,[21] had received glowing prophecies, a king of Phrygia had invaded Thessaly to kill him. With a glance at Basilius' abdication, Musidorus condemns the folly of all men who fear prophecy. On the other hand, the growing Pyrocles had received a forecast in

[21] See Denver E. Baughan, "Sidney's *Defence of the Earl of Leicester* and the Revised *Arcadia*," *JEGP*, 51 (1952), 38.

which only love was "threatened"; but it was promised to be "both [a] tempest and [a] haven" (p. 189).

In an intrafictional model of the *New Arcadia* itself, the education of the princes had consisted much in excellent patterns for imitation—"conceits not unworthy of the best speakers," devices that lent profit even to sports, "images of battles," the delight of heroic tales that later would be "converted to . . . knowledge" of princes, and exercises moving upward to "doing and suffering" (pp. 189–190). Like Evarchus, the growing boys thus imitated the idea of a prince; like Sidney's auditors in the *Defence,* they had been moved to such imitation by means of "speaking pictures . . . of lively knowledge." In Sidney's updated version of the Cyropaedia and of Plato's training for guardians, "no servile fear [or] violent restraint" was permitted to alter the princes' habit of governing, which arose from their natural command "of truth, whereon all the other goods were builded."

As they grew, not only did they pace one another in heroism but also initiated some of the identification characteristic of the *New Arcadia*. Friendship made them "more like than the likeness of all other virtues"; the younger "bore reverence full of love," to the elder, and he returned "delight [with] love." Pyrocles was as glad to learn chivalry from Musidorus as the latter was to teach and live it. Eventually, after they and their heroic virtues had come to maturity, a Macedonian siege of Byzantium had seemed to require their practice of such knowledge.

Instead of seeing limited martial service before Byzantium, however, the princes providentially had been led farther east. There, as in a gallery rather than from a mountain, they saw the "kingdoms of the world." The major part of the *New Arcadia* is given over to that almost infinitely instructive encounter. It is to guide the young lovers, along with the state, in finding a haven within the tempest of fortune and love. It can convert speaking pictures into foreconceits, thus confronting proceeding with pattern and loss with a "course like the sun" (p. 165).

"The shore's rude welcome": Masculine tyranny in Phrygia, Pontus, and Paphlagonia

In one of the *New Arcadia*'s vaulting symmetries, which replace the brisk dramatic structure of the *Old*, the entrance of the Greek princes into Asia almost duplicates the reader's vicarious entry into Arcadia. Not only does a shipwreck cast them ashore, but, earlier, the sea and sky which met them as they voyaged east had recapitulated the opening cosmic harmony of the *New Arcadia*. Similarly, the happy crew of the ship had recapitulated the original Arcadian state. Almost pastoral (and obviously emblematic) within the general community of feeling, the ship's company "all kept together like a beautiful flock, which so well could obey their master's pipe." The princes might see from such practice that "beauty and use can . . . well agree together" (p. 191).

Such perfect practice of perfect idea, assuring the young heroes that truth and beauty may be united by means of love (even as Sidney was assured that knowledge and action might be joined by delight), draws a feeling Neoplatonic tribute from both the experiencing and the narrating Musidorus:

And (O Lord) to see the admirable power and noble effects of love, whereby the seeming insensible lodestone, with a secret beauty (holding the spirit of iron in it) can draw that hard-hearted thing unto it, and (like a virtuous mistress) not only make it bow itself, but with it make it aspire to so high a love, as of the heavenly poles; and thereby to bring forth the noblest deeds, that the children on the earth can boast of [pp. 191–192].

But the young princes must suffer and do as well as observe. The entire *New Arcadia* is intent upon their coming to a "mournful stage for a tragedy." In recapitulation both of the initial loss at sea and of occasional political chaos in Macedonia and Arcadia, the mountainous, fortune-resembling seas rise "as in a tumultuous kingdom, [thinking] themselves fittest instruments of commandment" (p. 192). The tumult persistently images the chaos of a political "flowing kingdom," what with "tyranny of the wind and . . . treason of the sea" (p. 193). To such loss, the princes oppose fearless countenances and constant labor, forming patterns for the crew by which the men might learn to govern their natural "inward dismayedness." But the seas, running as blindly as fortune (p. 193), keep poetic justice: "lest the conclusion should not answer to the rest of the play, they were driven upon a rock." The sailors, left to the proceeding of their own passions, react with fear, despair, and Job-like curses; the princes, resorting to the pattern fixed by virtuous minds, cause "the passions of fearing evil . . . only to serve the rule of virtue" (p. 194). Even more notably, their two servants (Phrygian captives, but native-born Thessalians) offer up their own lives to save those of the princes. Such a sacrifice had been a tribute to the Fortune-surmounting love already celebrated by Musidorus. It now receives an echo from the Biblical praise of the man who would lay down his life for his friend and thereby forms an ideal Arcadia in action, despite the tides of outrageous fortune. The princes soon will be asked to do as much within the political tempests of Asia.

Even as a tempest intimating the chaotic environment inevitable to infected wits had begun the direct action in Laconia and Arcadia, so another storm now serves to initiate the Odyssean central section of the *New Arcadia*. It is more Homeric than Heliodorian. Although the general kind of incident of course suggests Hellenistic romance, the purposes and form of the section resemble those of the epic.

Sidney's extraordinary dispositions of narrative at first tend to obscure those purposes. To have had a disguised Musidorus attempt to recommend the past heroic Musidorus to a Pamela who herself knows enough of the past (and suspects enough of the present) to be able to assume part of the narrative herself and to interpret it in the present was complicated enough, but when Pyrocles and Philoclea also contribute narrative, auditive, and interpretative services, and when most of the past incidents clearly either reflect present circumstances or warn pointedly of those that may come, then the relationships of tale, teller, hearer, and intention or application, both past and present as well as particular and universal, become very dense indeed. Yet, as we have seen, the purposes and the structure that convey them are simple and shapely. Apart from Musidorus' recommending of his person and character to Pamela, his long account is a parallel to the adventures related by Odysseus in Homer.[22] Although the direction outward and the age of the two heroes might suggest a *Telemacheia,* the adventures themselves bear the same kind of moral and symbolic importance as those in the *Odyssey*. Somewhat like Homer's account of the Laistrygonians and the Cyclopes, about half the stories in the *New Arcadia* concern men in bad personal and public governing; and like the accounts of the Sirens and of Circe, about as many provide examples of erotic misdirection, mostly among women.

A relatedly simple pattern is seen also in the seemingly complex increase of persons involved in narrative and audi-

[22] If Sidney's design is compared with that in Homer, major redistributions are apparent. The *New Arcadia* differs from Chapman by uniting the *Iliad*'s "predominant perturbation" and the *Odyssey*'s "overruling wisdom"; by making the polytropic Odysseus into diatropic heroes; and by reversing the Odyssean regeneration by means of adventures. However, these polar differences in applicable time, action, and setting should not obscure similarities of structure and purpose. See George de F. Lord, *Homeric Renaissance: The Odyssey of George Chapman* (London: Chatto and Windus, 1956), pp. 21–50, 100–102.

tive action. What had appeared to be an extravagant and almost accidental swirl of digressions turns out to be a close design of cross-reflections. In such a presentation, the general audience is asked to realize at all times what each narrator-auditor-actor half sees, much of the time—that the adventures are monitory examples for himself and mankind.

As a shipwreck had brought Odysseus to Scheria, so another brings the princes to Asia. Their princely minds had sustained them as they counselled each other "how to labor for the better, and . . . abide the worse" (p. 195). Reversing the beginning of the *New Arcadia* wherein Musidorus was saved first, in Asia it is Pyrocles who is the first to reach shore. Far from being welcomed by shepherds or a Nausicaa, however, he is seized by the king of Phrygia, the first of the three sequential antitypes to the princes' own heroism. Somewhat resembling the three Corinthian emblems of erotic love in Book I, the three kings of Phrygia, Pontus, and Paphlagonia will represent and warn of fearful isolation, of inconstancy, and of ambitious ingratitude in monarchs.

The Phrygian anti-Cyrus is a collocation of selfish, jealous horrors: "wickedly sad, ever musing of horrible matters . . . fearful and never secure while the fear he had figured in his mind had any possibility of event," and afflicted with a "toad-like retiredness, and closeness of mind" (p. 196). Not only does he figure forth the danger of Basilian retirement, and also suggest Herod in having tried to kill the infant Musidorus, but furthermore he has produced a nation of informers and accusers. His people's "deeds were not only punished, but words corrected, and even thoughts by some means or other pulled out of them" (p. 197). It is a terrible parody of the proper interest of a monarch in his people's thoughts. Into this general state of "watchful fearfulness," which is imaged in the "stormy mind" of the king, the natural tempest has hurled the hero, Pyrocles.

True at least to his own hideous jealousy, the king determines the stranger's death. After discovering Pyrocles' close
relationship to the long-dreaded Musidorus, Phrygia's tyrant
wishes thus doubly to "quite [lose] the way of nobleness [in
favor of] the height of terribleness" (p. 197). The prince
meets this inhuman assault much as he has met the earlier
natural tempest, opposing to each a constancy that shows
"virtue in his sweetest growth." His virtue is matched with
an equal or greater goodness in Musidorus, however. Having
come ashore in neighboring Pontus, the elder cousin agrees
to surrender himself to the hate-choked king of Phrygia in
exchange for Pyrocles. Despite Pyrocles' protest, which had
produced a notable contention of sacrificial friendship,
Musidorus is duly delivered up to execution.

As the entire series of encounters demonstrates, a virtuous
will can often overmaster the floods of fortune. Odysseus-
like yet again, a disguised and servile Pyrocles enters into the
very household of the Phrygian executioner. At the moment
of the execution, he throws a sword to his cousin, saying,
"Musidorus . . . , die nobly." And the two princes turn to
face death like princes.

[At this point, praise for his cousin in the past causes the
narrating Musidorus of the present to betray himself, replacing the third with the first person and the past tense with the
present. However, the Penelope to his disguised Odysseus
only smiles in both encouragement and love, and when Musidorus "the more blushed at her smiling, . . . she the more
smiled at his blushing." Since his words are more important
than the picture, however, he returns her thoughts "from his
cheeks to his tongue" (p. 199).] *

Unlike the united heroes, the contentious body of soldiers
at the intended execution falls out with itself. Some volatile

---

* Brackets in the general text indicate "present" Arcadian inter-
ruptions within the internal narratives of the Asian past.

young Phrygians immediately raise the cry, "Liberty," setting off scenes like those of the French Revolution. Retreating from the resulting threat of "popular license . . . many-headed tyranny," a few wiser heads elect Musidorus regent. Justice has arranged to make fortune herself smile, in that "a scaffold of execution should grow a scaffold of coronation" (p. 201).

But the offer of a crown was of course a concealed test of Musidorus' magnanimity. He believed it "a greater greatness to give a kingdom, than get a kingdom," somewhat as Evarchus before him had given up all kingdoms except Macedonia. Instead, he establishes a good member of the Phrygian royal family on the throne, first having worked out constitutional guarantees that neither the governor nor the government could again "decline to tyranny" (p. 202). In that service, he had "set forth . . . his magnificence" even as he earlier had established his magnanimity.

In a second major encounter, the virtues of the Greek cousins are opposed by a cousin to the king of Phrygia, the tyrant of Pontus. The young princes had entered his kingdom in order to avenge their two servants (who, like the princes, had survived the tempest only to meet its cruel human counterpart in Asia). Whereas the lord of Phrygia had dwelt like a toad in constant "suspicion, greediness, or unrevengefulness," his cousin in Pontus is as selfish and inconstant as fortune. Like her accidents, his good deeds arise only from occasional caprices within the central vice; for example, he sometimes gives prodigally "not because he loved them to whom he gave, but because he lusted to give; punishing, not so much for hate or anger, as because he felt not the smart of punishment" (p. 202). His favorite, a man also possessed of fortune-resembling envy, had first smiled upon the Phrygian servants but then caused their imprisonment. With the king, any such alteration of favor announced "a downfall." When the Greek princes urge Pontus to deliver up the two servants, the king instead intemperately has the prisoners executed, all the while accusing the princes of treason against him. Although after a battle with the tyrant Pyrocles inclines to a commendable but dangerous pity, Musidorus sternly executes the unworthy monarch. As for the envious favorite of the king, he expires apoplectically at seeing the "honor done to the dead carcasses"!

Having demonstrated yet again "public actions, of princely, and (as it were) governing virtue"—including Pyrocles' parallel gift of the offered throne of Pontus to the tyrant's sister—the young Greeks turn to more "particular" trials (p. 204). Foremost among them is the subjugation of two giant brothers in Pontus, who oddly enough are less emblematic than their predecessors in the *Old Arcadia*. Possessed of savage strength, they obviously mirror to the cousins the possibility of a career of martial, not moral, power. These two gigantic Calibans think "nothing juster than revenge, nor more noble than the effects of anger"; perverting reason, they are sure that its glass registers bravery only when the actions are terrible. Although under a good king their strength might have been directed to the "public good," it now suffers under a "blind" judgment that makes "wickedness violent" (p. 205). Acting as a private, paired Hercules, the two princes put down such a possible image for themselves. In that heroic service, Pyrocles again demonstrates one major way of surmounting time and fortune. In a chain of courageous redemptions, a hero can "make one action beget another." His practice will bring him the proper fame of an Odysseus or Hercules, for he will have employed "those gifts esteemed rare in them, to the good of mankind."

However, despite their seeming similarity to "Ulysses and Aeneas" (p. 206) as well as to later knights errant, the cousins are not impelled "to heroical effects by fortune, or necessity."

By serving their "own choice, and working," they may seem to pursue only the directions of their own wills. In mastering fate and fortune of the kind seen in the kings of Phrygia and Pontus, they instead serve justice and mankind generally. They act more as redeeming examples than as mere national or cultural deliverers. Somewhat as the same geographical sites were to do for Christianity, each new city or state in Asia serves to "witness to another of the truth of their doings" (p. 206). In that description, which implies a speaking picture, Sidney obviously intends primary emphasis upon "truth" rather than "doings."

Their third major encounter in Asia Minor—probably their most famous, because it supplied Shakespeare with the most profound of his materials for *King Lear*—is therefore created for witness and meditation, more than action. It also increases the scope of reflective applicability for the present Arcadia. If the abdication of the Paphlagonian king mirrors Basilius' abdication, the opposing treatment of that king by a true son and a bastard can point the way for Musidorus and Pyrocles if, in the *New Arcadia,* they are again to be brought to trial by Evarchus. But of course, the mirror is also intended to serve a far more general audience; it intends the "good of mankind." Paphlagonia therefore demands humane rather than martial attention from the representative princes.

Like the characters in Shakespeare who are passionate but largely passive sufferers with Lear, the two Greek heroes suffer an "extreme and foul . . . storm" and "pride of the wind" as they cross Galatia. Driven to seek a "shrouding place" in the cleft of a rock, they overhear a son, Leonatus, tenderly conduct his blinded father away from an attempt at suicide. Before relating to them his father's story, the son begs them to "convey this afflicted prince to some place of rest and security"; such a deed would be "none of the least . . . among [their] worthy acts," especially "if either [of the princes has] a father, and feel[s] what dutiful affection is engrafted in a son's heart" (pp. 206–208).

After his son has finished a swift but complimentary history, the old king insists upon delivering up the proper record of his own life, one that will not palliate his wickedness. Taking witness of the sun, he grimly traces the parallel progress of his affection for a bastard son and his hatred for the true. The bastard, sliding in "poisonous hypocrisy, desperate fraud, smooth malice, hidden ambition, and smiling envy," had stirred the king to abandon his true son to death. Perhaps in warning against the too-easy pity of Pyrocles, the old king now excoriates his "cruel folly to [a] good son, and foolish kindness to [an] unkind bastard" (p. 209). The bastard son eventually had banished his father in rags, lacking even a hand "to guide [his] dark steps" (p. 210).[23] Reversing the parable of the prodigal son, however, the legitimate heir now performs for his father the "kind office" of guide and savior. (The listening Pamela, who at times fiercely resents her degradation because of Basilius' folly, might well take instruction from this Paphlagonian mirror.)

The narrative of "true natural goodness" (p. 206) must look to an opposed action, however, when the bastard son, Plexirtus (*twisting*), enters with his troops, intending to have his legitimate brother killed. Friendly soldiers from Pontus aid the princes and Leonatus. In a corrective reflection of the two giants of Pontus, two Paphlagonian brothers, valorous by nature but by environment devoted to the malevolent causes Plexirtus, force Musidorus and Pyrocles to "repeat their hardest lesson in the feats of arms" (p. 212) in order to overcome them. (These several sets of brothers are arranged in a vertical scale of heroism much as the three Corinthian couples in Book I were formed into

[23] See "A. D.," "Possible Echoes from Sidney's 'Arcadia' in Shakespeare, Milton, and Others," *N & Q*, 194 (1949), 555.

an ethical triad.) Thereafter, the old king having died from a Lear-like "stretching" of his spirits first in unkindness and then in consolation, those two brothers nobly serve Leonatus, the new king. Although both cousins now counsel him against pitying his prodigal brother, Leonatus nevertheless extends him a pardon. Such nearly Christian pity should serve as a warning to Pyrocles, on the one hand, who also is too easy in pity, but on the other suggest to Musidorus a tempering of justice with mercy. However, if the reconciliation of Leonatus with Plexirtus is shadowed by doubts, the following service of the two brothers to the Greek princes is not. In a proper Platonic distribution, timocrats for a time accompany and support the heroic sages.

In almost emblematic adventures which strikingly parallel some of the allegorical encounters of Spenser's knights, the two heroes have thus met and put down kings who figured secretive ire, inconstant cruelty, and "bastardly" selfish will. As if in themselves, they have similarly extirpated a paired emblem of gigantic brute force and then converted another paired emblem of undirected valor. If their "exercise" has involved an implied warning against too-easy pity, it has also included profound personal instruction in "true natural goodness," along with somewhat more objective directions for magnanimity and magnificence.

To this point, the two princes have adventured in a unitary masculine world of heroism. Somewhat like the blind king of Paphlagonia, they have needed only to choose the true prince as against the false, whether in being or in action. Arcadia, too, for whose present action these narratives serve more as mirror or prophecy than as exposition, has to this point received narrative examples of princeliness and its opposite. Such examples can serve Pamela well in her role as present princess and future governor. But now, as if anticipating the entrance of the princes into Arcadian love, the adventures turn principally to stories of Asian queens and the cousins' untried agon of love.

"A living image, and a present story of what Love can do": Feminine passion in Lycia, Iberia, and Armenia

Emblematic narratives of the kings of Asia were related by a prince who had been an actor. Along with Pamela, he is also one of the auditors to whom it best applies in the present. As the "histories" now turn to accounts of love, not only are the present temptations of the Arcadian princesses given continuous attention as they weave in and out among the narratives, but also the narrative burden itself is passed to the princesses and to Pyrocles,[24] to whom the narrative pictures now have perhaps the most home truths to speak.

Musidorus, the narrator for the mainly political tales of monarchy, opens the way into the largely ethical and erotic gallery by taking up the account of Erona of Lycia, who had been besieged by the king of Armenia. Although such a "history" had continued the political instruction of the princes as they attempted to reconcile heroism and love for the princes of the Asian kingdoms, it also mirrors the confusing present perplexities of love in Arcadia. Perhaps more applicable to Pamela than to the immediate narrator Musidorus, such tales have more still to tell to the dangerous passions of Gynecia and Philoclea.

[As if to emphasize the transition from heroism to love in both the adventures and the present action, Sidney has Pamela interrupt the narrative to indicate that she too knows of this story; she has heard it from Plangus, in the near present. The author also has Musidorus repeat his past heroic

[24] Walter R. Davis, "Thematic Unity in the *New Arcadia,*" *SP,* 57 (1960), 131, notes that whereas Musidorus had told of civil strife, Pyrocles turns to the psychology of passion.

magnanimity by celebrating his present holding of a lover's sheephook in place of a principality. Sidney arranges propagation as well as direct reception of the narrative by having Pamela repeat all of Musidorus' account to the lovesick Philoclea. Finally, in a luscious Marlovian interlude or prologue that precedes the immediate Asian action, he has Pyrocles spy on the bathing princesses. Although Sidney might have had Actaeon or Susanna allusively in mind, in practice he offers a lover's reversal of the heroic Odysseus with Nausicaa and insists again upon the value of the Asian mirror for the Greek action.

In one of his most notable extensions of love into landscape, Sidney presents Arcadia's river Ladon as a feminine circle moving in sweet purity between the masculine banks that would embrace it. Similarly, Philoclea resembles a goodly cypress that is reflected by that "running river" (p. 216). When the hidden and disguised Pyrocles trembles and leans upon a tree almost like a Daphne, Philoclea in turn, reacting to the chill water, is overcome with "a pretty kind of shrugging," even as the Ladon becomes "heated with love" (p. 217). Pyrocles projects upon the Ladon his own ardent desire; bubbles in the river mirror and then increase Philoclea twenty-fold. Although never divorced from the sensual, the ardor of Pyrocles is impelled to a Neoplatonic heroic fury, as Philoclea, love, and multiple images produce a Cyrus not only in him but from him: "so together went the utterance and the invention, that one might judge, it was Philoclea's beauty which did speedily write it in [his] eyes; or the sense thereof, which did word by word endite it in [his] mind, whereto [he] (but as an organ) did only lend utterance" (p. 218). His glorification of Philoclea considers her outward beauty to be the token of "fairer guests, which dwell within." For such spiritual attributes, in contradiction of Philoclea's own earlier complaint that her virgin vows were blotted,

Pyrocles finds that her "goodness [is] the pen, heaven paper is;/ The ink immortal fame doth lend" (p. 222).

Still within Arcadia and the present, after Pyrocles has made his blazon complete he is supplied with his opposite image in love. It is Amphialus, perhaps the most complex but most interesting character in the *New Arcadia*'s enlarged cast. He was introduced in the complaint of Helen in Book I. Although he is of "goodly presence" and is a "right manlike man" who might serve as a pattern, he would keep the glove belonging to Philoclea, which his hunting-dog (almost a mirror of himself) had seized. Although Amphialus intends it not as a rape of the glove but only as a token for his knightly service, and although he admires the "Amazon" Pyrocles for similar service to Philoclea, the enraged Pyrocles, all but acting a transversed Diana against an Actaeon and his dog, attacks and wounds the interloper. Thereafter, the pity he had shown in Asia Minor returns. Pyrocles apologizes, but promises that Amphialus may some day contest with "Pyrocles, prince of Macedon." He still encounters only the courtesy and amiability that should have made Amphialus a third to Musidorus and Pyrocles, not their enemy: "I would (answered Amphialus) I had many more such hurts to meet and know that worthy prince, whose virtue I love and admire, though my good destiny hath not been to see his person" (p. 224). Yet he is separated from the young princes precisely by his fortune-plagued "destiny" in love, which at many points resembles that of the Asian queens. It is forecast when the princesses, "Pamela with a noble mind, and Philoclea with a loving," reprove Amphialus with "sweet-graced bitterness" (p. 225) for his having intruded upon their bathing, while the scapegrace Pyrocles is not only fully accepted by the princesses but is also moved to hate the "melancholy" Amphialus, the more the latter reveals his love of Philoclea.

A second interruption causes Philoclea to recount the sim-

ilar recent meeting of Basilius with Plangus and to give
Pyrocles the written version of their debate. It is an adapted
form of the contest of Plangus with Boulon in the *Old Arcadia*'s Second Eclogues. Placed just here, it comments profoundly upon the lover's melancholy of both Plangus and
Amphialus, as well as anticipating atheistic arguments still
to come. Furthermore, the weight of its stoic and Christian
consolation importantly maintains the *New Arcadia*'s Basilius as a king, not a mere *senex*. To Plangus' cry, "Where was
first that cruel cunning found,/ To frame of Earth a vessel of
the mind,/ Where it should be to self-destruction bound,"
Basilius, speaking for the gods, had replied, "We think they
hurt, when most they do assist," men being "with inward
tempest blown/ Of minds quite contrary in waves of will." In
the *New Arcadia,* this verse also serves as a gloss for the fictional use of storms, shipwreck, and civil war; they reflect the
inward tempest of infected will against the erected wit. The
written lyric only teases the listening Pyrocles, however,
partly with desire to know more of Plangus after having
heard "something in [his travels] of this strange matter" (pp.
227–231), but mostly with desire to hear the story from Philoclea's warm lips.]

The narrative of Asian love is now significantly taken up
by Philoclea, who will be followed by Pamela and Basilius.[25]
As the three kings had offered negative examples to the
young princes, who had then acted against them in judicious,
redemptive heroism, so the three queens of Lycia, Iberia, and
Armenia appear in a negative emblematic procession, showing love's errors in both the public and private spheres. They
will represent error in choosing lovers; a lust amounting to
nymphomania; and a love directed almost entirely by politi-

[25] See Nancy Lindheim, "Retrospective Narrative," p. 181, and
Davis, "Thematic Unity," p. 130, for the central position of the Erona-
Plangus story, including its disposition among narrators and auditors.

cal hatred. Sidney arranges that these reflectors receive present comic support from lower Arcadia, too, when both Miso
and Mopsa offer the present young lovers their myths of love's
genesis.

The narratives begin in Lycia. There Erona, as a young
princess, had loathed Lycia's display of naked Cupids. She
had caused all such herms to be pulled down. Like Hippolytus or the *Old Arcadia*'s Musidorus, she is soon punished by
falling so deeply in love with a stupid, Dametan commoner
named Antiphilus that she refuses marriage with the king of
Armenia. Not even the mock execution of Antiphilus (anticipating those of Book III) shakes her love. The Armenian
monarch, resembling the cruel king of Pontus, therefore lays
waste her land and besieges the capital. He carries all before
him until Erona enlists the aid of Pyrocles and Musidorus.
[The narrative is broken here to permit Pyrocles' present
admiration for Philoclea's naming him in the "past."] Heroism can do much in martial aid for Erona, but can do nothing
against her degrading passion for an oaf who is so incompe-
tent in battle that he is easily overwhelmed by Armenia.
Much as Basilius had counselled Plangus in discussing fate,
Philoclea remarks of Erona, with perhaps some intimation of
applicability to herself, that although we call Cupid a god
we are in truth tyrannized because "our own thoughts seem
as a God unto us" (pp. 234–235). Although Lycia's queen
briefly debates whether to surrender to Armenia's lust in
order to save her lover's life, or let her lover die rather than
to dishonor their love, she is interested not so much in a
Solomon as a sinecure. Like Philoclea, who had recently
abandoned all issue of "what, and how," Erona flings the
issue to the two princes; it is they who must save and direct
her. They manage to kill the besieging Armenian king, but
in doing so they call down the implacable hatred of his sister, Artaxia, upon themselves and Erona. In her own marital

affairs, Artaxia will thereafter love only when a lover can serve her hatred.

[Just after Philoclea passes the burden of narrative to Pamela, their story of the second adventure in Asian love is temporarily suspended, although the certainty that Asia is a mirror for Arcadia continues; after inveighing against Asian torments of love, Philoclea adds, with a blush, "O most happy were we, if we did set our loves one upon another" (p. 237). They are interrupted by the alewife Miso, who has other thoughts about the ways of love, formed in part by her having been forced to marry Dametas. Fed up with their "tittle tattling . . . here is Cupid, and there is Cupid," she thrusts in with her own account of the genesis of love. Her comic prose proves once more that Sidney's characters speak in a various, not a uniform, style. The account itself is adapted from a serious description of an emblem in the *Old Arcadia:*

[My gossip] brought me into a corner, where there was painted a foul fiend, I trow: for he had a pair of horns like a bull, his feet cloven, as many eyes upon his body, as my gray-mare hath dapples, and for all the world so placed. This monster sat like a hangman upon a pair of gallows, in his right hand he was painted holding a crown of laurel, in his left hand a purse of money, and out of his mouth hung a lace of two fair pictures, of a man and a woman, and such a countenance he showed, as if he would persuade folks by those allurements to come thither and be hanged. . . . Well (said she) this same is even Love: therefore do what thou list with all those fellows, one after another; and it recks not much what they do to thee, so it be in secret; but upon my charge, never love none of them [pp. 238–239].

Having provided a rockbottom parallel with Polonius' advice to Laertes, she then adds a parallel with the written debate of Plangus and Basilius—the lyric "poor painters oft with silly poets join." It shows the princesses clearly enough in the present (supposing the emblematic Asian narratives have failed) that Love's mother can be a cow and the hundred-eyed Argus his father.

Yet one more lowly, but instructive, interruption delays the narratives of Asian love and heroism. Because lots for the order of speaking happen to fall to Mopsa, the company hears a fruitily romantic tale of love's genesis. A princess, says Mopsa, the fairest "that ever did eat pap" (p. 241), fell in love with a strange knight, and eloped with him. *And so* (for Mopsa uses narrative's most primitive connective), although he had forbidden her to ask of his origin, she had disobeyed. He had vanished on the instant. As Mopsa, a wretched descendant from Sir Thopas, continues her horrible mangling together of Cupid and Psyche with demon lovers and fairy aunts who offer the poor bride magical nuts, Philoclea at last cries mercy by promising Mopsa her own wedding gown, if only she will stop!

The two present comic reflectors of love having first deflated aristocratic love with cynicism but then unwittingly elevated it in implied contrast with Mopsa's ridiculous version of romance, Pamela is now permitted to return to the Asian narrative. For the first time, the future actively begins to be shaped from the pattern of past adventures and their present reflections. With some of the pleasure of Tom Sawyer listening to his own funeral sermon, Pyrocles wants to hear what the princesses will say about him—but also, "purposing . . . to succour her" (p. 242), he now learns directly of the present danger to Lycia's Erona.]

In the *Old Arcadia,* Sidney had introduced the story of Erona amidst the Eclogues and referred to it at several later junctures, hinting that it would be continued or expanded later: a sufficient indication that he felt it to be an important reflector or metaphor even for the direct, quasi-dramatic action of the *Old Arcadia*. In the *New*, it not only binds past, present, and future temporally and unites Asia with Greece geographically, but also, together with the story of Argalus and Parthenia, it commands central importance as a mirror for the young lovers. In this tale even more than the others, the public and private issues of humbly heroic constancy *versus* self-willed passion are joined. Those issues meet in the account of Plangus, who forms a bridge for the loves of Erona and Andromana even as his life is an example of erotic evolution.

The king of Iberia, still reigning in the present time, had been given a son, Plangus, by his first wife, "who both from her ancestors and in herself was worthy of him" (p. 242). For a time, the bereaved king had been both father and mother to the child. When the boy reached about the present age of Pyrocles, he, like the Phalantus of Book I, had persuaded himself that he was in love. He had chosen a married woman, Andromana, who dexterously took him to her bed. When his father, the king, discovered the affair, Plangus had nobly tried to show his father the woman's merit—but had managed only to be succeeded by his father. The older man had then played David to his son's Uriah by sending Plangus away to battle. Andromana, now a widow and acting far more shrewdly with the father than with the son, plays the old man like a fish until she marries him.

When Plangus returns from war, he honorably refuses to take up the affair with his new stepmother. Resembling both Potiphar's wife and Phaedra, she wreaks her scorned wrath upon him in several related ways—by rousing her husband's fear that Plangus will supplant him on the throne; by instituting whispering campaigns that make any virtue of Plangus appear a vice, so that "if he were magnificent, he spent much with an aspiring intent; if he spared, he heaped much with an aspiring intent" (p. 247); and by making the addled king believe both that Plangus wants to be co-regent, and that he intends to kill the king and marry the stepmother.

Like Paphlagonia's Leonatus before him, Plangus is at last so constant a son that he chooses exile in Armenia rather than disservice to his father. And there the narrative from the past reaches into the present, where it remains suspended: Armenia has now besieged Erona in Lycia, Plangus has recently sought the two princes in Arcadia in hope that they might save her, and Armenian Artaxia (*disorder*) hates the Greeks for killing her brother. In the equivalent situation within Arcadia, the two young princes (like Plangus) wander in loves that may turn them against Evarchus and their own honor; the princesses threaten to love beneath them or, perversely, to love their own sex, in something of the pattern of Erona with Antiphilus and of the stepmother with Plangus; Gynecia threatens to duplicate the Iberian stepmother's passion for a younger man; and Basilius, who already has all but deposed his daughters, threatens to scuttle all other concerns for love.

[Such a present reflection or extension of Lycia and Iberia into Arcadia is marked by Basilius' fulsome praise and Gynecia's lavish kissing of the disguised Pyrocles. The prince ruefully notes that whereas Musidorus is only slightly impeded in love, and that by the "shepherdish folks" of Dametas, he himself is beset by two commanding governors, who figure forceful "Love and Jealousy" (p. 252). It matters little that Gynecia, like Philoclea before her, deplores her fault. Pyrocles remains so entangled in her love that his song finds deficiency and excess of love actually to be one ("Let me be lov'd, or else not loved be"). He is at once waylaid by Basilius, who, like the king of Iberia, pleads the absolute privileges of an old man's lust. As the young prince had done in the *Old Arcadia,* he turns the request to his own advantage by asking that Philoclea plead her father's case—and, incidentally, be the unwitting pander to her own seduction. The eager Basilius cooperates by preventing Miso from even attending Philoclea as a duenna.

However, much as an idealizing Pyrocles had once watched her bathe in the Ladon, Philoclea comes upon him bathing Ladon with his tears. The ardor and constancy of his heroic love wrestles with his Iberian lustfulness. Similarly, his subsequent revelation of his true identity shares with the elevated and general past narratives the sense of being among "strange tragedies" that can portray "a living image, and a present story of what Love can do" (p. 258). Considering the two of them in the third person as if they were indeed the characters of a narrative as well as lovers speaking directly to each other, he says, with almost as much bitterness as praise,

Behold here before your eyes Pyrocles, Prince of Madedon, whom you only have brought to this game of Fortune, and unused metamorphosis; whom you only have made neglect his country, forget his father, and lastly, forsake to be Pyrocles: the same Pyrocles, who (you heard) was betrayed by being put in a ship, which being burned, Pyrocles was drowned. O most true presage [p. 259].

And as if he and Musidorus were once again in Phrygia, he pleads that her beauty "not be without pity."

It is as if the returned Odysseus had been certified by Penelope. Philoclea gradually comes to believe in a lover warm and real where there had been only a mysterious and shameful hope. Caught up again in the "shrugging kind of tremor" that she had earlier experienced with the Ladon alone, she candidly acknowledges her love, only charging him in turn, "Thy virtue won me; with virtue preserve me. Dost thou love me? keep me then still worthy to be loved" (pp. 260–261). In the *New Arcadia*, Pyrocles' fiery passion is always controlled ("commanded") by Philoclea's governing

reason and love of honor. A governed ardor is signalled also
by their mutual "promise of marriage" (p. 261), along with
Pyrocles' reflective awareness that "wickedness may well be
compared to a bottomless pit, into which it is far easier to
keep oneself from falling, than being fallen to give oneself
any stay from falling infinitely" (p. 262).

To distract Pyrocles, who eagerly would have preferred "a
more straight parley" than the internal narratives, Philoclea
directs him to return to the story of Asia. He can thereby
bridge the gap in related "history" between the time when
the princes left Armenia and when they entered Arcadia.
With unwitting application to Pyrocles' own passion, his first
tale will condemn the wayward Antiphilus.

After the cousins had restored Erona, her lover did not
"[hold] his affection" for her in the private sphere nor satisfy
"his ambition" by high advancement in the public (p. 262).
It is with this ethical and political anti-Cyrus, then, that the
third major sequence of narratives will commence.]

"Delight in myself": The self and love in Dido,
Andromana, and Zelmane

More than ever before, the theme for Asia (now concentrated mainly in Armenia) has become pride. Its primary
effect is shown in love, by two women, and in power, by
several rulers; its total opposite is pictured, in the end, by
the real Zelmane. Thus loss can be opposed by love. Pyrocles
is involved not only as narrator and critic but also as possible
present host to the past disease, unless he continues to act in
accordance with the meaning of Zelmane. Although the adventures now include men, they concentrate upon an an-
atomy of "feminine" passion. The "masculine" and "feminine" forms of pride, distantly reflective of Basilius and
Gynecia, are evident also in Pyrocles, a possibly prideful

young hero now effeminately disguised as an Amazon. Only when the third among these final narratives explains why, when assuming his disguise, Pyrocles had also taken the name "Zelmane," is he effectively placed in general opposition to both the masculine and feminine forms of pride, even though he is not yet fully delivered from them in the present.

The issue is joined when Pyrocles begins the story of the Armenian princeling Anaxius (*worthless; a lord*), "to whom all men would willingly have yielded the height of praise, but that [he must] bestow it upon himself [because of an] insupportable . . . pride." It is this man, and this possible pride in himself, that Pyrocles is seen to defeat at the very end of the *New Arcadia*. Lucifer, along with giants from Greek mythology, is close to Sidney's thought, for he says that "if it be true that the giants ever made war against heaven, [Anaxius] had been a fit ensign-bearer for that company." His pride is that of the warrior, with only "the sword and spear . . . judging of desert" (p. 263).

With almost equal amounts of competitiveness and disdain, Pyrocles notes that Anaxius had frequently bested his own present rival, Amphialus; yet Pyrocles' story somewhat ingenuously (and probably unwittingly) reverses the moral toward himself. He had wanted to go alone when he encountered Anaxius, "desirous to do something without the company of . . . Musidorus" (p. 263). Although Musidorus had always been to his younger cousin a "lively . . . image of virtue," the dependence had become galling to Pyrocles. With irritation, he asks himself, "How can my life ever requite unto him? . . . Without him I found a weakness, and a mistrustfulness of my self, as one strayed from his best strength, when at any time I missed him" (p. 264).

Alone, therefore, after departing Lycia, Pyrocles had ridden into a defile that in modern fiction would have symbolized the female. There he had come upon nine women stabbing a man with bodkins while the victim lay bound "with many garters" (p. 264). Obviously a symbolic rape by women of a Don Juan among men, the incident is a double warning to Pyrocles. In the past he had needed to avoid a libertine's pride (essentially "effeminate," to Sidney), even as in the present he must avoid abusing Philoclea's simple trust. The women, themselves now on the attack with an "over-mastering . . . manner of pride," intend to blind their victim, thereby creating from him an ironic Cupid. They would later have gone from a symbolic to an actual castration. That Pyrocles could have been such another Don Juan is stressed by their leader, Dido, after he breaks up the attack. "I see you are young," she hisses, "and like enough to have the power (if you would have the mind) to do much more mischief" (p. 265).

The hapless Don Juan, who (like Terence's hero) is named Pamphilus, had displayed the amiability in appearance and manners of a Pyrocles or a Philoclea. Indeed, softness and good nature were the first webs of his sexual snare. After he had gained his prey, however, he kept his several women on tenterhooks of jealousy, envy, and desire. Dido accurately describes such predatory, fashionable love when she says that she herself had come to love him out of a sense of competition but then had remained in play, "like them I have seen play at the ball, grow extremely earnest, who should have the ball; and yet every one knew it was but a ball" (p. 267). Her highly sophisticated wit then envisions Pamphilus' killing himself, in order that in his absolute inconstancy he be spared even the continued wedding of his soul with his body! The pride of this "effeminate" Pamphilus is not greatly different, in the end, from that of the masculine Anaxius; like rulers grown proud, "and in their pride foolish," they may strut their way among either warriors or women, "as if the planets had done enough for [them], that by [them] once he had been delighted" (p. 268). Anticipating the early Donne, Pamphilus likes to prove "it was no inconstancy to change from one love to another, but a great constancy; and contrary, that which we call constancy, to be most changeable" (p. 268).

This mangling comedy of pride, far more deadly than the mere affectation of Phalantus in Book I, is not yet quite over. Dido, the plaintiff against Pamphilus, finishes her plea by asking Pyrocles how Pamphilus could have charged her with want of beauty. "Many fairer?" she demands, incredulously. "I trow even in your judgment, Sir (if your eyes do not beguile me), not many fairer; and I know (whosoever says the contrary) there are not many fairer" (p. 269). What is more, when Pamphilus' friends rush in to conquer Dido, in a turnabout of fortune Pyrocles most unexpectedly finds himself helping her, until peace seems restored.

The episode colors the subsequent first major encounter of Pyrocles with Anaxius, for it initiates the conversion of the Greek prince from martial pride to patience. In their combat, Pyrocles, regretting that his opponent is "abased by his too much loftiness" (p. 270), is near victory, when Pamphilus is seen avenging himself upon Dido. In imitative punishment she is to be beaten, probably raped, and then killed. Pyrocles breaks away from Anaxius in order to aid her. Despite the clear knowledge that onlookers will judge him a coward—that although he "ran in [his own] knowledge after Pamphilus, . . . in all their conceits [he ran] from Anaxius, which as far as [he] could hear, [he] might well hear testified with . . . laughter and games" (p. 271)— Pyrocles serves her need rather than his pride.

In a sense, however, the miasma of pride only increases around Pyrocles. After she is freed, Dido leads him to her miserly father's castle. His Terentian name is Chremes, but he is munificent only in "sparing, in . . . unmeasurable

. . . sort [and] extreme dealing" (p. 273). His Pamphilian "miserable happiness, and rich beggary" makes the miser such that "any enemy could not wish him worse, than to be himself" (p. 274). He even plots the murder of Pyrocles in order to clutch the bounty offered by Artaxia, the hate-filled Armenian queen. When Pyrocles later is delivered by Musidorus from ambush in yet another defile, he learns never again to be injudiciously innocent. He also has learned to cherish, and even to emblematize or Christianize, the help of Musidorus: "who can fear that hath Musidorus by him?" (p. 276). It is a prevenient lesson in man's need for benevolent powers other than his own. As for Chremes and his pride, he at least remains true to his passion. As he is led away to the gallows, he laments not his death nor that of his daughter, but only the loss of his goods. And he dies, therefore, to the sound of "more laughter than tears" (p. 277).

Much as interest in these encounters centers upon Dido rather than Pamphilus, Anaxius, or Chremes, so in the Iberian court (to which the reunited princes next ride) it rests upon the queen, Andromana. In modern psychomedical Greek, she could as well have been named Nymphomania. She would seem at first glance to be the opposite of an Erona, who had once reacted puritanically against naked Cupids. However, in Sidney's world all forms of the passions of love, as they oppose reason, are likely to be one. The political effects clearly may be so, for Andromana is in complete control of her husband. To have a dominant wife may be lucky, says Sidney, if she is "heroical minded," but far otherwise if her power is "neither guided by wisdom, nor followed by fortune" (p. 278). By now, the effeminate vice of feminine control is so deeply imbedded in Iberian national life that it cannot be "unwound." Such a passion presents one more warning to both Philoclea and Pyrocles—especially to the latter, for he imitates an Amazon. The inconstant Andromana lusts for both the young princes at the same instant, her erotic will ranging with continual change. She speeds from the "suburbs of her foolish desires" straight to the capital, debating only whether the brownness of Musidorus or the red and white coloring of Pyrocles is more immediately delectable. As Dido had seen love as a competitive game, so Andromana tries to lead them to play "a request at tennis between us." The narrating Pyrocles draws the analogy and points the moral: "Which proceeding of hers I do the more largely set before you (most dear Lady) that by the foil thereof, you may see the nobleness of my desire to you, and the warrantableness of your favor to me" (p. 279). Keeping such an anti-Cyrus as Andromana in view will act to control the *Old Arcadia*'s luscious but darkling "assault" and "victory" between Philoclea and Pyrocles.

Rebuffed by the princes' reason as she had earlier been refused by Plangus' filial duty, Andromana's passion rises to fury. Her jailing of the princes anticipates the similar future action by Cecropia, although her agreement to free them if they submit to her desires also looks backward to the dilemma of Erona and the conquering king of Armenia. Their "noble minds" refuse such servile disservice to love (p. 280). As Pyrocles increasingly realizes, love, if properly entertained, will be an ally or image of virtue, not its enemy. Like the passions in tragedy, love may be medicinal even when it seems most agonizing: "Love . . . in the course of my life hath a sport sometimes to poison me with roses, sometimes to heal me with wormwood" (p. 281).

In a change of its Asian character, love brings both of those conditions into play when the young Iberian prince Palladius, in love with Zelmane (daughter to the Paphlagonian bastard, Plexirtus), frees the princes in order to please Zelmane. Love proving indeed to be wormwood to Palladius, he watches Zelmane turn from him to Pyrocles.

Because Zelmane was "poisoned with roses" in that love, the Pyrocles of the *New Arcadia* is far more serious than his counterpart in the *Old*. By taking the name "Zelmane" for his Amazonian disguise, Pyrocles not only marks his mental fealty to the memory of such a love and acts to prevent his betraying Philoclea's similar love for him, but also forms solemn bonds between the lovers in the present—for it was with "Zelmane" that Philoclea had first uneasily fallen in love.

When a week's emblematic tourney, which balances with tourneys in each of the other Books, is called to celebrate the wedding anniversary of Andromana with the Iberian king, all the narratives of Asian adventure move toward a conclusion, opening the way to the princes' actions in the present dramatic narrative.

Opposite the villainous Andromana, who is *de facto* ruler in Iberia, stands the Greek Helen of Corinth, many of whose knights have come to the Iberian jousts. Like Palladius and Zelmane, Helen is a positive emblem and example of royal love. As she is the paragon of earthly beauty, so her rule is "no less beautiful to men's judgments." Even the chivalric exercises of her reign had been educative, carrying Sidneian "riches of knowledge upon the stream of delight." Her court was therefore "the marriage place of Love and Virtue, and . . . herself . . . a Diana appareled in the garments of Venus" (p. 283). Such Elizabeth-like marriage of private or ethical with public or political "beauty" shows that folly need not be "the cause of vehement Love, nor reproach the effect." On the contrary, wisdom may consist in well knowing "what is worthy the loving," and goodness, in loving the object "so discerned" (p. 284). Helen's love may be tormented, for she has offered her affections to the always misdirected Amphialus, but it will never be inconstant or degrading.

Because Corinth wins in the first three days of the tourney,

Andromana releases the princes on the fourth day on condition that they contest on the side of Iberia. Like the two queens, the tourney is as much emblematic as "dramatic." [26] In the first tilt, an Iberian proclaims the Iberian seizure by passion: his device is to enter chained, led by a "Nymph." Opposing him for Corinth and representing its humble constancy is Philisides, who enters as a shepherd bearing the impresa of a sheep "marked with pitch, with this word, *Spotted to be known.*" Among the ladies watching was the "Star, whereby his course was only directed." Sidney with his own Astrophilian fiction having thus doubly entered into his Arcadian fiction, it is only fitting that Pyrocles should repeat Philisides' song, "O fool full gaily blest:/ Where failing is a shame, and breaking is his best," with the aside, "Thus I have digressed, because his manner liked me well" (p. 285).

In keeping with the *New Arcadia*'s entrance through loss into recovery, passionate Iberia wins two contests thereafter. The champion for the second is an Elizabethan "savage" man enslaved to love, carrying the impresa of a mill-horse and the "word" *Data fata sequutus* ("following the fate assigned"). Corinth then moves toward victory, led by knights who either display the "device" of having no device or who wear signs of chivalric rather than passionate love (the phoenix in fire, despair in ice). In the afternoon and following day, the two young princes for a time win for Iberia, but only in order to make their escape into Bythinia. When Andromana pursues them her own son, Palladius, is killed. The passionate monster in turn does away with herself.

[In sympathetic pity, Philoclea kisses the narrator. Led almost into an Iberian "rebellion" against honor, Pyrocles is instead commanded back to his obedience by her Corinthian "sweet . . . rigor" (p. 288).]

[26] See Yates, "Elizabethan Chivalry," pp. 4–25.

As the princes reach the coast and prepare to leave Asia Minor, they encounter several final un-heroic images—men who embody an ambitious pride that parodies heroism, and women whose ambitious lust parodies love. First, in a reflection of Andromana and Helen, they hear the girl Leucippe mourning that Pamphilus has again betrayed both her and Baccha. His lust had proved to be so impartially inconstant to either sacred or profane love that neither could "fetter his fickleness" (p. 290). Leucippe can only take herself to a nunnery, while the Cupid-resembling Pamphilus marries Baccha, "the most impudently unchaste woman of all Asia." Like a parodic captain with "brave soldiers," Baccha also draws hosts of lustful Bacchantes into her empire.

In contrast to those two women, although in a sense also uniting their possibilities within a Corinthian marriage of "love and virtue," Zelmane again appears. As if she and the Arcadian Pyrocles between them could use transvestitism to become one Tiresias and thus break down the isolative walls of gender, she comes to the princes dressed like a "young Gentleman" (p. 290). Like a tragic Viola, accepting the name Daiphantus (a name which, in a second tribute to the girl, Pyrocles had assumed in Laconia), she had entered into Pyrocles' service as a page. During that time reversing the recent position of Philoclea with a disguised "feminine" Pyrocles, Pyrocles himself had noticed that the supposedly masculine page's eyes had registered love, but would not understand them. Slowly, the little party makes its way from Bythinia, where the princes serve one last time in Asia as peacemakers, through Galatia, toward Thrace.

Just before crossing out of Asia, they meet their third set of mirrors in mere strength of arm—the brothers Tydeus and Telenor. They had helped the bastard Plexirtus in Trebisond, the kingdom which the good young prince Leonatus, his brother, had given him. Distrusting the two brothers thereafter, the Machiavellian Plexirtus had betrayed them into mistakenly attacking one another. As the brothers weaken into death, they sharply warn Musidorus and Pyrocles against man's placing "good will upon any other ground, than proof of virtue," "no man being good to other, that is not good in himself" (pp. 294, 295).

Having witnessed the emblem of friendship in those two brothers but also having observed the danger even to friendship of living by arms alone, Pyrocles next sees in the fading of Zelmane (because of despair over the cruelty of her father, Plexirtus, as well as love) the emblem of a wholly undemanding ardor. Love, whether in despairing sorrow over her father or concealed affection for Pyrocles, feeds on her damask cheek. The suffering "sorrow and pity" that Pyrocles comes to feel in return crowns all the doing he has accomplished in Asia. It fixes her pain forever with him. He can forget it only if he forgets humanity itself (p. 296). His sympathy is such that he "could willingly . . . have changed lives with her" (p. 298). His disguise in Arcadia, although initiated from passion, not only partly exchanges lives with Zelmane but also assures Philoclea that she will receive from him some of the deep respect and service that Pyrocles now associates with love. Similarly, when Musidorus takes the name "Palladius" upon entering Greece, he will attest in his love for Pamela some of the selflessness Palladius had shown for the real Zelmane. Pyrocles had continued "as full of agony, as kindness, pity, and sorrow, could make an honest heart," but he is ready to transfer most of that complex of feeling to Philoclea. The Arcadian princess in turn can extend and fulfill in her flourishing love all that Zelmane, who "somewhat . . . did resemble" her, had shown in her loving death (p. 299).

With one last burst of Herculean actions, which include Pyrocles' struggle with a monstrous beast in order to free

Plexirtus (as Zelmane had requested), the two young princes conclude their season in Asia. If positively they have given much, negatively they have also learned much that will be of permanent use to their public and private governance. Asia in its turn pays farewell tribute to them with an almost worshipful royal assemblage of rulers. From her kings the princes receive Homeric "highest honors" and "right royal presents" (p. 302). Because they magnanimously have accepted no crowns in Asia Minor, they bid fair to be magnanimous kings in their own provinces, one day.

In Greece, Arcadia had drawn them onward as if to one more heroic encounter, partly because in general "no prince could pretend height, nor beggar lowness" that could bar them from a country "so renowned over the world," but also because of the more particular fame of its pattern for heroes, in Argalus and Amphialus, and for heroines, in Pamela and Philoclea. Although Plexirtus had arranged for the princes' death at sea, like Hamlet they had learned of the plot. When in self-defense they had leaped to the attack, the ship, like many an Asian state and like the Laconia that they will soon encounter, had fallen to civil war and then to fire. Within the symbolic context of that loss, then, they had entered Arcadia.

Here the long account of the adventures in Asia closes, except for the Lycian epilogue that will be supplied by Basilius. It does not end without a wish that it might somehow be prolonged within actuality. If its poetry has not exactly made Arcadian life golden, it has delightfully shown where the gold of heroism and love may lie. Somewhat like Pamela earlier, Philoclea asks that the narrative music play on, in order to celebrate Pyrocles' meeting with *her*—"the best part of your story" (p. 307). Instead, he asks her to supply final knowledge of Erona's danger and Plangus' recent quest for the two princes. She pertly agrees to become narrator if he will give his word that his hands "shall be quiet auditors" (p. 307).

Both narrator and auditor, in whichever disposition, are at that moment called back to the immediately actual. Miso's intervening arrival is too solid for mirrors. Now they must face a present Iberia in Gynecia's passion, even though a present Corinth may also appear in their own love.

Although Basilius still has something more to relate, instructed present action will now almost replace instructive past adventures. Until modern readers have been naturalized to such a "landscape of the mind," the instruction may seem intrusive or digressive or both, whether it appears in the *Odyssey,* the central and final Books of *Paradise Lost,* or the dumb show and mirror play in *Hamlet.* But if a mirror is the thing in which a conscience is to be held and a will delightfully taught, Homer, Sidney, and Shakespeare probably would agree that a triple mirror is in itself a good thing. It can reflect at least three faces, including that of the reader who sees himself in seeing a character or group of characters also seeing themselves in present action, by means of seeing others in past actions. For Sidney, who has carefully changed his narrators as well as having their narratives be directed to other characters so that narrative will breed narrative and each Cyrus form at least one other Cyrus, it is in a sense a mistake to say that the principal action "resumes." From his point of view, a simultaneous meaning has merely been witnessed processionally on a related plane of action or a related dimension in time. As we have seen, many of the political and ethical concerns remaining from Asia Minor shadow forth and inform the present action in Arcadia, even as the pictures of Asia and Arcadia might in turn speak to Sidney's contemporary England.

The largely Arcadian portion of the action reopens upon

Gynecia, dreaming her Freudian dream of a thorny thicket that holds her from Pyrocles. Although she does not quite understand the dream, its implications appear at once in action. First, she cannot reveal Pyrocles' disguise and thereby thwart Philoclea without "thornily" thwarting herself. She finds jealousy to bear the "thorns" of the dream's picture. much as Philoclea's face will soon become for her the "image of death" (p. 310):

O Jealousy . . . the frenzy of wise folks, the well-wishing spite, and unkind carefulness, the self-punishment for others' faults, and self-misery in others' happiness . . . daughter of love, and mother of hate . . . [p. 309].

Less a phoenix in love than a jealous fury, she envisions herself (and perhaps her effect upon others) as a destructive flame: "My lovely joys to doleful ashes turn;/ Their flames mount up, my powers prostrate lie:/ They live in force, I quite consumed die" (p. 310). Although she drives Philoclea from Pyrocles with the look of a masterful Pallas to an Arachne, it is she who acts the spider, forcing the young lover to look upon "the storehouse of her deadly desires" (p. 310).

Such massive irregularity in the private Arcadia is paired almost at once with public rebellion. Although Cecropia had instigated this attack, like that of the animals in Book I, the passion of the mob had soon become self-feeding. It soon resembles that of the suitors in the *Odyssey*. The young princes act with contemptuous, partly Platonic severity toward this flood of tailors, butchers, millers, and painters, although Musidorus' use of a "two-handed sword" suggests that they are all the while the agents of a justice greater than the human. A similar use of the princes as ministers and scourges had appeared in the recent war at sea. Whether or not Sidney intended any connection, he considers that art may also be a proper stay against indecorum and immorality, even as words are a necessary part of the true hero's poly-tropic character. After showing his readers an anti-Cyrus in the rebel painter who wanted to portray centaurs and Lapiths, and who therefore had entered on the wrong side of the princes' combat in order to inspect not reasons but wounds, Sidney has him receive direct injuries, including the loss of his painting hands, for his trouble. In contrast, the heroic Pyrocles, mounting suddenly into the "judgment seat of the Prince, which . . . was before the gate," for the second time in the *New Arcadia* unlocks his word-hoard to allay a popular tempest. He also extends his Asian heroism directly into the heart of Arcadia. A good, almost English farmer helps him by reminding the mob that it was of old "counted wisdom, to hear much, and say little" (p. 314). When Pyrocles asks the crowd to state its grievances in order that its interested king may know and act upon them, the mob falls to selfish bickering: "no confusion was greater than of particular men's likings and dislikings: one dispraising such a one, whom another praised, and demanding such a one to be punished, whom the other would have exalted" (p. 315). Having with some secret satisfaction seen them turn their rage upon one another and thereby disperse if not diminish it, Pyrocles (with, it is to be hoped, some ironic sense of his own disguise) says that when men grow effeminate, women such as "he" may give counsel. Extending but also localizing the argument from the *Old Arcadia,* he declares that in the Prince rests their love and security; at Basilius' lodges are "harbored no Argians your ancient enemies, nor Laconians your now-feared neighbors. Here be neither hard landlords, nor biting usurers" (p. 316).

The justice of his case, together with his art, lets Pyrocles make words to be a picture of his mind. His gestures add dimensional shading. He thus affects the "rugged wilderness" of the mob's "imaginations," transforming their "roaring cries" first to "confused muttering" and then to shouts, "God save Basilius" (pp. 318–319). The pacific word-painting of Pyrocles stands in obvious contrast to the painter's image of wrath.

But Sidney is not yet finished with the issue of art and audience. Badly judging what he has seen, one Clinias inveighs against such alteration in "the many-headed multitude." Although Sidney approves that general complaint, he distrusts Clinias' reasons for complaining. Clinias is a sliding sophist, learned rather in "words than manners, and of words rather plenty than order." Although he, like Musidorus, has acted in tragedies, he has learned from them only the protean imitation of "many passions" (p. 319). He is well fitted by such imitativeness and by his native cowardice to serve as a spy and rumor-monger against Basilius. He shifts, of course, with the multitude; when it again applauds Basilius, he out-Herods its Herod. He cries out against any Giants that would pluck down such a Jupiter; he praises Basilius as the "Pelops of wisdom, and Minos of . . . good government" (p. 320). His rant is stopped by a blow from the disgusted honest farmer. Unhappily, that blow creates counter-blows ("as if Aeolus had broke open the door to let all his winds out"— p. 320), and only the post-Asian intervention of the princes prevents a general civil slaughter.

No Minos or Pelops, Basilius now errs as badly as the pitying Pyrocles had done in Asia Minor. He thanks the chameleon Clinias and accepts his version of the rebellion. Although the account itself has been taken over with only a few changes from the direct narrative of the *Old Arcadia,* those alterations cause over-protestation to stain the truth. Basilius, "that was not the sharpest piercer into masked minds" (p. 324) or disguised oracles, cannot distinguish mask and reality in Clinias any better than he could tell Dametas' stupidity from honest plainness. Bad art and bad reception of it contrast sharply with Pyrocles' heroic truth, both in the matter and in its expression.

In the present action, then, the governed love and heroism of Philoclea and Pyrocles, taught by Asian narratives, increasingly oppose the disordered passion and bad judgment of Gynecia and Basilius. If the reclaimed citizens over-react in holding that, in comparison with the two princes, "what examples Greece could ever allege of wit and fortitude were [now] set in the rank of trifles" (p. 325), their ideals or conceits have nevertheless been almost set right. Arcadia can thus be restored by the heroic means demonstrated in Asia. The counsellor Philanax tries to bring Basilius out of retirement by discounting the oracle. Repeating it, however, Basilius shows that for the time being he is indeed a poor piercer of disguise and self-deceit; he insists that "Zelmane" fulfills the oracle.

The present situation in Asia Minor at last is clarified by Basilius, who has been distracted from ardor to narrative art by Pyrocles—exactly as he himself had been distracted by Philoclea. What Basilius has to tell not only leads narrative of the past into a suspended plea for similar action in the present, but also should have mirrored the private and public horrors of blind love to the king himself.

"Much grieved (because much loving)":
  Possible redemption of love and state,
  in Plangus and Erona (and the princes)

Basilius' account reveals that in unfortunate Lycia, Antiphilus has now become the model of a bad king. As love was a tennisball for Dido, Lycia is only a tenniscourt to her base king, and the "game" of monarchy only a sway of changing passions. Two forces play at being anti-Cyrus, however. As the spy Clinias has worked upon Basilius in Arcadia, so in Lycia the flattering court drums up a false measure, to which Antiphilus' careless mind dances as to a "pretty . . . music" (p. 331). He comes to despise Erona and covet Artaxia—and with her, Armenia. Although the humiliated Erona tries to serve as their go-between (in somewhat the same service that Basilius had designed for Philoclea), Artaxia hates both of the Lycians relentlessly. She conceals her hatred only until she can strike, intending then to sacrifice both Erona and Antiphilus upon her brother's tomb.

In a final emblematic "picture" useful equally to politics and ethics, the base Antiphilus promptly goes to pieces under Armenian attack. The noble Erona, however, becomes only the stronger—showing, if Basilius, too, could learn, that "to the disgrace of men . . . there are women more wise to judge what is to be expected, and more constant to bear it when it is happened." She thus impresses an ideal upon the conquering Armenian Plangus, who can "perceive the shape of loveliness more perfectly in woe, than in joyfulness" (p. 333). Like the princes in Arcadia, Erona and Plangus now might have redeemed both love and the state. Although Plangus is unsuccessful in arranging the escape of Antiphilus, mainly because of the latter's crass cowardice, he does manage to seize a royal hostage, thereby staying Artaxia's hand temporarily. It is agreed, however, that if Pyrocles and Musidorus do not return for personal combat with Armenian knights, Erona will be burned. During the time when the desperate Plangus has sought the cousins in Greece, Artaxia has married Plexirtus. Now king of Armenia as well as Trebisond, he joins to her vows his own personal hatred of the two redemptive cousins. Not finding the princes in Arcadia, Plangus has hastened north to seek aid from Evarchus, although he is fearful that Erona must already have perished.

In completing the account, Basilius urges its moral upon

Pyrocles: "Consider . . . the strange power of love, and . . . exercise therein the true nobleness of . . . judgment." He of course asks it only in order that favor be shown "to the unfortunate historian" who has told the affecting tale (p. 338). As Sidney was to indicate in the *Defence,* mirrors from history may avail little, especially to blind Cupid or his blind victims. To all the Arcadians, therefore, a present lyric mirror is now offered: the Second Eclogues.

Coming after thirty chapters of coupled narrative, the eclogues seem far less integral in the *New* than their counterparts were in the *Old Arcadia.* Rightly so; but the even more integral adventures have assumed much of the former choric burden of the Eclogues. The poetry has been accommodated to the complex reflective system of the prose section, but by no means supplanted. The Eclogues begin with the debate of Reason and Passion, which now can mirror twice the narrative territory it had indicated in the *Old.* The dialogue of Musidorus with Dicus follows. In its new position, it not only comments upon the occasions of constancy in the past but also prepares the personal and theological constancy that is to come. In a collective framework, something of the same comment is conveyed first by the comically boisterous debate of Nico with Pas, then by the dizaine of Strephon and Klaius, and finally by the Echo song, hopeless of all merely material responses to spiritual aspiration. In keeping with other vicarious reporting in the *New Arcadia,* the penultimate lyrics were sung by "Lamon," who—in another of Sidney's explorations of mimetic art and sympathetic expression— "with great cunning, varying his voice according to the diversity of the persons" (pp. 348–349), could "well . . . express the passions" (p. 351). Unlike Clinias, who had altered roles selfishly, the creative Lamon embraces them all, with a kind of negative capability. Similarly, Philisides reflects in the echo song the melancholy that is felt by all young lovers and manifested in his own countenance. If the procession of emblematic Asian narratives has been well used, his question "Can fancies want eyes? or he fall that steppeth aloft?" (p. 352) must be answered, "No." On the other hand, if the Arcadians retire only "to meditate upon their private desires" (p. 353), then the answer from Philisides will unhappily apply: "Oft."

"In that sort flourishing":
The Third Book

Whereas the center of the *Old Arcadia* had offered complications of the love plot, the new Book III all but transcends that concern. Private affairs as such are surrendered into the massive, ceremonious military campaigns of Cecropia and Asia Minor against Arcadia. Those campaigns involve immense loss, of course, but even more importantly, they found heroism upon a patient serenity that masters suffering or loss and affirms faith. Like their reflective model, Parthenia, the two princesses now are tried not by illicit love but by physical death and the arguments of atheism, which supposedly would lead to spiritual death. Similarly, the two princes act not as secretive, often lustful Cupids but as the Miltonic "new" heroes they had proved themselves to be in Asia Minor.

In recapitulation of the opening of the work, the last brief period of freedom for Arcadia had served to prove the virtue of Pamela and Musidorus, just before their opposites—the vicious Cecropia [27] and the vacillating Amphialus—invade the setting. During that interval, Pamela had revealed the

[27] Upon Cecropia, see Tillyard, *The English Epic*, p. 297, and Alexander Brunet, *The Regal Armorie of Great Britain* (London: H. K. Causton, 1839), p. 58.

love she formerly had severely restrained, although maintaining even in that declaration her attitude of "noble favor, and chaste plainness." Her confession should have released the initial joyful springtide into their lives, but Musidorus cannot relinquish the ice of despair into the warmth of love without an over-reaction. As an archetypical "child of passion . . . never acquainted with mediocrity" (p. 354), his expression of love becomes reflectively absolute and seemingly uncontrollable. The advances he makes upon Pamela become as unreasoned as the rebellion that had lately afflicted the nation. She flinches, thinking the wine or roses of love to have been found poisoned. He is rejected as "unworthy . . . to love, or to be loved" (p. 355). Like the supposed father of such appetites, Musidorus is stricken to find himself "not only unhappy, but unhappy after being fallen from all happiness . . . his own fault, and his fault to be done to no other but to Pamela" (p. 355).

For a second suggestive three-day period, paralleling that of his earlier separation from Pyrocles, Musidorus berates himself. At last, regardless of what he feels to be his own low worth, he is unwilling to discard the nobility of the love he has felt. In a confessional elegiac he acts the Adam with God, striving in words "to show his sorrow, and testify his repentance" (p. 356). He looks in his heart and writes, after laboriously discarding any untruthful or falsely expressive statements.

Pamela, who in the *New Arcadia* often threatens to be a prig, C. S. Lewis' fierce Protestant,[28] or a cold emblem, is satisfactorily humanized again by Shakespearean humor when she comes to deal with his letter. At first, she believes it would contaminate her. In the end, however, she decides that she must open and read it, if only to "pick some further

---

[28] *English Literature in the Sixteenth Century Excluding Drama* (Oxford: Oxford Univ. Press, 1954), p. 342.

quarrel [with] him" (p. 357). Drayton as well as Shakespeare would soon relish such unwitting wit in his speakers. The elegy itself, after paying full tribute to her "gratefulness, sweetness, holy love, hearty regard," wrestles with the divine authority of Love, asking,

> Shall to the world appear that faith and love be rewarded
> with mortal disdain, bent to unendly revenge?
> Unto revenge? O sweet, on a wretch wilt thou be revenged?
> shall such high Planets end to the loss of a worm?
>
> . . . . .
>
> If that love be a fault, more fault in you to be lovely:
> love never had me oppressed, but that I saw to be loved.
> You be the cause that I loved; what Reason blameth a shadow,
> that with a body it goes? since by a body it is [p. 358].

Musidorus concludes with a history and confession of reason's yielding to passion, which in turn had yielded to violence; but as the spokesman for all such love, he demands, "But what's this for a fault, for which such fault is abolished,/ Such faith, so stainless, inviolate, violent?" (p. 359). It is quite certain that Pamela, too, would have come to a favorable verdict upon his "disputation between favor and faultiness" (p. 359), especially as it moves to explain the divine frenzy. However, a rival spring song, a false allurement, and real violence intervene.

Even while Basilius is in conference concerning Cecropia's part in the recent rebellion (for in the *New Arcadia,* the world never lets Basilius rest long in foolish ease), his sister again "invades" Arcadia. She sends in six Pyroclean Amazons seemingly acting a Primavera like that which initiated the *New Arcadia,* but actually enacting Winter. They are dressed in scarlet petticoats garnished with leaves; their heads are crowned with roses and gilliflowers; and they are sufficiently sunburned to offer feminine "eclogues" rivalling those of the shepherds. Although they appear to be like Pamela and true springtime both in their "graceful gravity" and "enticing soberness" (p. 360), they instead are an antimasque, from the lineage of Circe and the sirens.[29] In a false echo of Musidorus' recent elegy, they declare that their message from Love must be delivered by their "lovely persons" (p. 361). It is possible that the princesses would have rejected the unlikely troupe, entering as it has into royal territory forbidden to strangers, but Miso, her nose out of joint from having missed the male pastorals, insists upon the advertized performance. She especially recommends its delights, which seem to promise something of her own low version of love, to the princesses; their tolerating such a show will make the "honest country people know" that the princesses are "not so squeamish as folks thought of them" (p. 361).

The Arcadians, led on by Miso, follow the pleasant music to a banquet of sense. Although the wine is Bacchic, the princesses are far less on their guard than was Milton's Lady against Comus. They are easy victims to twenty men in arms, who capture and abduct the two princesses and the disguised Pyrocles. They are spirited away to a captive exile that almost exactly parallels their exile under Basilius' licentiousness.

From this point forward, inward battles of atheism and expediency against faith match the outward battles of Arcadia against a rebellious Argian faction. It is a vast emblem of an almost Manichean struggle. In it, the young lovers are perfected by suffering into an entirely new form of heroism, that of patience, even as their love is perfected toward a celestial level. Sidney could hardly have formed a more telling picture of the manner in which the ways of the world may not only be opposed by the ways of the spirit, but even be used by the spirit for its own perfecting.

[29] See J. F. Kermode, "The Banquet of Sense," *Bulletin of the John Rylands Library*, 44 (1961), 76.

When she is forced into the Argians' castle, Pamela is as adamant with her captor, her Argive aunt Cecropia, as she had been with her lover. She demands that death, if it be designed, come quickly. The niece's firm ethical control is matched by the aunt's more than Machiavellian pride and will. Cecropia's son, Amphialus—"an excellent son of an evil mother," but unwilling to assert his excellence if her evil inclines to his profit (p. 363)—is told that he can now take Philoclea: that, like the service of Cymoent for her son in *The Faerie Queene,* the raid has been a doting mother's present to her lovesick son. To his bemused questions, she supplies yet one more internal narrative.

Originally from Argos, she had married the younger brother of Basilius in the confident expectation that the old king, unmarried at threescore, could have no children and that, if necessary, he might be assisted to his grave with poison. Like a Richard II, she had suffered the prideful beams of her majesty to bless the populace:

Did I go to church? it seemed the very Gods waited for me, their devotions not being solemnized till I was ready. Did I walk abroad to see any delight? Nay, my walking was the delight itself; for to it was the concourse . . . my sleeps were inquired after, and my wakings never unsaluted. . . . And in this felicity wert thou born, the very earth submitting itself unto thee to be trodden on as by his prince [p. 364].

Her pride is lacerated when her husband dies—the victim, says Cecropia, of heavenly envy, although Hamlet's cherub might whisper of divine justice—and at almost the same moment Basilius marries Gynecia. The "hill of honor" (p. 364) suddenly becomes a slope of fortune. "Think then what my mind was," she demands, and at once demonstrates the terrible pride and wrath such an imagination can body forth. Her loss, though much less than that of the princesses, was insupportable to her, because "the fall is greater from [being] the first to the second, than from the second to the undermost" (pp. 364–365). At once, like eroding fortune, the fickle Arcadian court had washed away from her. As inflexible in wrath as Pamela is in virtue, however, Cecropia had resolutely told herself that in such distress "weeping becomes fools, and practice wise folks."

Her vengeful "practice" has already released wild beasts upon Arcadia's pleasant pastorals, a popular tumult upon the stable (if lapsed) monarchy, and six Amazons upon the Arcadian heiresses. In each case, she had fully intended death to the line of Basilius. If Fortune or providence had prevented the animals, and if their own loutishness destroyed the attack of the mob, in the present only her indulgence of her son's love has stayed Cecropia's hand. Still in parody of the captivity and submission to love attested by Musidorus and Pamela, she cynically thrusts Amphialus toward Philoclea, swearing "hate often begetteth victory; Love commonly is the instrument of subjection" (p. 365). When her son protests his romantic servitude to the captive princess, Cecropia anticipates in herself Macbeth's tribute to his wife. "Well (said Cecropia) I would I had born you of my mind, as well as of my body; then should you not have sunk under base weakness" (p. 366). When in courtly Sidneian complexity he answers, "I would not for my life constrain [her] presence, but rather would I die than consent to [her] absence," the reader half shares her tart judgment: "Pretty intricate follies" (p. 366). His difficulty is that of an erotic Atticus: he is eager to love, but yet afraid to support love, much as he is by inclination heroic, yet capable of self-serving anti-heroism. This frustrating mixture nevertheless is something of the lot mediate man was born for. It at least preserves the son from the mother's complete loss of humanity.

"Outward and inward eyes": Argian force
versus the princesses' constancy

Near the beginning of both the *Arcadias*, Pyrocles sings
of the defeat of his powers by "outward force, and inward
treason." In the portion of Book III that Sidney completed,
the ambitious outward force of Cecropia is paired with the
ill-managed, treasonable love of Amphialus against the princesses and, through them, against Arcadia. The political
opposition of Laconia in Book I is thereby paralleled by a
largely ethical opposition in Book III, between which has
stood the preparatory emblematic narratives of Book II. The
metaphors of "outward" and "inward" are employed structurally as well as emblematically. Not only does Amphialus
use "outward" nature and "inward" art to prepare his castle
for the Basilian siege, but also the physical battles on the
outside move in close parallel with the spiritual contest
within.[30] Finally, physical attacks upon the princesses mount
in scale with spiritual and psychological attacks, balancing
actual war with a form of psychomachia.

The contest begins when the pretender Amphialus, em-
phatically different from Musidorus, comes to address the
captive Philoclea. Whereas Musidorus had carefully weighed
his truthful inward rhetoric, Amphialus carefully chooses
his clothing for external expressiveness. He completes a black
costume with a collar of icy opals and fiery rubies, demon-
strating "the two passions of fear and desire, wherein he was
enchained" (p. 367). In what amounts to an unwitting
burlesque of Musidorus' recent elegy, he dares to tell the
imprisoned girl that *he* rests under *her* threat of execution,
for he is her "eternal slave" (p. 368). Like a Venus mourning

[30] For excellent commentary upon the structure of these episodes,
see Davis, *A Map of Arcadia*, pp. 126–129.

for her proper Adonis (p. 367), however, she sadly reminds him, "You call for pity, and use cruelty . . . you say I am mistress of your life, [but] I am not mistress of mine own. You entitle yourself my slave, but I am sure I am yours." Amphialus inhabits an ethical limbo. Although he hates her being imprisoned, he cannot bear to let her go, being "neither able to grant, nor deny" (p. 369). Before such unavailing respect and threatening desire, Philoclea begins to quake as if in the throes of death. It is a sad contrast with her delicate trembling at the Ladon or with Pyrocles. The wretched Amphialus can only make an awkward exit, "having the cold ashes of care cast upon the coals of desire" (p. 370). His mother later listens with "amazement" to his sorry tale, especially as a different kind of siege must now be expected from the pursuing Basilius and his army.

Unsuccessful in making love, Amphialus turns with almost visible relief to preparations for war. He seeks young men filled "with unlimited desires" who would profit from civil war, offering "to the ambitious, great expectations; to the displeased, revenge; to the greedy, spoil" (p. 371). He circulates a declaration of rebellion, a document that "from true commonplaces [fetches] down most false applications." For every act of rebellion it speciously pleads the cause of the commonwealth, declaring that "new necessities require new remedies" —such as the abduction of the princesses. Amphialus' rhetoric manages to create a number of anti-Cyruses, but as for himself, he lets time, the Fortune-serving "mother of many mutations" (pp. 372–373), sustain him while he further exercises his outward and inward eyes, in nature and art, to perfect his castle's fortifications and to dispose the defending troops. As the *Defence* advises, he instructs his men by example rather than precept (p. 374).

Although Sidney relishes the military acumen of an Amphialus, he is careful to show that jealous retirement by the

Argians is actually much worse than the fearful but luxurious exile of Basilius. Whereas the one was initiated in folly, the other springs from deceitful malice. Similarly, although Amphialus assigns his men with Machiavellian awareness and use of their limitations, he himself still labors under the assault of love. He finds it ironic that people should hold that idleness breeds love, for he finds that "inward guest" (p. 374) to be at the center of even his most furious business. Still irresolute in serving or jailing Philoclea, he is eloquent when alone but "dumb-stricken, when her presence gave him fit occasion of speaking" (p. 375). Unwisely, he turns for counsel to his mother.

Cecropia, judging love by her own expedient past, is impatiently sure that the princess can be brought to drink love's poison if only it is distilled in sweet liquor, "which she [herself] with little disguising had drunk up thirstily" (p. 376). She attacks Philoclea, who has been "left to a neglected chance, which yet could [not] unperfect her perfections" (p. 376). Suiting her Satanic, materialistic temptation to the simplicity and warmth of Philoclea's nature even as Amphialus had placed his men so that the defence might reap advantage from their weaknesses, she begins by pleading a use for the body other than grief. When Philoclea answers that whether or not tears become her eyes, they surely become her fortune, her aunt asks that the girl lend her her sensual ears, giving up her armed mind. She demands that Philoclea accept her as a "good angel" and take the proffered wine of love or marriage, even if it is not conveyed in the specific glass she fancied; if she accepts, the princess can then own the very castle in which she is imprisoned. Cecropia knows that she herself could not have resisted such an offer: "It is so manifest a profit unto you, as the meanest judgment must straight apprehend it: so far is it from the sharpness of yours, thereof to be ignorant" (p. 378).

When Philoclea unexpectedly answers that under these circumstances her heart is set upon "a virgin's life to [her] death," she thoroughly scandalizes the worldly Cecropia. The aunt argues that the body of a woman must serve love and generation; if it does not, it is only then that she is truly bereaved or imprisoned, for "man's experience is woman's best eyesight." The profit of marriage, she adds (echoing Miso), is that it frees lust from its inhibitions, providing "free delight . . . without the accusing of the inward conscience, or fear of outward shame" (pp. 379–380). But Philoclea, her mind inwardly staid on Pyrocles, finds all the argument to be so much "tedious prattle." Her thoughts, then, have lent only her ears to Cecropia.

Like a poisonous reptile, Cecropia sucks up "more and more spite out of her denial," even though concealing it for her son's sake. Amphialus meanwhile showers the imprisoned girl with music, presents, and letters, assuring her that if she dwells in bondage, it is "only knit in love-knots" (p. 381). Philoclea either disdains such burdens or converts them by imagination into tributes from Pyrocles.

Doubly galled, Cecropia expediently determines to win Pamela instead. She hopes from her a "beautiful gratefulness" in place of her sister's "disdaining beauty"—a judgment suggesting that she is no more capable than Basilius of piercing masks or defining character. Trying to suit her attack to the quarry, she eavesdrops before entering Pamela's cell. Unlike the weeping Philoclea, Pamela has been occupied with "deep (though patient) thoughts"—those such as might later serve Charles I in prison. She is sure that jail cannot keep out God. She prays only that injury not overmaster her; that a beam of the "all-seeing light" (p. 382) remain with her, despite all trials; and that, no matter what her own fate will be, Musidorus may be spared. A "speaking picture" of devotion, her right hand expressive of zeal and her left of humility, she might all but make Cyruses in heaven. On earth, even the stony Cecropia is for an instant abashed and disconcerted, partly from realizing now that only some image of virtue—which she herself entirely lacks—will be able to move Pamela. Her somewhat slack attempt to "invade [Pamela's] excellent judgment" and "bring her mind into servitude" (that is, into an agreement to have Amphialus) fails, beaten off by "the Majesty of virtue" (p. 384). It remains for her to fight more broadly on another day. She will then attack not Pamela but the God in whom Pamela places her trust and bases her knowledge.

Meanwhile, the lesser business of Mars without the castle complements that of the cold materialistic Venus within. As Basilian forces threaten the Argians, the ice of Clinias' cowardice is paired with the heat of Amphialus' courage, the Petrarchan metaphors having proved again the kinship of love and war. While Clinias trembles in cowardice, Amphialus, boiling with "choler" (p. 386), rushes some offensive troops out from the castle. Although he did not intend it, his first charge brings down a youthfully brave and handsome brother of Philanax, whose close friend at once follows him to death. Such beauty and bravery, resembling that of the two heroic cousins, serves to mock Amphialus. He would not have wished to be their enemy, yet remains so. He ranges further upon the attack like a tiger, confirming himself as a true son of the Cecropia who had released wild beasts upon Arcadia.

The battle, which had become Homeric with a catalogue of Arcadians slain and with the turn of its "tenniscourt" fortune after Philanax' counterattack (p. 390), gains a chivalric character when, after Philanax' capture, a knight in black armor enters to support the flagging Basilian cause. Amphialus is inevitably attracted to the newcomer, for as Venus "in two beautiful folks . . . stirs a desire of joining," so Mars leads the two heroes together with "desire of trial" (p. 393). During their bout, excellent minds guide their two lieutenant bodies—until the Black Knight is treacherously wounded by an old confederate of Amphialus. The protest by Amphialus against the dishonor done both knights is interrupted when he discovers that Basilius has placed troops in his rear. The day's work ends with Amphialus' return into his castle and the disappearance of the Black Knight. With Amphialus as with Cecropia, the Argians seem to win particular battles yet obscurely sense that they are losing both the outward and the inward wars. Philoclea, for instance, resolutely rejects "his good success [as] a pleasant monument of a doleful burial" (p. 399), whether it appears in a battle or a lyric. He is glad to spare Philanax' life and even to free him, at her request, but is greatly angered by that counsellor's probity and judgment when Philanax warns him that although Basilius is still "apt to forgive" (p. 401), in consideration of Amphialus' youth and his excuse of love, he will surely maintain and intensify the siege.

"The war of wickedness in her self": Self-serving atheism *versus* reasoned faith

With Amphialus gaining no perceptible "inward" advantage, Cecropia mounts a second major assault upon the princesses. With Philoclea, she urges merely a "duty" to repay Amphialus for freeing Philanax. With Pamela, she attacks the conviction that the cosmos proceeds from an orderly and benevolent design and will.

As she enters upon the elder sister, Cecropia finds her acting the orderly and benevolent artist, herself, as she works roses and lilies upon a purse. The materials she uses look "with many eyes upon her," and when she bites away loose thread her lips resemble the roses even as her hands reflect the lilies. Like the "ground" of her life, that of the design is "neither sullenly dark, nor glaringly lightsome" (p. 402). Despite the onslaught of fortune, even as she cares minutely for her designed creation so Pamela cares for the "dainty dressing of herself," as a creature within a greater design (p. 403). Witnessing such control, Cecropia is misled into expecting that it will be Pamela, not Philoclea, who can be won by the appeal of controlled cynicism.

Punningly "animated" by such a hope, Cecropia praises the beauty of the purse and its maker, only to receive the retort that physical beauty is never more than a "pleasant mixture of natural colors," which are found as frequently in beasts and minerals as in man. Cecropia, feinting toward Pico and doctrines of the *Defence* but actually lodging with Aphrodite, declares that "the beauty of human persons [is] beyond all other things [in that] to them only is given the judgment to discern beauty." Furthermore, that discernment is greater in women, the rival gift of strength having been given men. The prideful power for resistless command can be much the same, however, in love or in war. Women are therefore commanded to use their beauty in order to command in turn the "purpose for which it is created" (p. 404). Pamela replies much as she had before: that such "victories" by beauty testify either to the weakness of the victims or else to a quality so exalted that it should not be "defiled" in petty triumphs (p. 404). Cecropia, scandalized a second time, objects that she had meant to say only that beauty demanded love. When Pamela, playing for time in saying that Amphialus must get consent from a form of higher power—her parents—before she will hear his suit, lest she offend God, the major argument is joined.[31]

[31] See Danby, *Poets on Fortune's Hill*, pp. 52–53; D. P. Walker, "Ways of Dealing with Atheists: A Background to Pamela's Refutation of Cecropia," *Bibliothèque d'humanisme et renaissance*, 17 (1955), 252–

Devotion to God, sneers Cecropia, should be left to old folks. The springtime (even that which began the *New Arcadia*) is to be seized; heaven consists largely in youthfulness; and only love, not religion, warrants devotion. To these positive, if commonplace, recommendations of libertinism she then adds a hostile criticism of religion. Its "bugbears" serve only as opiates that keep servile men in subjection. Religion arose unreasonably from "fear . . . and fearful ignorance," for only man, among all the creatures in the cycles of creation and decay, "strives to things supernatural, [while losing] his own natural felicity" (p. 406). (The example of Basilius or of the beast-envying Musidorus must make the argument at least interesting to Pamela.) Epicurean wisdom lies in knowing that such wisdom is itself a "God," even as "heaven" is an untroubled contentment with things. If there are gods, Cecropia concludes, they, in their Olympian calm, could not possibly be interested in creatures so mixed and partial as men.

Although her argument might be medicinal for the superstitious Basilius, it is generally subversive. Pamela breaks into it with divine ardor. She commands silence in a woman who, while breathing, refuses to acknowledge the biblical giver of breath; reason, in a woman who does not see that cosmic cycles imply a designing will; admission of a cause, from one who has been brisk only in cataloguing effects; and a sense of eternity, from one who must base the operations of chance and material configuration (distantly like artistic "making," to Sidney) upon something other than chance. If the argument is made to move from nature, a God who produces the coherence of nature is implied; if from the harmony of opposites, the principle of harmony; if from political

277; Ronald B. Levinson, "The 'Godlesse Minde' in Sidney's *Arcadia*," *MP*, 29 (1931–32), 21–26; and William R. Elton, *King Lear and the Gods* (San Marino, Calif.: Huntington Library, 1966), pp. 35–55.

or philosophical analogies, a constitution that binds the many into a cooperative one. But, says Pamela, if the argument from nature in truth defines nature as "wisdom, goodness, and providence, which knows what it doth, then you say that, which I seek of you . . ." (p. 408). And finally, if the argument is made by a reasonable creature, how can it assume that the creation of which it is a part is without reason? Pamela dismisses related claims of chance, Fortune, and Epicurean materialism as "beastly absurdities." Like a true creature or the true state, or like true love in either or of either, she declares, "This world . . . cannot otherwise consist but by a mind of Wisdom, which governs it, which whether you will allow to be the Creator thereof . . . or the soul and governor thereof, most certain it is that whether he govern all, or make all, his power is above either his creatures, or his government" (p. 410). Having been once wounded by an absconding king and father, Pamela is probably twice shy of a *deus absconditus*. With fine apocalyptic fury, she concludes by warning Cecropia that the creator, if disdained or ignored, will at last with divine irony reveal himself "a Creator in thy destruction" (p. 410).

In Pamela's argument, Cecropia may have "found a truth, but could not love it" (p. 411). Her "disdainful pride" almost breaks through her "cunning dissimulation" entirely, wickedness at last having produced war even with her own expediency.

A corresponding outward war now nears the castle, for Basilius has turned from the sword to the mine. While the Basilian sappers work, however, Phalantus of Corinth challenges Amphialus to more heroically "martial matters." It is to be the last showing of true chivalry in the *New Arcadia*. Because all the future combat brings tragic suffering even to the victor, the ideal of heroism turns gradually to patience. But for one last moment, combatants meet not from hatred but from the wish to exercise arms "without any mislike of . . . person" (p. 413). They want only to be "known" in courage and to delight their audience. The challenge is accepted. Amphialus rejoices to find a friend, or enemy, of so noble a mind. The tourney for a brief, fading instant is once again a speaking picture of a princely valor and honor.

When they meet on an island beneath the castle, each knight has himself become a speaking picture. The brown horse of Amphialus is harnessed to suggest a tree in autumn, and the man is armed as if embraced in dark flames. His shield is painted with the torpedo fish. If his colors distantly suggest the "brown" of a Musidorus, those of his rival counter with the "red and white" of Pyrocles. Phalantus enters upon a white horse trimmed in red, as if of strawberries with cream. His armor, like the Amazonian dress of Pyrocles, is blue. His shield bears the heroic greyhound; his motto is "The glory, not the prey" (p. 416). Amphialus eventually wins, but their reintegrative good will to each other is so great that Phalantus will no longer fight for Basilius against such a noble foe. He seems to have been converted from the popinjay of Book I into a prince. He leaves for foreign adventures—and with him goes most of the splendid but incomplete old heroism.

Although this chivalric interlude has reminded readers of the honorable character of Amphialus, that honor in no way alters his general unluckiness. The victor of the lists remains the victim in love, carelessly mastered by the uninterested Philoclea. Amphialus anxiously displays to her his challenge and triumph over all who blaspheme against love. One among them says that love is "the bewitcher of the wit, the rebel to Reason, the betrayer of resolution, the defiler of thoughts, . . . the curse of life, and reproach of death"; another holds that women are "the oversight of Nature, the disgrace of reasonableness, the obstinate cowards, the slave-born tyrants, the shops of vanities, the gilded weathercocks" (p. 419). He never quite sees that her captivity is a greater "blasphemy": but then, even the two princes have sometimes found it hard to tell ardor from lust. The world of chivalry and friendship evidently is simpler than that of love and ethics.

Even chivalry grows increasingly questionable, however, as its aims and results suddenly diverge. The seeming luck of Amphialus in winning personal combats with individual Arcadians alarms Basilius into sending for Argalus. Sidney apparently intended to have the emblematic Corinthian couples from Book I appear in a close parallel in Book III, although they would now manifest the tragic cost of Argian hatred rather than the scale of love. The fine love of Argalus and Parthenia here is broken by irrelevant martial honor; the possible love between mediate Helen and Amphialus will have to arise from the mangled body of Amphialus; and the converted Phalantus is not even present when his luckless, unloving Artesia is executed for treason. Partly because these six people now figure in the principal action and therefore no longer receive internal narratives, they now do not command the same kind of emblematic authority they had in Book I. Sidney might have altered Book III, had he lived and returned to it, so that the structural parallelism would appear in manner as well as matter. In any case, in the calling up of Argalus, Cecropia's warfare destructively breaks into the peaceful life of the Corinthian couple. Book III's current of loss thus sweeps away the most perfect of Book I's images of marriage.

The marriage had been so tempered that it imaged not only an almost perfect private love but also its public extension in the state:

A happy couple, he joying in her, she joying in herself, . . . because she enjoyed him: both increasing their riches by giving to each other; each making one life double, because they made a double life; one, where desire never wanted satisfaction, nor satisfaction never bred satiety; he ruling, because she would obey; or rather because she would obey, she therein ruling [p. 420].

Together, they might have remained an emblem of human happiness. Separated, they soon serve as warning against an excessive sense of honor in the two young princes and against excessive surrender to grief by the princesses.

In a time so troubled, it was perhaps unlikely that "coupled joys" could continue unchallenged, even though they never cease to indicate the ends toward which Arcadia and the Arcadian lovers should move. Even as Argalus is interrupted, he is reading of the heroic Hercules. After checking Basilius' summons, he believes that he must proceed to enact Hercules. If his honor is dear to him, he says, it must be dear also to his wife. Although she fearfully attempts to hold him from battle, he plays the Hotspur. He is more in love with the tyrant, honor, than with the servant, love. Sidney has swiftly and characteristically reversed our expectations, to say nothing of the recent combat of Amphialus and Phalantus, by causing honor, that once had pled its freedom before the tyranny of love, to become in its turn the tyrant. Argalus intemperately challenges the victorious Amphialus, and of course is accepted.

Bearing Parthenia's sleeve as a token, her husband rides to combat in armor significantly knotted with a woman's hair. On his shield are two palm trees, signifying loving union, together with the word "In that sort flourishing" (p. 423). Having abandoned his strength in love, however, he is no match for the martial Amphialus. His veins filled "with spite instead of blood" (p. 424), he soon is severely wounded. Although Parthenia tries to save him, and although Amphialus seeks his friendship rather than his death, Argalus continues the struggle with his own aggrieved sense of honor until he is killed by it.

The desolate Parthenia can only writhe in agony. Her fall from joy seems to her a punishment by God. Grief threatens to bring her to Cecropian atheism, despite her husband's dying insistence that his death will somehow serve "Him, whose wisdom and goodness guideth all" (p. 427). His death does release her into a "desperate yielding to sorrow"—an affecting proof of love, yet a warning to Pamela and Philoclea to resist this passion even as they have previously resisted the passions of fear and love. Meanwhile, even the praise given to the victim only serves, obliquely, to exalt the victor. Reversing the situation of his late enemy, however, Amphialus' honor still contrasts painfully with his failure in love. Even Spenser could hardly have created a more telling illustration of the deficiency of passional excess as opposed to the plenitude possible from the reasonable, harmonizing governance of a mean.

If in some ways Book III of the *New Arcadia* is a nostalgic farewell to heroic chivalry in favor of the "new heroism," the process is hastened by the arrival of two forms of the anti-hero. Anaxius and his two brothers from Asia Minor will now dominate the close, even as the immediate foreground is occupied by the lout Dametas and the wily coward, Clinias. They are comic reflectors of heroism, much as Miso and Mopsa were comic reflectors of love in Book II.

The reduction of chivalry by burlesque and mock-heroism in Dametas (or, on the other hand, the partial restoration of chivalry by means of its contrast with his inane parody) begins with his going to battle not to serve love or his lord but only to escape from his ill-favored Miso. In something of the same reversal, even as "the speech of heaven doth often beget the mention of hell" (p. 428), the glory of Amphialus is shown in the dispraise of Dametas' Argian rival,

Clinias. As also happens with their descendants in *Twelfth Night,* such dispraise is used to whet Dametas to combat. His letter of challenge apes the lofty style. Having berated Clinias as "the very fritter of fraud, and seething pot of iniquity," it hobbles on toward grandeur: ". . . I will out of that superfluous body of thine make thy soul to be evacuated" (p. 429). "Dumb-stricken with admiration," a young gentleman suffocating with laughter bears away the challenge, hoping at least that the comedy will relieve Basilius' settled melancholy. It does. When Clinias refuses, Dametas is half Chauntecleer, half Falstaff: "[He] began to speak his loud voice, to look big, to march up and down, and in his march to lift his legs higher than he was wont, swearing . . . that the walls should not keep the coward from him, but he would fetch him out of his cony-berry" (p. 430).

Sidney anticipates in his chivalric fool some of the ridicule Cervantes would heap upon chivalry, for in imitating heraldry Dametas manages to construct only a reductive parody. His device, for instance, is a plow from which oxen are loosed, *with* a sword surrounded by amputated limbs, *and* a mound of pens, inks, and books. Unlike those who would leave devices clouded in mystery, Dametas hastens to explain his. The farm implement means that he has abandoned the plow for the sword; the writing implements mean that his bloody deeds will surely be "historified." The word that he somewhat lamely adds is a triumph of Delphic ambiguity: "Miso mine own pigsnye, thou shalt hear news o' Dametas."

To his horror, his challenge to Clinias is returned. Although Dametas tries to deflect it by saying that he is now in no humor for reading letters, his friends force him to read of himself as a "filthy drivel," along with other "thundering of . . . threatenings" quite unlike the addresses of Phalantus and Amphialus (p. 431). On his way to the encounter, poor Dametas becomes an Astyanax to himself, for the "clashing of his own armor [struck] miserable fear into him" (p. 432). The charge (which is begun by Dametas' horse, much to his master's dismay) "jogs" Dametas so abruptly that he reins in the steed, which promptly leaps and bucks its way straight toward Clinias. The wretched Clinias manages to make his own steed stumble, first over his own lance and then over the scrambling Dametas. After seeing his enemy in turn pinned by a horse lying on its back, kicking slowly like an overturned beetle, Dametas should have triumphed. However, Clinias survives to push him all the way into the water, while the grave counsellor to Basilius sometimes bawls that he is dead and sometimes threatens to tattle all this trouble to Basilius. Dametas manages to win only when he begins to flail about with his farmer's fists. Similarly, he abandons the instruments of chivalry for the small knife he has used for slitting calves' throats. Adapting his own character to the knife, Clinias lies under Dametas with a suitably "sheepish" countenance. Dametas, crowing over such an enemy, thus brings the "combat of cowards" (p. 434) to an end.

This combat of cowards is a terrible parody of the bout of Amphialus and Phalantus, and as such helps to deliver a kind of *coup de grace* to the unitary value of chivalric heroism. If realism in love has always threatened it, the *New Arcadia*'s increasing emphasis upon tragic patience will at the least cause that virtue to weigh heavily in the scales with simple chivalry. The princes' coming good government and quasi-Christian ethics will reduce chivalry to a purely occasional, or complementary, value.

In the present, however, spreading forces of outward brutality and inward treason force all the action, Argian as well as Arcadian, toward a convergent, common resolution. Although the *New Arcadia* itself was unfinished, the given action for Book III is all but complete.

"To dance to his own music": Last battles

It had been an article of faith in the *Old Arcadia* that folly and error were self-punishing. Altered into the context of the *New,* the article holds that loss, treason, and brutality finally erode their own positions, leaving their adherents to violent death unless some kind of restoration toward the ideal takes place. On the other hand, those who endure the attack may at last begin to construct a golden world, having all the while been sustained by the ideal that countered brazen fortune, expediency, and atheism. Thus, as the Argians go under, Amphialus is brought to a near-death that seems to promise a new life; Pyrocles triumphantly defeats a united outward and inward attack by Anaxius; and even Basilius is offered a new, "plain" oracle to replace the one that had been instinct with superstitious loss and irresponsibility.

The last movement begins with internal Argian treason. The coward Clinias, already an Arcadian traitor, feels his defeat by Dametas so strongly that he turns his secret treason smilingly upon his host, Amphialus. He is matched with the Artesia of Book I, a woman now of his own mind. Because she previously assisted in the abduction of the princesses, Artesia was certain that Amphialus would now take her. When that lovesick prince still disdains her ambitious affections, she too moves to serpentine deceit.

Her chosen agent for creating treason will be Pyrocles. In a way, she is even suited to him. Her "disdain to be disdained" finds a companion in the "spite and disdain" that almost choke the prince, who lies helpless in jail while Philoclea suffers (p. 436). Reason has temporarily given way in him to a circling sorrow that both feeds and consumes itself. "Figures of rhetoric" only serve to inflate "the injuries of misfortune, against which [he] would often make invective declamations, methodized only by raging sorrow." His rea-sonless excesses evidently are not wholly unlike those of Dametas and Clinias. Fortunately, however, he has sufficient reason left to be self-analytical and suspicious of Artesia, "using [his] own bias to bowl near the mistress of her own thoughts" (p. 437). Tempting the temptress, he so works upon her "ill-concealed discontentment" that she agrees to bring him armor. Still not wholly unlike Dametas, Pyrocles in his old heroism trusts that he alone can perform "any-thing, how impossible soever, which longing Love can per-suade, and invincible valor dare promise" (p. 437). Clinias would not risk single-handed treason in his part of the double plot, however. Having arranged to poison Amphialus, he hurries to inform the princesses, certain that every other person will be as complicitously dishonorable as he is. Philo-clea, who can "find no hiding place" for treason in her "clear mind," merely refuses him. Pamela, "in whose mind Virtue governed with the scepter of Knowledge" (p. 438), denounces him publicly. The conspiracy having collapsed, Clinias is executed and Artesia locked away to await a terrible later employment.

As the anti-heroism of cowards and sly traitors has supplied one kind of foil for the new heroism, so brute force, although at times somewhat too closely resembling heroism, sets an-other. Such a foil is now developed at length in the newly arrived Asian Anaxius. Although Sidney praises the courage in such a man, he develops him into a terrible yet ridiculous *miles gloriosus*. His strength being "guided by pride, and followed by injustice," he cannot distinguish between "valor and violence." Like much of the purely chivalric ethos that develops around the siege (which has attracted a full con-gress of knights and soldiers of fortune), he esteems "fear and astonishment righter causes of admiration than love and honor" (p. 439). Treacherous attack without warning was to be expected of such a man. It of course endangers the entire Basilian line. In the long run, however, the Thrasonian Anaxius—the opposite even in name of Basilius' good Philanax—presents a greater threat to his friend Amphialus than to any supposed enemy.

The Asian newcomer turns out to be stuffed with vainglorious Asian pride. He brushes away his host's noble welcome, wishing there were more kings about Amphialus so "that what Anaxius can do, might be the better manifested." He cannot risk visiting the princesses, he says, because he knows that any lady infallibly must love him. When Amphialus permits this bravo full freedom to "dance to his own music" (pp. 440–441), his yielding of Argian governance to such mindless brawn is a new, and worse, version of Basilius' yielding Arcadia up to Dametas or Philanax. However, Anaxius may at least provide a useful negative example to Pyrocles. That prince sometimes has thought that he, too, could singlehandedly perform whatever "longing love can persuade, and invincible valor dare promise" (p. 437).

Set instructively against such monomania is the emblematic harmony of an orchestra, hired by Amphialus to serenade Philoclea. "[Enriching] itself in travail" like the princesses, its sounding of cornets to viols and voices brings to all "unpossessed minds" the union of Cyrus with Cyruses or of a male suitor with feminine beauty. The song itself, however, is a despairing statement of *contemptus mundi*, lamenting the present alienation of Amphialus from any but destructive uses of the four composing elements.

In somewhat the same way, history alone, with its "dark forgetfulness," can do no more than bury "unnamed numbers" during the next day's battle, whereas three armored knights receive the full propagative treatment of poetry. In habits respectively of white, green, and black, they are "beams of . . . valor" (p. 443) to the dispirited Basilians.

When Anaxius is duly wounded in combat with them, he charges all heaven with the overthrow of so indispensable a creature. In the Basilian camp there now appears his total opposite—a newcomer who will not even be known, but who is called the Knight of the Tomb. His trappings of the sepulcher share as complements an impresa showing a beautiful child with two heads, one of which is dead, and a motto reading "No way to be rid from death, but by death." Anaxius' chivalric power of arms and lust for life could hardly be more utterly countered. The suicidal intent is wrong, and the cause is dubious; there is no question, however, about the new-heroic contest and its resultant kind of death.

Amphialus, who might utilize power and lust as flamboyantly and selfishly as Cecropia and Anaxius, finds himself of the new knight's party not only in honor but in grief. He gently says that there is "more cause of affinity than enmity between them" (p. 445). In their opening career, Amphialus even turns aside his lance from his "infriended enemy" (p. 446). When the Knight of the Tomb reviles him, however, Amphialus swells in a "spiteful rage" that soon dispatches the enemy. When the stranger's headpiece is lowered, Amphialus feels anew the horror of a life in which blindly good intentions always manage to speed heroic arrows straight into the hearts of those whom he would love. As in the past the Argians had imprisoned his beloved Philoclea, so now he finds that he has butchered the almost perfect Parthenia. The "red and white" of her outward beauty declines into gore splotched on a pallid neck. If she had offered a pattern of beauty of Pyrocles, she now presents only a corpse to Amphialus.

The appalled victor cringes in "grief, compassion, and shame, detesting his fortune, that made him unfortunate in victory" (p. 447). In anticipation of the two princesses' torments, on the other hand, Parthenia can make of death what poor Amphialus can in no wise make of life: the partly tragic, partly Christian reconciliation of life with death, love with war, and fortune with time. In words suggesting those of a Christian martyr, she breathes:

O sweet life, welcome . . . now feel I the bands untied of the cruel death, which so long hath held me. And O life, O death, answer for me, that my thoughts have not so much as in a dream tasted any comfort, since they were deprived of Argalus. . . . And, O God hide my faults in thy mercies, and grant (as I feel thou dost grant) that in thy eternal love, we may love each other eternally [p. 448].

Acting as a new oracle, she had recently shown her own un-comprehending companions the way of martyrdom, saying "that she should have her heart's desire in the battle against Amphialus" (p. 448). Although Sidney would have recom-mended patience in preference to a near-suicide, her death is finally judged to be not so much terrible as heroic. Filled with "the rarely-matched-together . . . pity [and] admira-tion" which Sidney uses as the heroic equivalent of Aris-totle's tragic emotions, mourners make a Cyrus of Parthenia, and a heroic poem from the materials of tragedy. In this way, "honor [can now] triumph over Death." The bodies of Parthenia and Argalus are all but canonized as "blessed re-liques of faithful and virtuous love" (p. 449). Marble "im-ages" of the lovers would have been supplied with an epitaph that Sidney himself did not live to write, but which would have served as a "word" to the fictive statuary's version of an "impresa." Although Sidney is never even half in love with easeful death as such, he obviously recommends the honor of Parthenia over the blind old-heroic "honor" of pride and aggression.

Now more than ever hated by the Basilians, but hating

himself far more, Amphialus despairingly breaks his sword. His rejection of chivalry, together with his inward suffering, brings him to a tragic pitch. In his agony he can only think that his past mistakes guarantee "a presage of following misery." He is borne down as heavily by victory as Pyrocles by defeat. With Philoclea, although he remains literally the jailor and she the slave, he so strongly wishes it otherwise that their roles are almost reversed. When with sorrowful courtesy he reports to his mother, "Lust may well be a tyrant, but true-love . . . is a servant," she snorts with irritated contempt. All women, she insists, want to be overpowered—by force, if need be: "No, is no negative in a woman's mouth." As he is masterful in war, she says, so should he be in love: "Love is your general: he bids you dare: and will Amphialus be a dastard?" (pp. 450–452). She presents a verbal gallery of women like that in Kalander's house, but all of hers are downright grateful for rape. As for Philoclea, "if she weep, and chide, and protest, before [her body is] gotten, she can but weep, and chide, and protest, when it is gotten" (p. 453). Her entire speech is a piece of bravura worthy of Don Juan, Pamphilus, or perhaps the princes in the *Old Arcadia*. In the *New*, however, it was opposed absolutely by the initial tributes of Klaius and Strephon to Urania. They are echoed now by the hapless Amphialus: "Did ever man's eye look through love upon the majesty of virtue, shining through beauty, but that he became (as it well became him) a captive? and is it the style of a captive to write *Our will and pleasure?*" (pp. 451–452).

The promising final debate between Amphialus and Cecropia is severed by the arrival of a new Basilian challenge. Amphialus' sigh admits that most of the obloquy of his present challenger, the "forsaken" knight, is true. In arming himself, he again predicts the ending of the old chivalric ways in love and heroism. He dresses in ragged black. His shield depicts night and the sun "with a shadow," upon which is a word signifying that he "only was barred from enjoying that, whereof it had his life." He carries into battle not the conventional ribands of love but Philoclea's knives, the only "token of her forward favor" (p. 455). His rival (later revealed to have been Musidorus) is also clothed in black. The catoblepta is his impresa; its word, "The moon wanted not the light, but the poor beast wanted the moon's light." In the long run, chivalry itself is being eclipsed by almost Christian qualities.

Somewhat as Amphialus had been "infriended" with Parthenia, so the two knights might now almost be Klaius and Strephon. They are like "two sons of sorrow, and were coming thither to fight for their birthright in that sorry inheritance" (p. 455). It is therefore more nearly a double tragic agon than a knightly battle.

Having been self-wounded too many times in the twisted proceeding of his honorable intentions, Amphialus "fairly" asks, "Good knight, . . . because we are men, and should know reason why we do things, tell me the cause, that makes you thus eager to fight with me." When he is told that the cruelty he has exercised upon the princesses is to blame, he once again reveals his inability to act in accordance with his honorable reasons and feelings. He takes refuge in sophistical evasion, claiming again that it is their beauty which must "inforce Love to offer this force" (p. 455). Each knight in large measure mistaking the other, choler replaces conference. The "game of death" is played out once more. Love and hatred, in terrible paradoxical company, spur the combatants. After coming again and again to stalemate, each lashes himself onward with memories of his past heroic victories. In martial rapture, courageous wrath becomes almost idealistic, its very perversity "barring the common sense from bringing any message of their case to the mind . . .

making the mind minister spirits to the body" (p. 460). In their grim but affecting union in hatred, which is as "unsecret as love" (p. 461), they are bound almost as closely as they wish to be bound with the princesses. What is more, their near-deaths in battle seem to promise a regeneration into peace.

When each of the combatants is near death, the brothers of Anaxius break into the battle from Amphialus' side, only to be met immediately with equal opposition from that of Basilius. The two knights who aid Musidorus are armed significantly, one as if in a pleasant garden and the other as if in Urania's heaven, with the motto "The best place [is] yet reserved" (p. 462). The entire armies of both sides then rage into battle, while the bleeding single combatants are removed for surgery.

Like the armed battle without the walls, the intellectual and moral battle within has also come to stalemate. Concerned lest Amphialus' increasing despair, which recognizes that to Philoclea he is "neither . . . a faithful coward, nor a valiant rebel, but both rebellious and cowardly" (p. 464), may lead him to death, Cecropia hastens to usurp his action. She quickly displays the princesses and Pyrocles on a high tower; unless the siege is lifted, she informs Basilius, the three will be beheaded. The "sight" also presents a speaking picture of the varieties of princely character, for Pamela retains "sweetness [with] majesty," willing to die "rather than to have life at other's discretion"; Philoclea enriches "nobleness with humbleness," feeling only that fear which is "a kindly child to her innate humbleness"; and Pyrocles remains at this time "the true image of overmastered courage, and of spite that sees no remedy" (pp. 465–466). Like Amphialus himself, the guards over the three prisoners "misliked what themselves did, and yet still did what themselves misliked" (p. 466).

A desperate conference concerning the prisoners, structurally reminiscent of the Ramistic debates of the *Old Arcadia*, takes place in the camp of Basilius. The good man Kalander, newly arrived, pleads with the father in Basilius: they should lift the siege on the grounds that "the winning of time is the purchase of life, and worse by no means than their deaths can befall unto you" (p. 467). Philanax counsels the prince far more austerely, saying that a promise by the enemy will be broken; afterwards, not only will the prisoners be killed but also the army may easily be defeated. "You are a Prince, and a father of people," urges Philanax. In his role as father to the entire nation, he must put down "all private conceits, in comparison of what for the public is profitable" (p. 468).

Basilius might have wavered between the two for a time, had not the passion-driven Gynecia arrived to plead with neither the father nor the prince, but with the would-be lover. "Straitly besieged" by his recalled passion for the Amazon, Basilius once again abdicates. He relinquishes most governmental powers to Philanax, discharges the soldiers of the siege army, and (again) retires to a castle. There he plans to negotiate with Cecropia—but only for the release of his lover. (It is likely that after having almost recreated Basilius as prince and general during the siege, Sidney felt the need to reduce him again, in order that the second half of the *New Arcadia* might return to the private and ethical affairs of Arcadia as its major concern. Obviously, one large segment, reaching from the initial abdication to this repetition, is coming to a close, but just as obviously, a large unit in which Basilius will figure with some dignity is opening out from the repetition of the oracle.) Basilius' selfish passion is almost disastrous in the immediate public issue, of course, for it serves only to free Cecropia from any last inhibitions in tormenting the princesses.

Her past oratory having failed to overwhelm the moral terrain of the princesses, whether of the Petrine "brave . . . rock" of Pamela's determination or the Davidian "sweet rivers of clear virtue" in Philoclea (pp. 469, 470), Cecropia now attacks them in their flesh. Intent on reducing them like Lears or captive Christs, she swiftly removes all their service, fills the nights with sudden noises, and brings in old hags who hate youth and beauty to help her scourge Philoclea. Cecropia increasingly resembles "a fury that should carry wood to the burning of Diana's temple" (p. 471). When the sun hides behind clouds as if for a crucifixion, weeping Eros also pleads to be deaf as well as blind, in order not to hear what such oppression can do. As Pamela earlier had prayed for a quick death, so Philoclea now asks with dignity if one death is not enough for her to suffer. Otherwise, her new-heroic armor of silence and patience is proof against such attack, no matter how painful and protracted the "tedious tragedy." Unlike Pyrocles, who still twists under the horror of "senseless Fortune," Philoclea can rest her mind partly upon him, partly upon things otherworldly.

Even more notably, when Pamela is brought under similar torture she becomes the manifestation in which "virtue took a body to show his (else inconceivable) beauty" (p. 472). Like a Christ, she bears the onslaught "with so heavenly a quietness, and so graceful a calmness" that she can tell Cecropia, "I know thy power is not unlimited. Thou mayest well wrack this silly body, but me thou canst never overthrow" (p. 472). Although Sidney has thus brought his characters up to the threshold of Christianity, he carefully maintains the chivalric theme as well. Pamela claims due honor as a prize for her new heroism, thereby so radically shifting the meaning of "honor" that it now suggests Milton's Samson, not Shakespeare's Hotspur. "Assure thyself," she tells Cecropia, "both my life and death, shall triumph with honor, laying shame upon thy detestable tyranny" (p. 473). Victory over "their doing [will be gained] with her suffering," for the trial attests her strength in virtue more than theirs in power. Through the "counsel of virtue," which produces the "comfort of love," she even triumphs over her own grief at being lost to Musidorus (p. 473).[32]

Such a reconciliative, tragic triumph is possible also to the audience. If the princesses in felicity had propagated one kind of Cyrus, the same women under trial present victories that can propagate another. Both of their victories so vex Cecropia, "owly-eyed in the night of wickedness" (p. 475), that she rushes to the "last part of the play"—the imitated death of each of the princesses, while the other with Pyrocles is an enforced audience. She claims that the deaths will be a kind of justice, a recoil which demonstrates "that despising worthy folks was more hurtful to the despiser, than the despised" (p. 475). She manages only to teach Philoclea, who is supposed to see her sister executed first, that death for either of them is better than "such a base servitude" (p. 475). Raging in frustration, Cecropia promises Philoclea that she will be with her sister that day in death.

The "tragedy" begins with the forced opening of the prisoners' window curtains. They see a lady executed. Fainting, Philoclea gasps, "Pamela my sister, my sister Pamela . . . I would I had died for thee" (p. 477). Even so would Musidorus have offered his life for his friend's, in Phrygia. Meanwhile, Cecropia weighs how to "make a profit of this . . . late bloody act" (p. 478). Because it has been in part a play (although a prisoner really has been executed), Cecropia watches to see if she has managed to catch the conscience of

[32] See Danby, *Poets on Fortune's Hill*, pp. 69–70, and also his *"King Lear* and Christian Patience," *Cambridge Journal*, 1 (1948), 305–320, along with Margaret Greaves, *The Blazon of Honour: A Study in Renaissance Magnanimity* (London: Methuen, 1964), p. 93.

a prince. But Pyrocles, too, is being tempered beyond the old heroism. He knows that love and valor alone are almost helpless in adversity. Although his courage "still [rebels] against [his] wit, desiring still with force to do impossible matters" (p. 479), the threat of Philoclea's death leads him into earnest meditation, across a Dark Night as black as his mind.[33] He can still falter, thinking as he does that the imprisoning forces must be small when seen "from the high top of affection's tower" (p. 480), but at least he now considers how best to fight wiles with wiles. If he must now be womanlike of mind for the first time, the princesses and Cecropia —the one for good, the other for evil—have supplied him with almost absolute models. He therefore believes that Philoclea should appear to yield slightly to Amphialus, as Penelope had seemed to yield to the suitors, in order to bargain for Pyrocles' freedom and, thereafter, his revenge.

But Pyrocles still must learn the simplicity of clear virtue. When he opens the scheme to Philoclea, she rejects it as swiftly as she had earlier rejected the treason of Artesia and Clinias. She demands: "Shall my tongue be so false a traitor to my heart, as to say I love any other but Pyrocles? . . . hath thy love so base alloy, my Pyrocles, as to wish me to live [by falsehood]? For dissimulation, my Pyrocles, my simplicity is such, that I have hardly been able to keep a straight way; what shall I do in a crooked?" (p. 481). And asking (as Pamela had asked of Musidorus) only that he remember her, Philoclea remains constant to herself. She too is led away to what appears to be her execution.

Fury for a time repossesses the only half-converted Pyrocles. He inveighs against "tyrant heaven, traitor earth, blind providence," demanding again as he had once demanded of love, "Hath this world a government?" He challenges its

[33] See Chew, *The Virtues Reconciled*, p. 115: one version of Hercules' choice is that between repentance and despair.

purblind doomsters—if they exist—to heap all misery upon him for a speedy obliteration. Unlike the princesses, who resisted possession by a suicidal passion, he even tries to kill himself. He thus joins the wounded Musidorus and Amphialus in a virtual death, resembling the seeming losses that had initiated the book. A voice intervenes, seeming to cry to him (as to other Elizabethan princes), "Revenge, revenge" (p. 483). Sidney does not settle the question, whether a good angel actually spoke or whether it was merely a comfort to Pyrocles to believe that one did. Whatever the case, a cherub (internal or external) has seen his ways and saved him for heroic anger toward Cecropia, and loving memory for Philoclea. His life will now recapitulate his service to the first Zelmane, whose name and memory he preserves. With gentled grief he can now look upon the whole world much as Klaius and Strephon had once looked upon the vacant Arcadia:

Thou hast done thy worst, world, and cursed be thou, and cursed art thou, since to thine own self thou hast done the worst thou couldst do. Exiled beauty, let only now thy beauty be blubbered faces. Widowed music, let now thy tunes be roarings and lamentations. Orphan virtue, get thee wings, and fly after her into heaven; here is no dwelling place for thee [p. 484].

Although he retains his cold resolution for vengeance, most of his old-heroic fury has been purged. In considering his will, he concludes, "Wishing power (which is accounted infinite) what now is left to wish for? She is gone, and gone with her all my hope, all my wishing" (p. 485).

Near dawn, however, a second good "angel" visits him. Upon hearing renewed outbursts from him, she rebukes him in much the homely way of Musidorus at the time of the younger prince's assuming his Amazonian disguise: "For most part of this night I have heard you . . . and have heard nothing of Zelmane, in Zelmane, nothing but weak wailings, fitter for some nurse of a village, than so famous a creature as you are" (p. 486). Offering hope that Philoclea somehow is alive, and continuing to chaff him upon letting his mind be estranged from his senses (with some implication that the original Zelmane would have been stronger), she ignores his dismissal of such argument as "woman's philosophy, childish folly" (p. 486). When in staring through darkness into morning light he sees (or seems to see, ideally) "the very face of Philoclea" (p. 487), his frenzy leads him to think her an angel indeed, and once more to demand, "Why should unjustice so prevail? Why was she seen to the world, so soon to be ravished from us? Why was she not suffered to live, to teach the world perfection?" (p. 487). Somewhat like Odysseus when meeting a similar question from Telemachus, she replies, "Do not deceive thy self . . . I am no angel; I am Philoclea." The proof reverses that of the first Easter. With a last internal narrative, Philoclea supplies an epilogue for the grisly "play" Cecropia had produced: it was the traitor Artesia, not Pamela, who had been executed, and Philoclea's head had been shown through—not on—an Herodian dish of gold. Amphialus, his moral sight gradually clearing even as the general night of Arcadian rebellion had fled away, had given the princesses partial freedom. He himself at last had sworn vengeance upon his mother.

Even Pyrocles' commitment to vengeance, then, has been assumed by a divinity. The freeing of Pamela follows that of the two younger lovers, with whom grief is beginning to alter into "a few April drops . . . scattered by a gentle Zephirus among fine colored flowers" even as reason replaces the shipwrecking "tide . . . of imagination" (p. 490). Pamela's princely "high heart" in "just disdain" reveals to Amphialus for the first time not only their savage treatment by Cecropia but also their implacable enmity to him: "I do not more desire mine own safety," she tells him levelly, "than thy destruction." The gentler Philoclea somewhat more reluctantly adds "that she had the same cause as her sister had" (p. 491). It is now Amphialus who must choke out in mingled prayer and protest, "O God," as he sweeps the castle, his sword drawn, looking for Cecropia. When he finds her on the leads, he curses her for being fit only to bring forth such an anti-Cyrus, such a monster of unhappiness, as himself. She backs away, frightened more by his look than his sword—and plunges to her death. It is as if the fall usually emblematic of fortune had somehow become the act of unchanging justice. A partial justice promptly returns to the state, at least, the Argian tyranny having ended with Cecropia.

But the castle remains transfixed in the self-castigation of Amphialus. He now must curse himself for the death of his mother along with those of his friend Philoxenus, the perfect Parthenia, and his page Ismenus, as well as for his rebellion against a kindly uncle and his complicity in the imprisonment and torture of Philoclea. Resembling Pyrocles in despair but finding no saving grace, he attempts suicide, which he would complete with Philoclea's knives. As he lies bleeding, near death, his people are overwhelmed by this latest, true, but nontragic "pitiful spectacle, where the conquest was the conqueror's overthrow, and self-ruin the only triumph of a battle." They now think of him as almost a Caesar: "everybody thinking, their safety bled in his wounds and their honor died in his destruction" (p. 494). There is none of the public relief and joy that had been felt at the death of Cecropia. In his way, Amphialus has received a hero's reward. Presumably Sidney himself would have wished a heroic rest (whether in a reformed life or in death) to the perturbed spirit that had been so afflicted within a "person full of worthiness" (p. 494).

The cause of the Amphialans has all but collapsed, of course. However, like Pyrocles before him, the proud, would-be earthshaker Anaxius can at least cry havoc upon individual persons. He is stopped for a moment by the suppliant Helen of Corinth. Her outpouring of grief for Amphialus, closely resembling that of Parthenia for Argalus, is stanched when a "wise gentleman" urges her to remember her "greatness, wisdom, and honor." With counsel like that with which Philoclea had returned Pyrocles to reason, the advisor dryly suggests that she take Amphialus to a surgeon "rather than only show herself a woman lover in fruitless lamentations" (p. 497).[34] Having once herself helped Parthenia to a medicinal cure, Helen accedes. As she removes the litter bearing the severely wounded Amphialus through both lines of battle, heroic lamentations follow them. The elegy given to Basilius in the *Old Arcadia* now considers Amphialus a "shepherd high," asking that "Your doleful tunes, sweet Muses, now apply." It asks myrrh, earth, and echo to mourn "such a saint," "virtue's treasure," "Man." Moving like Pyrocles to a complaint against the world's government, the long poem mourns that "the minds, which over all do climb,/ . . . Must finish then by death's detested crime" (pp. 498–501). If that estimation of the world is correct, then justice, bountifulness, and goodness were delusions as brief as life. Having mentioned the general healing power of Aesculapius, however, the lyric, by an inference as much moral as physical,

34 Rosemary Syfret, ed., *Selections from Sidney's Arcadia* (London: Hutchinson, 1966), p. 216, assumes that Amphialus will recover and marry Helen. See also Tillyard, *The English Epic*, p. 308, for the assumption that Musidorus and Pyrocles will come to a patience matching that of the princesses. The four principals, along with Amphialus, may all have been intended to experience the Orphic *glykipikron*, or bittersweet, movement from "death" into new life. Cf. Edgar Wind, *Pagan Mysteries in the Renaissance* (New Haven: Yale Univ. Press, 1958), pp. 129–140.

for an instant finds another vein. Like the two shepherds with Urania and like his people with Basilius in the *Old Arcadia,* the mankind-representing Amphialans celebrate the pattern of a Governor:

> Shepherd of shepherds, whose well-settled order
> Private with wealth, public with quiet garnished.
> While he did live, far, far was all disorder;
>
> . . . . .
>
> Far was homestrife, and far was foe from border.
> His life a law, his look a full correction:
> As in his health we healthful were preserved,
> So in his sickness grew our sure infection [p. 502].

The assigned tribute of the people for Amphialus also oddly anticipates that of England for Sidney himself—"a young man, of great beauty, beautified with great honor, honored by great valor, made of inestimable valor by the noble using of it" (p. 502).

Anaxius' departing threat to execute the princesses shocks them from easy hope back into patience. Having come to know delusive fortune like an old acquaintance, Pamela can say, "Sister . . . you see how many acts our tragedy hath." She acts the good Stoic schoolmistress to Philoclea, reminding her that death is at worst only a "bug-bear" (p. 503). However, if fortune has been at work on the negative side with Anaxius, it also has brought the Black Knight (Musidorus) safely back to health.

What is more, Pamela's beauty makes an ironic conquest of her new captain, Anaxius. Pyrocles, now with a "resolute staidness" purged from rival tensions of excessive "anger, kindness, disdain, or humbleness," calls Anaxius firmly to an accounting not with valor but with virtue. Having accused him of weakness and cowardice both in having acted as executioner to the princesses and in having proved of little help to Amphialus, Pyrocles, like Pamela with the once over-ardent Musidorus, declares his captor "unworthy to be counted a Knight, or to be admitted into the company of Knights" (p. 505). He almost reveals his identity in order that the judicial challenge be taken seriously. Anaxius turns away from the seeming woman, however, to fondle the womanly Pamela, even as his two brothers erotically badger Philoclea and "Zelmane." Disdainfully, Pamela informs Anaxius that his present comedy of love is even worse than his previous tragedy of violence. And, indeed, comedy suddenly begins to envelop and humble the three neo-Odyssean suitors. Thus Anaxius would be far more agreeable to her as a hangman, Pamela tells him, than a husband.

Although the two sisters prepare for death rather than defilement, the young Pyrocles, now shrewdly battling for time like an Odysseus, urges them to demand Basilius' assent to Anaxius' wooing. In characteristic manner, Anaxius sends a letter to Basilius pompously recommending himself as a son-in-law. It is almost as remarkable as that of Dametas. If accepted, he promises not only to protect Basilius in his quiet course but to "give him the monarchy of the world"; if rejected, on the other hand, Basilius would soon see that Anaxius' "will [was] not to be resisted by any other power" (p. 509). Anaxius' sychophant servant flatters him into believing that he truly is at the least an Alexander, whose glory must make Arcadia "think the heavens opened, when [it] heard but the proffer" of marriage to Pamela. "Anaxius gravely allowed the probability of [the] conjecture" (p. 509), but Basilius, distracted by "the fear of Anaxius' might, the passion of his love, and jealousy of his estate," seeks to rise beyond conjecture; Arcadia's harried king therefore returns to Delphos for the guidance of Apollo.

The *New Arcadia* at this halfway point seems to have intended a wholesale conversion of the remaining materials from the first half of the *Old*. This time, the priestess of

Apollo is possessed with a poetic, "true," Brunovian sacred fury. She speaks with the plainness, clarity, and "resolute staidness" that are now associated with the noble lovers. Basilius is to deny his daughters to Anaxius, "for that they were reserved for such as were better beloved of the gods." He is to remain in contemplative exile until such time as "both Philanax and Basilius fully agreed in the understanding of the former prophecy: withal, commanding Philanax from thence forward to give tribute, but not oblation, to human wisdom" (p. 510). In these few lines, Sidney almost reverses the *Old Arcadia*'s conception and use of the oracle. There, it had always bespoken the foolish, private credulity of the king, which Philanax had rightly opposed with human reason. Now it is Philanax, with his trust in purely human wisdom, who is reproved. Despite his foolish abdication, the king has in his way sought Urania. Following the path Pamela had recommended to Cecropia, the counsellor leaves off "reasoning in things above reason," having come to prefer truth "before the maintaining of an opinion." No longer does he try to persuade Basilius "from that which he found by the celestial providence directed" (p. 510). He instead fortifies the two Arcadian lodges. They, too, will no longer be gardens of exile but outposts of defense.

Although Sidney fully credits the conversion of Philanax, he makes haste to show that even a doctrine of higher wisdom is open to the perversions of human folly. When Anaxius' flattering servant tells his lord that he should marry neither of the mere human princesses, being already "enrolled among the demi-gods," Anaxius ponders for only a second before agreeing that there must be "another wisdom . . . above, that judged so rightly of him" (p. 511). He therefore determines to take Pamela by force. He and his brothers swagger toward the three prisoners so rapt with thoughts of Venus that the "loudest trumpet [of Mars] could scarcely

have awaked [them]" (p. 511). And, indeed, even at that instant Musidorus is marching upon the castle. Within, the
Dametas-like brother smacks his lips in approaching the disguised Pyrocles, promising "her" that mating with such a
demi-god will create progeny rivalling that of Jove and
Alcmena. Dryly advising him, "I should never be apt to bear
children" (p. 513), Pyrocles routs and kills him. Within the
operations of justice, the first brother has become a sacrifice to Proserpina, a goddess "angry . . . against ravishers"
(p. 514). Again resembling Odysseus in Ithaca, Pyrocles brings
the second brother, Lycurgus, to his knees. When sued for
pity, the once too-pitying Pyrocles starts to respond to such
an "image of humane condition" (p. 515) until he sees Philoclea's garter and jewel—the jewel having been his own present to the princess—on Lycurgus' arm. He then acts the
resolute executioner.

These events, all so "contrary to all his imaginations,"
drive Anaxius into familiar charges against heaven. Although
they resemble the recent laments of Pyrocles and Amphialus,
the context has changed utterly. Whereas the earlier outcries
strove to understand the clouded ways of "celestial providence," Anaxius' blasphemy only bemoans his family's righteous punishment. When he in turn confronts Pyrocles, the
character of the combatants expresses in moral as well as
physical terms the weakness of Anaxius and the recently
achieved strength of Pyrocles: "strength against nimbleness;
rage, against resolution; fury, against virtue; confidence,
against courage; pride, against nobleness" (pp. 516–517).
Their opposition is like that of Iras with Odysseus, Goliath
with David, or Milton's Harapha with Samson. As their battle
surges and eddies, it is expressed in Sidney's chosen thematic
images of tide and shipwreck.

For the last time in the *New Arcadia,* two men who are
heroic in arms, even if otherwise as different as night and

day, join in the strange companionship and mutual knowledge of combat. Gradually, the "time, distance, and motion" in which each moves and which he in part determines is so well known to the other that had they been "fellow counsellors, and not enemies, each knew the other's mind, and knew how to prevent it"—that is, how to anticipate it (p. 517). But such limited combative knowledge must yield to the surer private, public, and even divine knowledges of Philanax and Basilius with Apollo. Once again, Sidney's ode to chivalry also becomes its elegy.

The *New Arcadia* reaches the point of a promising increase in Pyrocles' fortunes, as with "gay bravery" and Odyssean "divers feignings" he brings Anaxius first to cry out against the "spiteful God" (p. 518) who envies his fortune and then to leap away from an attack: "whereat ashamed, (as having never done so much before in his life)"—and with these words, the Pyroclean Sidney himself supposedly took up the sword in place of the pen, leaving behind him the noble question, whether a Cyrus in history might not be as true and propagative of Cyruses as one in his own fictional making. Certainly his immediate "audience" in England would have agreed that he had made his life a heroic poem, which the *Defence* had said might teach and move men to the most high and excellent truth.

As for what more might have been done with the *New Arcadia*,[35] the oracle is silent. It seems likely that the two sets

[35] The major single study of the *New Arcadia* is that of Walter R. Davis, *A Map of Arcadia: Sidney's Romance in Its Tradition* (New Haven and London: Yale Univ. Press, 1965). Among other studies devoted largely to the *New Arcadia* are these: D. Coulman, " 'Spotted to Be Known,' " *JWCI*, 20 (1957), 179–180; Walter R. Davis, "Thematic Unity in the *New Arcadia*," *SP*, 57 (1960), 123–143; Elizabeth Dipple, "The Captivity Episode and the *New Arcadia*," *JEGP*, 70 (1971), 418–431, and "Metamorphosis in Sidney's *Arcadias*," *PQ*, 50 (1971), 47–62; K. D. Duncan-Jones, "Sidney's Urania," *RES*, 17 (1966), 123–132; Alan D. Isler, "Sidney, Shakespeare, and the 'Slain-Notslain,' " *UTQ*,

of young lovers would have been joined by a restored, mediate Amphialus and Helen; that a Book IV might have presented a gallery of favorable "pictures" of government and love, balancing the admonitory failures in Book II, while keeping the thread of Dametas' folly and Gynecia's lust for Pyrocles; and that a final Book would have brought about a general, reconciliative "resurrection" after trial, together with a prophecy of future harmony for the children of Arcadia, Thessaly, Macedonia, and Corinth. But we will know nothing exactly of what Sidney might have done for an ending. It was left to him instead to make a good end, like that for which his princes at their best had readied themselves. The modest Sidney probably would have contended that such a "unity" argued "constancy in the everlasting governor . . . each thing being directed to an end, and an end of preservation: so proper effects of judgment, as speaking and laughing, are of mankind" (pp. 407, 409).

---

37 (1968), 175–185; Ronald B. Levinson, "The 'Godlesse Minde' in Sidney's *Arcadia*," *MP*, 29 (1931–32), 21–26; Nancy R. Lindheim, "Sidney's *Arcadia*, Book II: Retrospective Narrative," *SP*, 44 (1967), 159–186; Irving Ribner, "Machiavelli and Sidney: The *Arcadia* of 1590," *SP*, 47 (1950), 152–172; Constance M. Syford, "The Direct Source of the Pamela-Cecropia Episode in the *Arcadia*," *PMLA*, 49 (1934), 472–489; Myron Turner, "The Heroic Ideal in Sidney's Revised *Arcadia*," *SEL*, 10 (1970), 63–82; and D. P. Walker, "Ways of Dealing with Atheists: A Background to Pamela's Refutation of Cecropia," *Bibliothèque d'humanisme et renaissance*, 17 (1955), 252–257.

For incidental discussion of technical questions similar to those in the *New Arcadia*, see Roman Jakobson and Morris Halle, *Fundamentals of Language* ('s-Gravenhage: Mouton & Co., 1956), pp. 71–82, and Wolfgang Clemen, *Shakespeare's Soliloquies* (Cambridge: Cambridge Univ. Press, 1964), pp. 10–22. In *English Tragedy Before Shakespeare*, tr. T. S. Dorsch (New York: Barnes & Noble, 1961), p. 31, Clemen notes that actors in works resembling the *New Arcadia* were called *interlocuteurs* and *entreparleurs*.

List of References Cited

A Book of Masques, in Honor of Allardyce Nicoll. Cambridge: Cambridge Univ. Press, 1967.

Anderson, D. M. "The Trial of the Princes in the *Arcadia,* Book V." *Review of English Studies,* n.s. 8 (1957), 409–412.

Baldwin, T. W. *Shakespeare's Five-Act Structure.* Urbana, Ill.: Univ. of Illinois Press, 1947.

Barnes, Catherine. "The Hidden Persuader: The Complex Speaking Voice of Sidney's *Defence of Poetry.*" *Publications of the Modern Language Association,* 86 (1971), 422–427.

Baughan, Denver E. "Sidney's *Defence of the Earl of Leicester* and the Revised *Arcadia.*" *Journal of English and Germanic Philology,* 51 (1952), 35–41.

Benz, Ernst. *The Eastern Orthodox Church: Its Thought and Life,* tr. Richard and Clara Winston. Garden City, N.Y.: Doubleday, 1963.

Berger, Harry, Jr. "The Renaissance Imagination: Second World and Green World." *The Centennial Review,* 9 (1965), 36–78.

Bradbrook, M. C. *Shakespeare the Craftsman.* New York: Barnes and Noble, 1969.

Brie, Friedrich. *Sidneys Arcadia: Eine Studie zur Englischen Renaissance.* Strassburg, 1918.

Briggs, W. D. "Political Ideas in Sidney's *Arcadia.*" *Studies in Philology,* 28 (1931), 137–161; and 29 (1932), 534–542.

Brooke, Tucker. "Sidney and the Sonneteers," in *A Literary History of England,* ed. A. C. Baugh. New York: Appleton-Century-Crofts, 1948.

Brunet, Alexander. *The Regal Armorie of Great Britain*. London: H. K. Causton, 1839.

Bruno, Giordano. *The Expulsion of the Triumphant Beast*, tr. and ed. Arthur D. Imerti. New Brunswick, N.J.: Rutgers Univ. Press, 1964.

Bucher, Francois. "Medieval Landscape Painting: An Introduction," in *Medieval and Renaissance Studies*, ed. John M. Headley. Chapel Hill, N.C.: Univ. of North Carolina Press, 1968, pp. 119–169.

Buxton, John. *Elizabethan Taste*. London: Macmillan, 1963.

Caspari, Fritz. *Humanism and the Social Order in Tudor England*. Chicago: Univ. of Chicago Press, 1954.

Cassirer, Ernst. *The Individual and the Cosmos in Renaissance Philosophy*, tr. Mario Domandi. Oxford: Blackwell, 1963.

Challis, Lorna. "The Use of Oratory in Sidney's *Arcadia*." *Studies in Philology*, 62 (1965), 561–576.

Chastel, André. "Le tableau dans le tableau," in *Stil und Überlieferung des Abendlandes*. Berlin, 1967, I, 15–29.

——. *The Age of Humanism*. New York: McGraw-Hill, 1963.

Chew, Samuel. *The Virtues Reconciled: An Iconographic Study*. Toronto: Univ. of Toronto Press, 1947.

Clemen, Wolfgang. *English Tragedy Before Shakespeare*, tr. T. S. Dorsch. New York: Barnes & Noble, 1961.

——. *Shakespeare's Soliloquies*. Cambridge: Cambridge Univ. Press, 1964.

Clements, Robert J. *Picta Poesis: Literary and Humanistic Theory in Renaissance Emblem Books*. Roma: Edizioni di Storia e litteratura, 1960.

Cody, Richard. *The Landscape of the Mind*. Oxford: Oxford Univ. Press, 1969.

Cook, Albert S., ed., Sidney's *Defence of Poesy*. Boston: Ginn, 1890.

Coulman, D. " 'Spotted to Be Known.' " *Journal of the Warburg & Courtauld Institute*, 20 (1957), 179–180.

"D. A." "Possible Echoes from Sidney's 'Arcadia' in Shakespeare, Milton, and Others." *Notes & Queries*, 194 (1949), 554–555.

Danby, John F. *"King Lear* and Christian Patience." *Cambridge Journal,* 1 (1948), 305–320.

——. *Poets on Fortune's Hill.* London: Faber and Faber, 1952.

Davidson, Clifford. "Nature and Judgment in the *Old Arcadia." Papers on Language and Literature,* 6 (1970), 348–365.

Davis, Walter R. "Actaeon in Arcadia." *Studies in English Literature,* 2 (1962), 95–110.

——, and Richard A. Lanham. *Sidney's Arcadia.* New Haven and London: Yale Univ. Press, 1965.

——. *Idea and Act in Elizabethan Fiction.* Princeton: Princeton Univ. Press, 1969.

——. "Thematic Unity in the *New Arcadia." Studies in Philology,* 57 (1960), 123–143.

Dipple, Elizabeth. "Harmony and Pastoral in the *Old Arcadia." English Literary History,* 35 (1968), 309–328.

——. "Metamorphosis in Sidney's *Arcadias." Philological Quarterly,* 50 (1971), 47–62.

——. "The Captivity Episode and the *New Arcadia." Journal of English & Germanic Philology,* 70 (1971), 418–431.

——. "The 'Fore Conceit' of Sidney's Eclogues." *Literary Monographs,* 1 (1967), 3–47.

——. " 'Unjust Justice' in the *Old Arcadia." Studies in English Literature,* 10 (1970), 83–101.

Dowlin, Cornell March. "Sidney's Two Definitions of Poetry." *Modern Language Quarterly,* 3 (1942), 573–581.

Duhamel, P. Albert. "Sidney's *Arcadia* and Elizabethan Rhetoric." *Studies in Philology,* 65 (1948), 134–150.

Duncan-Jones, Katherine D. "Sidney's Urania." *Review of English Studies,* 17 (1966), 123–132.

Durling, Robert M. *The Figure of the Poet in Renaissance Epic.* Cambridge, Mass.: Harvard Univ. Press, 1965.

Edelstein, Ludwig. "The Function of Myth in Plato's Philosophy." *Journal of the History of Ideas,* 10 (1949), 463–481.

Eliot, T. S. *The Use of Poetry and the Use of Criticism.* New York: Barnes and Noble, 1933.

Else, Gerald F. *Aristotle's Poetics: The Argument.* Cambridge, Mass.: Harvard Univ. Press, 1957.

Elton, W. R. *King Lear and the Gods*. San Marino, Calif.: Huntington Library, 1966.

Empson, William. *Seven Types of Ambiguity*. 3rd ed. New York: New Directions, 1966.

Fleming, John V. *The Roman de la Rose: A Study in Allegory and Iconography*. Princeton: Princeton Univ. Press, 1969.

Fletcher, Angus. *Allegory: The Theory of a Symbolic Mode*. Ithaca, N.Y.: Cornell Univ. Press, 1964.

Fraser, Russell A. "Sidney the Humanist." *South Atlantic Quarterly*, 66 (1967), 87–91.

Genouy, Hector. *L' 'Arcadia' de Sidney dans ses rapports avec l' 'Arcadia' de Sannazaro et la 'Diana' de Montemayor*. Paris, 1928.

Gilbert, Allan H. "The Function of the Masques in *Cynthia's Revels*," *Philological Quarterly*, 22 (1943), 211–230.

Gombrich, E. H. "Icones Symbolicae," *Journal of the Warburg & Courtauld Institute*, 9 (1948), 163–192.

Grabar, André. *Byzantium from the Death of Theodosius to the Rise of Islam*, tr. Stuart Gilbert and James Emmons. London: Thames and Hudson, 1966.

Greaves, Margaret. *The Blazon of Honour*. London: Methuen, 1964.

Greenlaw, Edwin A. "Sidney's *Arcadia* as an Example of Elizabethan Allegory," in *Kittredge Anniversary Papers*. Boston and London: Ginn, 1913; repr. New York: Russell and Russell, 1967.

Greville, Sir Fulke. *Life of Sir Philip Sidney*, intro. Nowell Smith. Oxford: Oxford Univ. Press, 1907.

Hadas, Moses, tr. Heliodorus, *An Ethiopian Romance*. Ann Arbor, Mich.: Univ. of Michigan Press, 1957, p. viii.

Hamilton, A. C. "Sidney's Idea of the 'Right Poet.'" *Comparative Literature*, 9 (1957), 51–59.

Hanford, J. H., and S. R. Watson. "Personal Allegory in the *Arcadia*." *Modern Philology*, 32 (1934), 1–10.

Hazlitt, William. "Lectures on the Dramatic Literature of the Age of Elizabeth," *Works*, ed. P. P. Howe. London and Toronto: Dent, 1931. Vol. VI.

Heiserman, A. R. *Skelton and Satire*. Chicago: Chicago Univ. Press, 1961.

Heltzel, Virgil B. "The Arcadian Hero." *Philological Quarterly,* 61 (1962), 173–180.

Heninger, S. K., Jr. "Metaphor as Cosmic Correspondence," in *Medieval and Renaissance Studies,* ed. John M. Headley. Chapel Hill, N.C.: Univ. of North Carolina Press, 1968, pp. 3–22.

Herrick, Marvin T. *Comic Theory in the Sixteenth Century*. Urbana, Ill.: Univ. of Illinois Press, 1964.

Hyman, Virginia R. "Sidney's Definition of Poetry." *Studies in English Literature,* 10 (1970), 149–162.

Isler, Alan D. "Heroic Poetry and Sidney's Two *Arcadias*." *Publications of the Modern Language Association,* 83 (1968), 368–379.

——. "Sidney, Shakespeare, and the 'Slain-Notslain.'" *University of Toronto Quarterly,* 37 (1968), 175–185.

——. "The Allegory of the Hero and Sidney's Two *Arcadias*." *Studies in Philology,* 65 (1968), 171–191.

Jakobson, Roman, and Morris Halle, *Fundamentals of Language*. 's-Granvenhage: Mouton & Co., 1956.

Joyce, James. *Ulysses*. New York: Viking, 1961, p. 209.

Jusserand, J. J. *The English Novel in the Time of Shakespeare*. London: Unwin, 1890; repr. New York: AMS Press, 1965.

Kalstone, David. *Sidney's Poetry: Contexts and Interpretations*. Cambridge, Mass.: Harvard Univ. Press, 1965.

Kermode, J. F. "The Banquet of Sense." *Bulletin of the John Rylands Library,* 44 (1961), 68–99.

Kimbrough, Robert, ed. *Sir Philip Sidney: Selected Prose and Poetry*. New York: Rinehart, 1969.

Krouse, F. Michael. "Plato and Sidney's *Defence of Poesie*." *Comparative Literature* 6 (1954), 138–147.

Lebel, Maurice, tr. *Un Plaidoyer pour la Poesie*. Quebec: Presses de l'Université Laval, 1965.

Lechner, Sister Joan Marie. *Renaissance Concepts of the Commonplaces*. New York: Pageant, 1962.

Levinson, Ronald B. "The 'Godlesse Minde' in Sidney's *Arcadia.*" *Modern Philology,* 29 (1931–32), 21–26.

Lewis, C. S. *English Literature in the Sixteenth Century, Excluding Drama.* Oxford: Oxford Univ. Press, 1954.

Lindheim, Nancy R. "Sidney's *Arcadia,* Book II: Retrospective Narrative." *Studies in Philology,* 44 (1967), 159–186.

Lipsius, Justus. *Two Books of Constancy,* tr. Sir John Stradling, ed. Rudolf Kirk. New Brunswick, N.J.: Rutgers Univ. Press, 1939.

Lord, George deF. *Homeric Renaissance: The Odyssey of George Chapman.* London: Chatto and Windus, 1956.

Malloch, A. E. " 'Architectonic' Knowledge and Sidney's *Apologie.*" *English Literary History,* 20 (1953), 181–185.

McIntyre, John P., S.J. "Sidney's 'Golden World.' " *Comparative Literature,* 14 (1962), 356–365.

Marenco, Franco. *Arcadia Puritana.* Bari: Adriatica, 1968.

———. "Double Plot in Sidney's 'Old Arcadia.' " *Modern Language Review,* 64 (1969), 248–263.

———. "Per una nuova interpretazione dell' 'Arcadia' di Sidney," *English Miscellany,* 17 (1966), 9–48.

Masai, Francois. *Plethon et le platonisme de Mistra.* Paris: Les Belles Lettres, 1956.

Mehl, Dieter. "Emblems in English Renaissance Drama," in *Ren. Drama,* n.s. 2, ed. S. Schoenbaum. Evanston, Ill.: Northwestern Univ. Press, 1969, pp. 39–57.

Miller, Perry. *The New England Mind: The Seventeenth Century.* New York: Macmillan, 1939.

Mills, Laurens J. *One Soul in Bodies Twain.* Bloomington, Ind.: Principia, 1937.

Moffet, Thomas. *Nobilis: Or a View of the Life and Death of a Sidney,* tr. V. B. Heltzel and H. H. Hudson. San Marino, Calif.: Huntington Library, 1940.

Myrick, Kenneth O. *Sir Philip Sidney as a Literary Craftsman.* Cambridge, Mass.: Harvard Univ. Press, 1935.

Nelson, John C. *Renaissance Theory of Love: The Context of Giordano Bruno's Eroici furori.* New York: Columbia Univ. Press, 1958.

Nelson, Norman E. "Peter Ramus and the Confusion of Logic, Rhetoric, and Poetry." Univ. of Mich. Contrib. in Mod. Phil., No. 2 (April, 1947).

O'Connor, John J. *Amadis de Gaule and Its Influence on Elizabethan Literature.* New Brunswick, N.J.: Rutgers Univ. Press, 1970.

Olney, Henry. In *Elizabethan Critical Essays,* ed. G. Gregory Smith. London: Clarendon, 1904, I, 149.

Ong, Walter J. *Ramus: Method and the Decay of Dialogue.* Cambridge, Mass.: Harvard Univ. Press, 1958.

Orgel, Stephen K. "Sidney's Experiment in Pastoral: The Lady of May." *Journal of the Warburg & Courtauld Institute,* 26 (1963), 198–203.

Ostrogorsky, George. *History of the Byzantine State,* tr. Joan Hussey. New Brunswick, N.J.: Rutgers Univ. Press, 1957.

Partee, Morriss Henry. "Sir Philip Sidney and the Renaissance Knowledge of Plato." *English Studies,* 51 (1970), 411–424.

Patterson, Annabel M. "Tasso's Epic Neoplatonism." *Studies in the Renaissance,* 18 (1971), 105–133.

Perkinson, R. H. "The Epic in Five Acts." *Studies in Philology,* 43 (1946), 465–481.

Porphyry, tr. Thomas Taylor. London, 1823.

Ransom, John Crowe. *The New Criticism.* Norfolk, Conn.: New Directions, 1941.

Ribner, Irving. "Machiavelli and Sidney: The *Arcadia* of 1590." *Studies in Philology,* 47 (1950), 152–172.

———. "Sir Philip Sidney on Civil Insurrection." *Journal of the History of Ideas,* 13 (1952), 257–265.

Ringler, William A., Jr., ed. *The Poems of Sir Philip Sidney.* Oxford: Oxford Univ. Press, 1962.

Robertson, Jean. "Sir Philip Sidney and His Poetry," in *Elizabethan Poetry,* ed. John R. Brown and Bernard Harris. New York: St. Martins Press, 1960.

Rose, Mark. *Heroic Love.* Cambridge, Mass.: Harvard Univ. Press, 1968.

———. "Sidney's Womanish Man." *Review of English Studies,* 15 (1964), 353–363.

Rosenblat, Angel, ed. *Amadis de Gaula*. Buenos Aires: Editorial Losada, 1963, p. 12.

Rowe, Kenneth T. "Romantic Love and Parental Authority in Sidney's *Arcadia*." Univ. of Mich. Contrib. in Mod. Phil., No. 4 (April, 1947).

Rudenstine, Neil L. *Sidney's Poetic Development*. Cambridge, Mass.: Harvard Univ. Press, 1967.

Samuel, Irene. "The Influence of Plato on Sir Philip Sidney's *Defense of Poesy*." *Modern Language Quarterly*, 1 (1940), 383–391.

Shepherd, Geoffrey, ed. Sidney's *Defence of Poesy*. London: T. Nelson, 1965.

Sidney, Sir Philip. *Correspondence with Hubert Languet*, tr. Steuart A. Pears. London: W. Pickering, 1845.

——. *Works*, ed. Albert Feuillerat. 4 vols. Cambridge: Cambridge Univ. Press, 1965–1967.

Smith, Hallett. *Elizabethan Poetry*. Cambridge, Mass.: Harvard Univ. Press, 1964.

Soens, Lewis, ed. Sidney's *Defence of Poesy*. Lincoln, Nebr.: Univ. of Nebraska Press, 1970.

Spencer, Theodore. "The Poetry of Sir Philip Sidney." *English Literary History*, 12 (1945), 251–278.

Struever, Nancy. *The Language of History in the Renaissance*. Princeton: Princeton Univ. Press, 1970.

Syford, Constance M. "The Direct Source of the Pamela–Cecropia Episode in the *Arcadia*." *Publications of the Modern Language Association*, 49 (1934), 472–489.

Syfret, Rosemary, ed. *Selections from Sidney's Arcadia*. London: Hutchinson, 1966.

Thompson, John. *The Founding of English Metre*. New York: Columbia Univ. Press, 1961.

Thorne, J. P. "A Ramistical Commentary on Sidney's *An Apologie for Poetrie*." *Modern Philology*, 54 (1956–1957), 158–164.

Tillyard, E. M. W. *Shakespeare's Last Plays*. London: Chatto and Windus, 1951.

——. *The English Epic and Its Background*. New York: Oxford Univ. Press, 1954.

Turner, Myron. "The Heroic Ideal in Sidney's Revised *Arcadia.*" *Studies in English Literature,* 10 (1970), 63–82.

Tuve, Rosemond. *Elizabethan and Metaphysical Imagery.* Chicago: Univ. of Chicago Press, 1947.

——. "Imagery and Logic: Ramus and Metaphysical Poetics." *Journal of the History of Ideas,* 3 (1942), 365–400.

Venezky, Alice S. *Pageantry on the Shakespearean Stage.* New York: Twayne, 1951.

Walker, D. P. "Ways of Dealing with Atheists: A Background to Pamela's Refutation of Cecropia." *Bibliothèque d'humanisme et renaissance,* 17 (1955), 252–277.

Wickham, Glynne. *Early English Stages: 1300 to 1600.* Vol. 1. London: Routledge, 1959.

Wind, Edgar. *Pagan Mysteries in the Renaissance.* New Haven: Yale Univ. Press, 1958.

Woolf, Virginia. " 'The Countess of Pembroke's Arcadia,' " in *Collected Essays.* London: Hogarth, 1966, I, 19–27.

Wright, Celeste Turner. "The Amazons in Elizabethan Literature." *Studies in Philology,* 37 (1940), 433–456.

Yates, Frances. "Elizabethan Chivalry: The Romance of the Accession Day Tilts." *Journal of the Warburg & Courtauld Institute,* 20 (1957), 4–25.

——. "The Emblematic Conceit in . . . Bruno's *Gli Eroici furori.*" Journal of Warburg & Courtauld Institute, 6 (1943), 101–121.

——. *Theatre of the World.* Chicago: Univ. of Chicago Press, 1969.

Zandvoort, R. W. *Sidney's Arcadia: A Comparison Between the Two Versions.* Amsterdam: N. V. Swets and Zeitlinger, 1929.

Zolbrod, Paul G. "The Poet's Golden World," unpublished dissertation, U. of Pittsburgh, 1967.

Zouch, Thomas. *Memoirs of the Life and Writings of Sir Philip Sidney.* New York: Wilson & Son, 1808.

Index